LIFE HISTORY OF
DR. BHIMRAO AMBEDKAR

LIFE HISTORY OF DR. BHIM RAO AMBEDKAR

Dharam C. Vyas

2008

CYBER TECH PUBLICATIONS
4264/3, Ansari Road, Daryaganj, New Delhi-110002 (India)
Ph.: 011-23244078. Fax: 011-23280028
E-Mail: cyberpublicationsdelhi@yahoo.com

LIFE HISTORY OF DR. BHIM RAO AMBEDKAR

Dharam C. Vyas

First Edition **2025**

Published by :

G.S. Rawat for **Cyber Tech Publications**
4264/3, Ansari Road, Daryaganj, New Delhi-110002 (India)
Ph.: 011-23244078. Fax: 011-23280028
E-Mail: cyberpublicationsdelhi@yahoo.com

Printed at : **Amit Enterprises**, Maujpur, Delhi, (9810878184)

Preface

Buddha was the first religious leader, who expounded peace and equality in the history of man. Five precepts (Panchsheeel) of Buddha's life are principles of building world peace the precepts Panchsheel based on Buddha's life would help to build world peace and harmony among the Nations. Our humanity is cultivated through our emotions. Each day we should look not only to be moved by others, But also to move them through kindness, patience and caring. Said Venerable Master Hsing Yun: It is my hope and prayer that we will always live a happy, joyful, peaceful life based on non-violence, truth, equality, love and compassion, this great message of Buddha is relevant today. The second great religion that originated in India is Buddhism. Ironically though Buddhism flourished overseas; in the land of its birth it was till recently nonexistent. It received a lease of life after independence, when Dr. B.R. Ambedkar decided to embrace Buddhism. A significant section of the scheduled castes followed Dr. Ambedkar and they today constitute an overwhelming portion of the adherents of Buddhism in India today. But they do not form part of the two traditional sects of Buddhism *viz.*, (Mahanayana and Hinayana) and are generally termed as Neo-Buddhists (Nava-Baudha). The history of Buddhism in India starts with that of its founder Gautama Buddha who lived in the 6th century BC.

Buddha was born in the Shakya clan that belonged to the warrior (Kshatriya) caste. His father was Shudhodana and his mother Maya. Before Buddha was born his mother had a dream in which a white elephant descended from heaven and entered her womb. Buddha was said to have been born in a grove named Lumbini near the ancient town of Kapilavastu. At birth the name given to him was Gautama, probably after the more ancient Vedic seer to whom some of the hymns in the Rig Vedá are ascribed. Buddha was also known as Siddhartha which means 'he whose aim is accomplished'

—Author

Contents

1

THE HISTORY OF GANDHI AND AMBEDKAR IN WORLD

INTRODUCTION

Mohandas Karamchand Gandhi (1869-1948) led India's struggle for independence from colonial rule and committed his life to the social reconstruction and regeneration of India. Bhimrao Ramji Ambedkar (1891-1956) fought to eradicate India's internal apartheid manifested in the pernicious caste practice of untouchability and was committed to a vision of modernized India free of caste and colonial oppression.

Both were champions of untouchables or dalits, both considered untouchability the most shameful smear on the Indian social fabric and both thought that social reform in India ought to precede political freedom. Both were also highly charismatic national leaders who carried the masses with them. Historian Judith Brown's comment that masses reacted to Gandhi "with a mixture of religious adulation and millenniary anticipation" could apply as well to Ambedkar. They have both been compared reverentially to the Buddha and were hailed as prophets of their times. Further, their respective paternal honorific—*Bapu* for Gandhi and *Baba Saheb* for Ambedkar—testify to the affection of their followers.

Yet during their lifetimes, as has been well documented, they differed fundamentally on many social and political issues and occasionally even fought bitterly about their respective roles as champions of Dalit masses. These quarrels are now part of national lore. D.C Ahir in his book *Gandhi and Ambedkar*, succinctly sums up the most common nationalist perception of their differences:

Gandhi christened victims of untouchability as Harijans, Children of God. Ambedkar, however, wanted to see his people as full-fledged "Children of the Soil" with equal rights and privileges and not merely as "touchables" under the guise of another name.

Ambedkar's biographer Dhananjay Keer characterized the differences between them as a clash of titans. As he dramatically put it: "Gandhi and Ambedkar were temperamentally what Vashishtha and Vishwamitra or Voltaire and Rousseau were to each other". From the late 1920s to the 1940s, the differences between them were serious enough to be manifested not only at national, but also international forums such as the two Round Table conferences in London in the 1930s and the famous meeting with the King Emperor, where the apocryphal Dalit narrative has the King infinitely more impressed with Ambedkar than with Gandhi:

Gandhi, with his ascetic mind and khadi apparel, stood exposed before the August Assembly by a man comparatively younger in age, but full of irreverent audacity, and who spoke with a cultivated ferocity and the fervour of an iconoclast.

Other depictions of the same event portray Gandhi in an admirable light and simply make no reference to Ambedkar. For instance, Viscount Templewood's *Nine Troubled Years*, gives us this account of Gandhi's meeting with the King Emperor:

When the conversation was drawing to an end, the King, the most conscientious of monarchs, evidently thought it was his duty to warn Gandhi of the consequences of rebellion. Just, therefore, as Gandhi was taking leave, His Majesty could not refrain from uttering a grave warning. 'Remember Mr. Gandhi, I won't have any attacks on my Empire'. I held my breath in fear of an argument between the two. Gandhi's *saviour faire* saved the situation with a grave and deferential reply. 'I must not be drawn into a political argument in Your Majesty's palace after receiving Your Majesty's hospitality'.

Templewood's is an eyewitness account for he escorted Gandhi to meet the King Emperor.

Comparison here is not to create any dissonance but to compare their respective achievement from a nationalist matrix. It is rather to widen the lens beyond the nationalist framework and cast the two personages, not as two political leaders and social reformers who differed on Indian societal arrangements, but rather as interlocutors of modernity on the world stage. The history of the Indian nation-state focus on their differences, while a world-historical approach shows deep points of convergence between them. World history, in other words, provides a different optic on the same set of historical events. As Geoffrey Barraclough put it in his *History in a Changing World*, "World history cuts into reality at a different angle from other types of history; and because its angle is different, it cuts across the lines they have traced" (cited in Stuchtey and Fuch, 2003: 44).

Attempt is to place Gandhi and Ambedkar on the stage of world history is based not so much on arguments to do with their respective global legacies after their deaths, as on a mining of their political vocabularies to unearth a critical mass of articulations demonstrating a cosmopolitical sensibility, one that invested deeply in the affective politics of living in and connecting with a larger world.

Two propositions are needed to be argued in this proposition. One, the tense relationship between Gandhi and Ambedkar can be recast as a dialogic exchange between two idioms of non-European cosmopolitanism—nonviolence as hybridized Hindu life-practice, and democratic development as a non-hierarchical Buddhist orientation to life. Two, the sharp differences between them notwithstanding, both Gandhi and Ambedkar, along with other nationalist leaders from Asia and Africa, were engaged in projects of world democratization in the era of the decline of modern European colonialism.

In his birds eye view of what he called "the short twentieth century", *Age of Extremes 1914-1991*, historian Eric Hobsbawm talks of the importance of the 1930s as a crucial decade in the democratization of not just the third world, but the globe as a whole. The imperial powers—France, Britain—were besieged by both economic and political woes in the form of the Great Depression and the emergence of fascism in Europe. With the globalization of industrial capitalism in the age of Empire, these developments adversely impacted on the already disgruntled colonies:

The Great Slump of 1929-33 shook the entire dependent world. For practically all of it the era of imperialism had been one of continuous growth, unbroken even by the world war from which many of them remained remote.... The Great Slump changed all this. For the first time the interests of dependent and metropolitan economies clashed visibly, if only because the prices of primary products, on which the Third World depended, collapsed so much more dramatically than those of the manufactured goods which they brought from the West. For the first time colonialism and dependency became unacceptable even to those who had hitherto benefited from it...for the first time...the lives of ordinary people [in the colonies] were shaken by earthquakes plainly not of natural origin, and which called for protest rather than prayer. A mass basis for political mobilization came into existence. (Hobsbawm, 1995: 213-4)

The mobilization of colonized masses in Asia and Africa under an anti-imperialist umbrella throughout the thirties was paralleled by the mobilization of both liberal and socialist regimes in Europe under an anti-fascist umbrella. These developments had the radical impact of catapulting democratic impulses of various hues onto the world stage and for enabling, perhaps, for the first time in world history, a democratic political vision that was truly global. To paraphrase Hobsbawm, in the 1930s one could see the emerging outlines of a mass politics of the future that would envelop the globe. As modernity's interlocutors among their mass followers, both Gandhi and Ambedkar were key participants in this emergent global democracy.

GANDHI AND AMBEDKAR IN WORLD HISTORY

Attempts to write about India, especially modern India, from the perspective of a world historical model is bound to attract much skepticism, not least because till recently such a model was scaf-folded to a narrative of European imperial formations. India in such a formulation entered "world" history as a British colony and as a "footnote" to the history of Britain. World history was interpreted as the globalization of European domination from the late eighteenth to mid twentieth century. One early expression of this is found in David Thompson's "What is World History":

> One feature of recent history is the spread of European power and influence throughout the world, and the manifold consequences of this both for Europe and for the other five continents. The result today is a world in which any momentous event anywhere really matters, within a relative short time, to all other parts of the world...a war, breaking out initially between groups of nations in Europe, tends to spread until it entangles nearly every other people on the globe. It seems possible, therefore, for the historian of world history not to write the history of the continents separately.

In spite of his claims that world historians could now write about all continents together, the structure of Thompson's book relegates decolonization in Asia and Africa to a chapter in the final stages of his book. Since Thompson there have been many attempts to redress this Eurocentric bias in theorizations of world history (Pomper, 1998, Stuchtey and Fuchs, 2003). Nevertheless, in the context of India, there is still much skepticism about these efforts. For instance, historian Vinay Lal notes that, while in recent times, there has been a widening of India's "world" horizon", not only through the history of the

Indian diaspora since World War Two, but also through globalization discourses that see India and China as major global economic and political players in the twenty-first century, world history even today is not much more than "the history of the West energizing the rest of the world".

While one does not doubt his proposition that the West is far from being provincialised even in current attempts to write world history, many recent projects re-imagine colonial histories in a global context by breaking out of the "nations and empire" mould or the "coloniser's model of the world" and refocussing attention on cultural traffic among imperial centres and colonies. This has had the effect of bringing together the mundane and monumental aspects of imperial systems in intricate networks of not only trade, military power and politics, but also cultural practices, social formations and knowledge-making. Tony Ballantyne and Antoinette Burton use the metaphor, "webs of empire" to describe these networks. As they put it, "the web...conveys something of the double nature of the imperial system. Empires, like webs, were fragile and prone to crises where important threads were broken or structural nodes destroyed, yet also dynamic, being constantly remade and reconfigured through concerted thought and effort". (Ballantyne and Burton, 2005: 3)

While Ballantyne and Burton's focus on the networked nature of empires does to some extent counter Vinay Lal's pessimism that world history invariably re-centres the West, there is one aspect of Lal's analysis that has a bearing on this attempt to read Gandhi and Ambedkar from a world historical perspective. Lal draws our attention to India's extensive connections with the world in pre-colonial times and highlights the makings of another kind of world history for India, one that connected her to vast regions in Asia, Africa and the Mediterranean through both trade and cultural-religious enterprises. He cites Janet Abu-Lughod's monumental work on the pre-European expansion of world systems in the second millennium in which India was part of a vast trading network. The Coromandel Coast in the southeast, the Malabar Coast in the south west and the ports of Gujarat in western India had active trade connections expanding from southeast Asia to eastern Africa, the Persian Gulf and the Mediterranean. The Gujarati trading class, to which Gandhi belonged, had a long pre-colonial history of extensive contacts with the world:

Classical sources suggest that Gujarati merchants may have been present in Eygpt in remote antiquity, and their presence in the ports of the Persian Gulf and the Red Sea, along the Arab littoral, and on the east coast of Africa, where there seems to be some evidence of Indian settlements from around the tenth century, is well documented. By the late Middle Ages, they appear to have gained dominance in the trade with East Africa, and obtained control over the ports...along the Coromandel coast.

Apart from trade, other world historical connections of pre-colonial India included those related to the spread of Buddhism in China, Sri Lanka and southeast Asia much before Christianity and Islam, and what the renowned Indologist, Sheldon Pollock, has called "the Sanskrit Cosmopolis". The millennium-long temporal stretch of this latter from AD 300 to 1300 had an awesome political and cultural reach from Afghanistan in the West to Vietnam and Central Java in the east. According to Pollock, the cosmopolis was a "new kind of vast zone of cultural interaction, what some might name an ecumene" (Pollock, 1996:199). But since the dominance of empire-led world history, the Sanskrit cosmopolis has remained a little known world cultural formation. Further, India's pre-colonial links with vast swathes of Asia and Africa are now mediated through an epistemology that foregrounds the history of European colonialism and the rise of the West as normative. In short, the insertion of India into a world history dominated by the making of European empires has had the effect of shrinking the horizon of India's total historical contact with the world to the history of its relationship with the West.

Can then one effectively bypass this conundrum in reading two modern Indian figures against a world historical background? Not wholly perhaps, but the conundrum can be tackled if one argues for the world historical provenance of both Gandhi and Ambedkar not just in terms of British imperialism, but also in terms of traces of India's pre-colonial links to the world that their respective cosmopolitical projects carry. The rest of assessment will place Gandhi and Ambedkar in world history precisely in these terms. The argument here is that Gandhi's peripatetic life and work in the context of his genealogy in the old global Gujarati thalassocracy, and Ambedkar's attempts to revive Buddhism in India and reconnect with the rest of the Buddhist world, when inserted into a narrative of their interventions in global democracy in the age of Empire, unsettle assumptions of modern India being engulfed by an Euro-American dominated world history.

The "world" of Gandhi and Ambedkar has to distinct orientation. First, their deep engagement with world events during the period of empire and focus on their commitment to global democracy. Second, is an endeavour to trace the vernacular and cosmopolitan idioms of their respective political projects—*nonviolence* as a vernacular Hinduised life-practice in Gandhi and *democratic development* for Ambedkar as a non-hierarchical Buddhist orientation to life. These can be read productively in complementary rather than in oppositional terms for both Gandhi and Ambedkar offered resistance to the oppositional way in which the discourse of "normative modernity" (Ganguly, 2005: ix) reads the *vernacular* in relation to the *cosmopolitan*, with the later invariably valorized over the former. In doing so, It can be argued for the provenance of these two thought figures in the domain of a "critical modernity" that bears witness to not just the achievements but the horrors of colonial modernity's civilizing mission, and that continues to carry traces of pre-colonial modes of connecting with the world. The reading is, in the final analysis, post-colonial in the complex historicist sense of the term, intertwining discrepant temporalities and articulating the pull of the vernacular and the push of the cosmopolitan in one single gesture.

CONVERSING DEMOCRATICALLY IN THE AGE OF EMPIRE

Gandhi was asked to comment on the future of India in the context of the Allied struggle in World War Two. In a global democratic gesture linking nationalist struggles in the colonies with the western world's fight against European fascism, his response categorically connected the democratic future of India to a world free of both fascism and colonialism:

Of what value is freedom to India if Britain and France fail? If these powers fail, the history of Europe and the history of the world will be written in a manner no one can foresee.... [At the same time] by doing justice to India, Britain might ensure victory of the Allies because their cause will then be acclaimed as righteous by the enlightened opinion of the world. (Gandhi, 1987: 309)

Throughout his political career, Gandhi never thought of India's freedom from colonial rule in isolation from world events. Empire, he believed, needed to be challenged globally, not merely nationally or territorially. As noted by many Gandhian scholars his early experience of the colonial racial divide in South Africa was the crucible that honed his cosmopolitical vision of a world free of all forms of inequities and bondage. Percesing through his voluminous corpus of books, letters and essays, one finds evidence of a mind constantly at pains to address colonial, communist and fascist excesses in all corners of the globe—Turkey, South Africa, Palestine, Israel, Germany and Russia.

One of the earliest manifestations of Gandhi's commitment to take the fight against imperialism onto the world stage can be seen in his mobilization of Indian masses on behalf of the Caliphate of the defeated Ottoman Empire in World War One. According to the Treaty of Versailles, the British as victors of the War had promised not to abolish the Caliphate claimed at the time by the Ottoman Emperor in Turkey. The Caliphate symbolized for the Muslim world, even if in a tokenistic way, a spiritual and temporal authority uniting the Muslim *Ummah*. So as to ensure that the British kept their promise, an already besieged global Muslim leadership appealed to Indian Muslim leaders to join forces with them and keep up the pressure on colonial authorities.

Hence was launched the Khilafat Movement in India to which Gandhi mobilized the masses and provided his wholehearted support, convinced as he was of the necessity to resist the juggernaut of British colonial authority decimating all non-Western political and sociocultural formations. The Khilafat Movement's three primary objectives were: to preserve the Turkish Caliphate, to maintain the unity of the Ottoman Empire within its 1914 frontiers and to maintain Islamic protection over the Holy Places of Islam including Palestine (Minault, 1982). The movement, which did not gain the desired momentum from the very beginning, suffered its fatal blow when, in 1924, Turkey's new secular republican leader, Kemal Ataturk overthrew the Ottoman Sultan himself and relinquished the Turkish state's claim to a universal Caliphate.

In most accounts of this movement Gandhi's role is seen in strategic terms as a bargain with the Indian Muslims, pledging his support for this pan-Islamic movement in return for their support towards Hindu-Muslim unity in his call for *Swaraj* or total freedom on home ground. This is broadly the thrust of Gail Minault's argument in her fine and detailed account of the movement, *(The Khilafat Movement: Religious Symbolism and Political Mobilization in India 1982)*.

However, if one turns from this nationalist focus and places Gandhi's articulations on Khilafat within the wider ambit of an imperial globalism taking shape in the early years of the twentieth century, one begins to trace a dialogue between Gandhi and the world that has hitherto not been audible in this specific context. Why does Gandhi, for instance, say in his *Young India* essay of 10 March 1920 that "the Khilafat Question has now become a question of questions"? That, "it has become an imperial question of the first magnitude?" (Gandhi, 1920: 145). Why does he refuse to equate the Jallianwallah Bagh massacre in 1919 with the international importance of the Khilafat Movement, as when he says, "However grievous the wrong done in the Punjab, it is after all a domestic affair...the Punjab grievance does not arise out of the peace [the Versailles Treaty] terms as does the Khilafat question.

We must isolate the Khilafat question if we wish to give it its proper value"? (Gandhi, 1919: 140-1) Surely statements such as these cannot be read purely in instrumentalist terms as trying to "win over" Indian Muslims to his nationalist cause. In fact, his relegation of the Amritsar massacre to a "domestic" concern could hardly have endeared him to the masses, either Hindu or Muslim. A clue to Gandhi's global orientation in the matter of the Caliphate lies in his invocation of a rich Islamic pre-Europe-dominated geopolitical and geo-cultural space and time that was now under threat of extinction from the modernizing machinations of a colonialist-capitalist enterprise:

> *The Great Prelates of England and Mohammedan leaders combined have brought the question to the fore. The Prelates threw down the challenge. The Muslim leaders have taken it up. (Gandhi, 1920: 145)*

In a fascinating recent reading of Gandhi in the context of the Khilafat Movement, Faisal Fatehali Devji notes Gandhi's resistance to the rhetoric of liberal interest and state arbitration in arguing the case of the Ottoman Empire (Devji, 2005: 86-7). He cites these words of Gandhi to make his case:

> *"Oppose Turkish misrule by all means, but it is wicked to seek to efface the Turk and with him Islam from Europe under the false plea of Turkish misrule.... Was the late war a crusade against Islam, in which the Mussalmans of India were invited to join? (Gandhi, 1921: 190)"*

Devji offers a reading of the Gandhian stance in terms of "prejudice" and a "politics of friendship" towards Islam and

Muslims that are not reducible to either the rhetoric of nationalist brotherhood or the rational rhetoric of liberal interest. To that extent he upholds Gandhi as an exemplary articulator of the limits of liberalism in the context of empire, a relationship brilliantly explored by Uday Mehta a few years ago in his book *Liberalism and Empire* (1999). While such a reading provides another fillip to this attempt to situate Gandhi in a dialogical relationship with the imperial world, it is another comment that Devji makes merely to his main argument that has a more significant bearing to place Gandhi in a world historical context.

It also relates to a point made in an early part of this essay about pre-colonial world historical formations that a Eurocentric world history has all but erased from collective global memory. Devji refers to Gandhi's "antiquated geographical imaginary", derived from pre-colonial Indian Ocean trade routes dominated by Arabs and Gujaratis, that ever so often impinged on his readings of British imperial territoriality (Devji, 86). So much so that Gandhi's rhetoric in his early writing subconsciously linked his passages to London and subsequently South Africa in a continuum with journeys of the old Gujarati thalassocracy rather than in terms of the routes of colonial capital. These old Islamic routes were part of his collective history that he could not orient himself out of simply because the European imperial order charted and controlled them in different ways.

It will be prudent to read Gandhi's conception of his and India's involvement in the Khilafat movement in terms of his vision of a clash between old Islamic world formations and a new imperial globalism dominated by Europe. The clash may have been decisively settled in favour of the latter, but no historicist account of Europe's triumph over pre-modern life worlds, can take away from the reality of their survival in some ready-to-hand ways in collective imaginaries across vast swathes of the non-European world. The complexity in globalising Gandhi, however, is not so easily resolved by marking his orientation towards Islamic world formations at a time of their imminent ruin. For Gandhi was as eloquent and forceful in identifying himself as a serious player in the British Empire and in world events as a whole. As he put it famously in 1920, "I serve the Empire by refusing to partake in its wrong" (1920: 192). His creticism of communism with its high-handed statism, of Zionism with its dispossession of Palestinians or of anti-colonial nationalism with its elitist stance towards the masses can certainly be read in this light.

The carnage of World War Two evoked in turn exasperation and anguish from him. "Europe seems to be heading for another war. It's not sufficiently exhausted", he told Louis Fischer after the atomic Holocaust in Hiroshima and Nagasaki (Gandhi, 1987: 581). In his personal correspondence with Mira Behn he expressed sorrow at the bombing of London.

He coped with his anguish by occasionally comparing the War with the epic battle in the *Mahabharata* and drawing on the message of the *Bhagavad Gita* to be philosophical about victory and defeat. His letter to Rajkumari Amrit Kaur on 25 May 1940 is reminiscent of Krishna's exhortation to Arjuna not to grieve over the death of his loved ones in the war:

> *Why should you feel depressed? The Allies seem to be losing everywhere. These are the fortunes of war. You must not grieve over these things. The slaughter is awful but it is part of the game. All parties know what is what.*

The War was a prime test of his ethical stance on the non-negotiable nature of nonviolence. The atrocities of Nazi Germany on the one hand and the threat to India's borders through Japanese invasion on the other, demanded more than just a pacifist response. His writings are scattered with his thoughts on the Nazi persecution of Jews. Obviously not able to imagine that the sheer monstrosity of anti-Semitism and the venality of the Nazi bureaucratic machine far exceeded the excesses of British rule in India, Gandhi urged the Jews to resist Germans nonviolently, through *Satyagraha*, just as the Indians did in South Africa. In 1938 he wrote in the *Harijan*:

"If there ever could be a justifiable war in the name of and for humanity, war against Germany to prevent the wanton persecution of a whole race would be completely justified. But I do not believe in any war.... If I were a Jew and were born in Germany and earned my livelihood there, I would claim Germany as my home even as the tallest gentile German might.... The Jews of Germany can offer satyagraha under infinitely better auspices than the Indians of South Africa. The Jews are a compact homogeneous community in Germany. They are far more gifted than the Indians of South Africa. And they have organized world opinion behind them. I am convinced that if someone with courage and vision can rise among them to lead them to nonviolent action...what has today become a degrading manhunt can be turned into a calm and determined stand offered by unarmed men and women possessing the strength of suffering given to them by Jehovah. (cited in Mehta, 1976: 166)"

In response to the panic among members of the Indian National Congress about an imminent Japanese invasion of the east coast of India, Gandhi pleaded with the INC to exercise restraint and not think in terms of an armed conflict. A troubled Nehru wrote:

"The approach of the war to India disturbed Gandhi greatly. It was not easy to fit in his policy and program of non-violence with this new development. Obviously civil disobedience was out of the question in the face of an invading army or between two opposing armies. Passivity or acceptance of invasion was equally out of the question. What then?"

In 1942, Gandhi had already dispatched his trusted lieutenant Mira Behn to Orissa to "prepare" as Mira Behn put it, "the masses for nonviolent, noncooperative resistance to the probable Japanese invasion of the east coast" (1949: 335) From Orissa Mira Behn sent a detailed report to Gandhi on *The Question of Invasion and Occupation by the Japanese* (1949: 336-40). The report outlined nonviolent strategies that the people of Orissa would be persuaded to adopt in the event of an invasion. The course of history did not allow Gandhi to have his way, not only because the Japanese did not get beyond India's North East, but also because negotiations with Nehru and Congress compelled Gandhi to "swallow the bitter pill" and accept that the "primary function of the provisional government of free India would be to throw all her great resources in the struggle for freedom against aggression and to cooperate fully with the United Kingdom in the defence of India with all the armed and other forces at her command".

While Gandhi went along temporarily with Nehru's pragmatic position that India's cooperation in regard to the Japanese invasion would expedite her freedom from British rule, he remained convinced of the long term efficacy of his nonviolent stance in resisting world wide colonialism and bondage. Tied to this commitment was his very radical vision of democracy that plumbed the very depths of what it was to be human in those fraught times. Calling himself a "born democrat", he added; "I make that claim, if complete identification with the poorest of mankind, longing to live no better than they, and a corresponding conscious effort to approach that level to the best of one's ability can entitle one to make it" (cited in Nehru, 1948: 189).

It is worth reading this radical Gandhian democratic gloss on the ethicality of being poor retroactively into a recent exposition of the "poor" as "the common denominator of life, the foundation of the multitude" found in Michael Hardt and Antonio Negri's *Empire* (2000: 156). What kind of democracy was Gandhi espousing and why was identifying with the poorest of mankind such a radical gesture that unsettled discourses of liberal democracy then circulating in the colonies? Hardt and Negri's exposition on the poor helps us answer these to some extent:

In each and every historical period a social subject that is ever-present and everywhere the same is identified, often negatively but nonetheless urgently, around a common living form.... The only non-localizable "common name" of pure difference in all eras is that of the poor. The poor is destitute, excluded, repressed, exploited—and yet living!.... This common name, the poor, is also the foundation of every possibility of humanity (2000: 156).

For Gandhi to live democratically was not merely a matter of reaping the benefits of electoral politics and representative government. It meant putting oneself in touch with the very root or foundation of what made humanity possible—the condition of being poor, bereft, destitute, a condition of pure difference in all eras and yet a common living form.

To turn now to Ambedkar's links with the world in the age of empire, by even the most sympathetic of accounts he did not command the presence that Gandhi did in the global order of things. Nevertheless, over his lifetime he displayed a unique cosmopolitical sensibility, one forged during his graduate study days in New York and London during World War One, when he began to imagine perhaps for the first time in the history of India's untouchable castes, the dalits, the possibility of a genuine global democratic revolution that would link Dalit freedom from the shackles of untouchability to the overthrow of racism against coloured and black people across the world.

Ambedkar's intervention on behalf of Indian dalits, in fact, can be inserted in any twentieth century political and legal narrative of the global passage of the notion of rights from "civil rights" to "human rights". Even though he would later make fine distinctions between caste and race, this aspect of his legacy has remained with the Dalit movement and was given global articulation at the UN Conference on Racism in Durban in 2001. Ambedkar's biographer, Dhananjay Keer, notes the impact on him of the Fourteenth Amendment declaring freedom of African Americans when he was a student of John Dewey and Edwin Seligman from 1913-1916.

Keer also notes how affected Ambedkar was by the death in 1915 of the African American reformer and educator, Booker T. Washington. What did not happen, however, was the quick transformation of the student into a revolutionary, and this in spite of the presence of the Indian Gadar Party revolutionary leaders such as Lala Har Dayal and Lala Lajpat Rai in New York at the time. Ambedkar preferred to concentrate on his studies at the time. After three years at Columbia University, he proceeded to the University of London to do his doctorate.

But he could not maintain his detachment from colonial politics for long. His doctoral thesis called *The Problem of the Rupee,* which he submitted to the University of London in 1922, caused a furore for it offended his imperial examiners and they demanded that he rewrite it. In the thesis Ambedkar argued that in the final settlement of the currency problem the exchange rate between the rupee and the pound was manipulated to the greater advantage of the pound and that this would lead to further impoverishment of Indians. While his pragmatism made him revise the thesis to some extent, he refused to modify his conclusions and stood his ground. A few weeks earlier he had spoken passionately to the students' union at his University about the responsibilities of the colonial government in India. His paper was later circulated among University staff and students and it evoked an alarmed response from Professor Harold Laski who commented on the "revolutionary nature" of Ambedkar's exposition.

Unlike anarchist tendencies in Gandhi's response to nation-making, Ambedkar's academic training in law, economics and political science oriented him towards arguing for the importance of the constructionist role of the state. He researched liberal democratic frameworks and aspired to a form of representational governance that spoke the language of identity-based politics. This implied, for him, not just recognition of minoritarianism on the basis of religion, but also of caste. The untouchables, he argued, could never hope to participate in nation-making unless they had special political representation.

This was the basis of his disagreement with Gandhi who aspired to a non-fragmented Hindu constituency and who believed that the untouchable cause could be redressed through revolutionary transformations in the domain of civil society.

Gandhi could not conceive of a political scenario where the untouchables stood *outside* Hindu representation, even though the social reality through millennia was precisely that the untouchables were located *outside* the bounds of Hindu sociality. Gandhi was steadfast in his conviction that his commitment to and identification with the destitute, which constituted the cornerstone of his democratic vision, would be sufficient to transform Hindu society and eradicate untouchability.

Ambedkar's social-scientific and legally trained mind was deeply suspicious of Gandhi's emotive and sentimental take on the problem of untouchability, especially when Gandhi announced in the same breath that he was and would always remain a *Sanatani Hindu*. Theirs was a critical dialogue on competing visions of representational democracy and resolution of minoritarian questions—liberalism, socialism Marxism, anarchism—in the era of fledging nation-building in the colonized world. The rest of twentieth century politics would continue to resonate with these meta-themes and agonistically witness radical manifestations of democratic life forms across the post-colonial world.

For more than half his life, Ambedkar negotiated the dialectic between nation and the world through conversations on democracy with Indian nationalist leaders, with the colonial government and with the vast tomes of political, social and legal philosophy in which he immersed himself from his early youth. But he eventually found his home in the world by recuperating for India a link with a pre-colonial world historical formation in the form of Buddhism.

His conversion to Buddhism in terms of a vernacular cosmopolitical act that drew on the cosmopolitical genealogies of the non-Christian world while at the same time resisting both antiquarianism and indigenism (Pollock, et.al. 2000: 582). Ambedkar's renewal of India's connections with the world through Asia, which, as we saw in earlier, were severed with the advent of colonial rule. Ambedkar's determination to lead untouchables out of the Hindu fold and into a more egalitarian religion, Buddhism, was tied to a desire to bring Buddhism back to the land of its birth and make India once again an important node, if not the central one, in Asian Buddhist transnationalism. For this purpose, all through the late 1940s right up to his death in 1956, he travelled to many parts of Buddhist Asia—Sri Lanka, Burma, Tibet and Japan—in order to forge spiritual alliances and bring to life once again an Asian world formation that could converse with modernity in tongues both sacred and secular.

His dialogic uptake on Marxism through the teachings of the Buddha was the substance of his intervention at the World Buddhist Conference in Kathmandu in 1949 and again in 1956. He spent many days in Sri Lanka in 1954 to specifically study Sinhalese Buddhist practices. He subsequently attended the Rangoon World Buddhist Conference.

In these years, he also frequently conversed with an English monk, Denis Lingwood (Sangharakshita), who was then based in a monastery in northeastern India. His letters to Sangharakshita exhorted the young English monk to take the message of Buddha to the western world. Sangharakshita subsequently founded the Friends of the Western Buddhist Order (FWBO) in the UK in 1969 which now has branches all over the world. In one of those recursive ironies that so characterize world history, after Ambedkar's death in 1956, the role of FWBO has been critical in keeping Buddhist religious practices alive among neo-Buddhist dalits in India, especially in Maharashtra, Ambedkar's home state.

THE PRECARIOUSNESS OF VERNACULAR COSMOPOLITICS

To bring together various lines that have so far traced the world historical provenance of Gandhi and Ambedkar on to a conceptual matrix, "vernacular cosmopolitanism" Bhabha's assertion that the phrase best applies to the orientation of embattled leaders and thought figures of the non-White, non-Western world—Du Bois, Gandhi, Ambedkar, Fanon, Morrison—

who attempt to "translate between cultures and across them in order to survive, not in order to assert the sovereignty of a civilized class or the spiritual autonomy of a revered ideal" (Bhabha, 2002: 23-24) in reading Gandhi and Ambedkar, the thinkers have explore the phrase a little further both conceptually and historically.

The term at first glance is an oxymoron. For "vernacular" connotes an affiliation to a domain that is local, finite, while "cosmopolitan" invokes an orientation to a world larger than one's own immediate *habitus*.

How then does one yoke them together? What does this oxymoronic adjacency generate? Before any attempt to answer these questions, it will be wise to note that the origins of the word "vernacular" lie in the term "verna" which etymologically denotes the language of slaves in Roman Republics. The circulation of the term "varna" in the Indian context further complicates its meaning, for in Sanskrit *varna* literally means "colour".

A philological reading of "vernacular", one that traces its embeddedness in historical practice, cannot help carrying signs of subjugation—slavery of course, but also racial subjugation if *colour* is refracted on to *race* in the age of Empire. The passage of meaning from subjugation to a finite, local boundedness is not hard to imagine. So, what does its yoking together with "cosmopolitanism"—a term that connotes a "world" orientation facilitating a free crossing of boundaries—achieve in the context under discussion?

One yokes them together, in order to mark critical moments of historical conjunction when historically disenfranchised "small" narratives engage in dialogue with firmly entrenched "world-enveloping" ones to generate radical transformations in both. So that, for instance, liberalism when translated or carried over to the domain of the colonized through the lexicon of Gandhian *ahimsa* or Ambedkarite-Buddhist *dhamma*, becomes a term loaded with plural histories of the indivisual self and its relationship with community and the State.

In the domain of Empire, liberalism, as Uday Mehta has shown, repeatedly confronts its limits in other non-European political narratives and is willy-nilly forced to hybridize itself. Again, notwithstanding the "ancient" cultural repertoire from which Gandhi and Ambedkar draw their political lexicon, their own deployment of predominantly "vernacular" Hindu and Buddhist terms is shot through with modern hybrid genealogies that bespeak the historical and cultural permeability of modernity's multiple practices. Such a reading breaks through the dichotomy of a modernizing cosmopolitanism and a vernacular traditionalism. Let us briefly illustrate this argument with examples from the writings of Gandhi and Ambedkar.

In enunciating his principle of nonviolence through terms such as *ahimsa, satyagraha and* sarvodaya ("nonviolence", "truth-force" and "welfare of all"), Gandhi is constantly at pains to foreground the "vernacular" connotative force of these concepts, to highlight that they are not exactly recuperable in English through terms such as "passive resistance". On June 11, 1917, he writes to an English friend, Esther: "You may not know that the *Gujarati* for passive resistance is truth-force. I have variously defined it as truth-force, love-force or soul-force" (Gandhi, 1987: 23-24). In 1914, he writes about truth-force and soul-force in the *Indian Opinion*:

> *"It is totally untrue to say that it is a force to be used only by the weak so long as they are not capable of meeting violence by violence. This superstition arises from the incompleteness of the* English *expression. It is impossible for those who consider themselves weak to apply this force. Only those who realize that there is something in man which is superior to the brute nature in him, and that the latter always yields to it, can effectively be Passive Resisters. This force is to violence and, therefore, to all tyranny, all injustice, what light is to darkness."*

Gandhi's emphasis on the power of the *Gujarati* term *satyagraha* which the English translation cannot convey, however, does not prevent him for invoking Socrates, Christ,

Tolstoy, Thoreau, Ruskin, Emerson, and many ancient Indian philosophers, to account for its complex etymology. In doing so, he seeks to distil into his Gujarati use of the term the combined connotative force of global registers of nonviolence available to him as his peripatetic inheritance and training. In this issue of the journal, Leela Gandhi's paper discusses yet another aspect of the complex etymology of Gandhian nonviolence and locates some early influences on Gandhi in a radical fringe late Victorian animal-welfare and vegetarian movement. During his student days, Gandhi imbibed from this movement a critique of imperial masculinity, a resistance to modern forms of governmentality and a regard for multiple forms of relationality that included strangers in radical ways.

Leela's argument is not only that these can be read as constituting part of the vocabulary of Gandhian nonviolence, but that their very "integrity" and "organicity" can themselves be read under the comprehensive sign of *ahimsa*. Each gets translated into the other. This resonates strongly with the line of argument pursued, that the vernacular cosmopolitics of a Gandhi or an Ambedkar is about generating transformation in the assured global registers of the politic through their translations into and from myriad *petit* registers.

Ambedkar's mining of Buddhist discourse to seek in it points of convergence and dialogue with modern political philosophy, especially Marxism, socialism and liberalism, can be seen precisely in terms of such a vernacular cosmopolitical practice. It can be noted that, like Gandhi, he wrote in a register that was truly vernacular, truly accessible to ordinary men and women who invested so much faith in him. He did not allow his specialist training in legal and political philosophy and his vast erudition to come in the way of writing in an accessible manner. One very good example is his attempt to read the principles of the French Revolution into Buddha's social message in terms of four rhetorical questions:

Did the Buddha teach justice?

Did the Buddha teach liberty?

Did the Buddha teach equality?

Did the Buddha teach fraternity?

He then goes on to impatiently mark a lacuna in esoteric traditionalist interpretations of Buddha's message by adding, "These questions are hardly ever raised in discussing the Buddha's Dhamma" (2002: 218). His famous ahistoricist comparison of Marx and Buddha, written in a register suspect to academic specialists, was actually delivered at a World Buddhist Conference in 1956 with the express intention of translating a possible dialogue between the two thought figures to the world at large in terms of a truly inclusive ethics of universal humanity. What is significant about this piece of writing is not so much Ambedkar's successful demonstration through a series of syllogisms that Buddhism has ethically more to offer than Marxism in terms of a democratic world order, but its subtext that the world is that much poorer for not taking into account (or merely dismissing as traditional) other legitimate and ethical ways of dwelling democratically on earth in the present.

Previously Ambedkar's place in world history has been analysed, not only in terms of his attempt to forge along with Gandhi a democratic vision for India and the world in the age of Empire, but also in terms of his efforts to re-establish India's links with the Asian world through Buddhism. His translational cosmopolitical efforts were thus, directed, not just westwards towards Euro-American life-worlds, but also towards an aspired Buddhist cosmopolis that would be truly global in its reach and vision.

Likewise, Gandhi's nonviolent resistance to the imperial regime was an effort to globalize the forces of soul, truth and love through acts of active translation in disparate tongues and registers, especially those disenfranchised by the British imperial machine. In spite of drawing deeply from the wellsprings of India's spiritual heritage, neither was antiquarian, nor indigenist in his response to the horrors of colonialism. In treading the faultlines of seismic political and cultural upheavals in the twentieth century, especially from the side of the vanquished, both were acutely aware of the precariousness of their cosmopolitical vision. But they were equally convinced of the sheer urgency of their moral and political enterprise in an age that stood at the threshold of a global democratic revolution of the kind never witnessed before.

GANDHI'S AMBEDKAR

'Inside every thinking Indian there is a Gandhian and a Marxist struggling for supremacy,' says noted historian and biographer Ramachandra Guha in the opening sentence of this publication. A significant portion of the book expands on this salvo. In short, it examines and discusses all those who comprise the life of thinking Indians today. Exclusive extracts from the book released.

Mahatma Gandhi was not so much the Father of the Nation as the mother of all debates regarding its future. All his life he fought in a friendly spirit with compatriots whose views on this or that topic diverged sharply from his. He disagreed with Communists and the bhadralok on the efficacy and morality of violence as a political strategy. He fought with radical Muslims on the one side and with radical Hindus on the other, both of whom sought to ,build a state on theological principles. He argued with Nehru and other scientists on whether economic development in a free India should centre on the village or the factory. And with that other giant, Rabindranath Tagore, he disputed the merits of such varied affiliations as the English language, nationalism, and the spinning wheel.

In some ways the most intense, interesting and long-running of these debates was between Gandhi and Ambedkar. Gandhi wished to save Hinduism by abolishing untouchability, whereas Ambedkar saw a solution for his people outside the fold of the dominant religion of the Indian people. Gandhi was a rural romantic, who wished to make the self-governing village the bedrock of free India; Ambedkar an admirer of city life and modern technology who dismissed the Indian village as a den of iniquity. Gandhi was a crypto-anarchist who favoured nonviolent protest while being suspicious of the state; Ambedkar a steadfast constitutionalist, who worked within the state and sought solutions to social problems with the aid of the state.

Perhaps the most telling difference was in the choice of political instrument. For Gandhi, the Congress represented all of India, the Dalits too. Had he not made their cause their own from the time of his first ashram in South Africa? Ambedkar however made a clear distinction between freedom and power. The Congress wanted the British to transfer power to them, but to obtain freedom the Dalits had to organise themselves as a separate bloc, to form a separate party, so as to more effectively articulate their interests in the crucible of electoral politics. It was thus that in his lifetime, and for long afterwards, Ambedkar came to represent a dangerously subversive threat to the authoritative, and sometimes authoritarian, equation: Gandhi = Congress = Nation.

Here then is the stuff of epic drama, the argument between the Hindu who did most to reform caste and the ex-Hindu who did most to do away with caste altogether. Recent accounts represent it as a fight between a hero and a villain, the writer's caste position generally determining who gets cast as hero, who as villain. In truth both figures should be seen as heroes, albeit tragic ones.

The tragedy, from Gandhi's point of view, was that his colleagues in the national movement either did not understand his concern with untouchability or even actively deplored it. Priests and motley shankaracharyas thought he was going too fast in his challenge to caste—and why did he not first take their permission? Communists wondered why he wanted everyone to clean their own latrines when he could be speaking of class struggle. And Congressmen in general thought Harijan work came in the way of an all-out effort for national freedom. Thus Stanley Reid, a former editor of the Times of India quotes an Indian patriot who complained in the late thirties that "Gandhi is wrapped up in the Harijan movement. He does not care a jot whether we live or die; whether we are bond or free."

The opposition that he faced from his fellow Hindus meant that Gandhi had perforce to move slowly, and in stages. He started by accepting that untouchability was bad, but added a cautionary caveat—that inter-dining and intermarriage were also bad. He moved on to accepting inter-mingling and inter-dining (hence the movement for temple entry), and to arguing that all men and all varnas were equal. The last and most far-reaching step, taken only in 1946, was to challenge caste directly by accepting and sanctioning intermarriage itself.

The tragedy, from Ambedkar's point of view, was that to fight for his people he had to make common cause with the British. In his book, Worshipping False Gods, Arun Shourie has made much of this. Shourie takes all of 600 pages to make two points: (i) that Ambedkar was a political opponent of both Gandhi and the Congress, and generally preferred the British to either; (ii) that Ambedkar cannot be called the "Father of the Constitution" as that implies sole authorship, whereas several other people, such as K. M. Munshi and B. N. Rau, also contributed significantly to the wording of the document. Reading Worshipping False Gods, one might likewise conclude that it has been mistakenly advertised as being the work of one hand. Entire chapters are based entirely on one or other volume of the Transfer of Power, the collection of official papers put out some years ago by Her Majesty's Stationery Office. The editor of that series, Nicholas Mansergh, might with reason claim co-authorship of Shourie's book. In a just world he would be granted a share of the royalties too.

Practised in the arts of overkill and over-quote, Shourie is a pamphleteer parading as a historian. He speaks on Gandhi only as "Gandhiji" and of the national movement only as the "National Movement", indicating that he has judged the case beforehand. For to use the suffix and the capitals is to simultaneously elevate and intimidate, to set up the man and his movement as the ideal, above and beyond criticism. But the Congress' claim to represent all of India was always under challenge. The Communists said it was the party of landlords and capitalists. The Muslim League said it was a party of the Hindus. Ambedkar then appended a devastating caveat, saying that the party did not even represent all Hindus, but only the upper castes.

Shourie would deny that these critics had any valid arguments whatsoever. He is in the business of awarding, and more often withholding, certificates of patriotism. The opponents of the Congress are thus all suspect to him, simply because they dared point out that the National Movement was not always as national as it set out to be, or that the Freedom Struggle promised unfreedom for some. But how did these men outside the Congress come to enjoy such a wide following? This is a question Shourie does not pause to answer, partly because he had made up his mind in advance, but also because he is woefully ill-informed. Consider now some key facts erased or ignored by him.

That Ambedkar preferred the British to the Congress is entirely defensible. Relevant here is a remark of the 18th-Century English writer Samuel Johnson. When the American colonists asked for independence from Britain, Johnson said: "How is it that we hear the greatest yelps for liberty among the drivers of Negroes?" Untouchability was to the Indian freedom movement what slavery had been to the American struggle, the basic contradiction it sought to paper over. Before Ambedkar, another outstanding leader of the lower castes, Jotiba Phule, also distrusted the Congress, in his time a party dominated by Poona Brahmins. He too preferred the British, in whose armies and factories low castes could find opportunities denied to them in the past. The opening up of the economy and the growth of the colonial cities also helped many untouchables escape the tyranny of the village. The British might have been unwitting agents of change; nonetheless, under their rule life for the lower castes was less unpleasant by far than it had been under the Peshwas.

Shourie also seems unaware of work by worthy historians on low- caste movements in other parts of India. Mark Juergensmeyer has documented the struggles of untouchables in Punjab, which under its remarkable leader Mangu Ram, rejected the Congress and the Arya Samaj to form a new sect, Adi-Dharm, which was opposed to both. Sekhar Bandyopadhyay has written of the Namasudras in Bengal, who like Ambedkar and his Mahars, were not convinced that a future Congress government would be sympathetic to their interests. And countless scholars have documented the rise of the Dravidian movement in South India, that took as its point of departure Brahmin domination of the Congress in Madras: the movement's founder, E. V. Ramaswami "Periyar", also fought bitterly with Gandhi.

The leaders of these movements, and the millions who followed them, worked outside the Congress and often in opposition to it. Enough reason perhaps for Shourie to dismiss them all as anti- national. Indeed, Shourie's attitude is comparable to that of White Americans who question the patriotism of those Blacks who dare speak out against racism. For asking Blacks to stand up for their rights, men of such stature as W.E.B. Du Bois and Paul Robeson were called all kind of names, of which "anti-American" was much the politest. Later, the great Martin Luther King was persecuted by the most powerful of American agencies, the Federal Bureau of Investigation, whose director, J. Edgar Hoover, equated patriotism with acquiescence to White domination.

Much of the time, Shourie writes as if there is a singular truth, with him as its repository and guarantor. Time and again he equates Ambedkar with Jinnah as an "accomplice of Imperial politics". He dismisses all that Ambedkar wrote about Hinduism "caricature" and "calumnies". Not once does he acknowledge that there was much truth to the criticisms. There is not one admission here of the horrendous and continuing sufferings of Dalit as the hands of caste Hindus that might explain and justify Ambedkar's rhetoric and political choices. For Shourie, the fact that Ambedkar disagreed long and often with Gandhi is proof enough that he was anti-national. He even insinuates that Ambedkar "pushed Gandhi to the edge of death" by not interfering with the Mahatma's decision to fast in captivity. Of the same fast other historians have written, that by threatening to die Gandhi blackmailed Ambedkar into signing a pact with him.

Somewhere in the middle of Worshipping False Gods, the author complains that Ambedkar's "statues, dressed in garish blue, holding a copy of the Constitution—have been put up in city after city." However, this aesthetic distaste seems rather pointless. For the background to the statues and the reverence they command lies in the continuing social practices of the religion to which Shourie belongs. If caste lives, so will the memory of the man who fought to annihilate it. The remarkable thing is that 50 years after independence, the only politician, dead or alive, who has a truly pan-Indian appeal is B. R. Ambedkar. Where Gandhi is forgotten in his native Gujarat and Nehru vilified in his native Kashmir, Ambedkar is worshipped in hamlets all across the land. For Dalits everywhere he is the symbol of their struggle, the scholar, theoretician and activist whose own life represented a stirring triumph over the barriers of caste.

Shourie's attacks on Dalits and their hero follow in quick succession the books he has published attacking Communists, Christians and Muslims. Truth be told, the only category of Indians he has not attacked—and going by his present political persuasion will not attack—are high-caste Hindus. Oddly enough, this bilious polemicist and baiter of the minorities was once an anti-religious leftist who excoriated Hinduism. To see Shourie's career in its totality is to recall these words of Issac Deutscher, on the communist turned anti-communist.

He brings to his job the lack of scruple, the narrow-mindedness, the disregard of truth, and the intense hatred with which Stalinism has imbued him. He remains sectarian. He is an inverted Stalinist. He continues to see the world in black and white, but now the colours are differently distributed... The ex- communist... is haunted by a vague sense that he has betrayed either his former ideals or the ideals of bourgeois society... He then tries to suppress the guilt and uncertainty, or to camouflage it by a show of extraordinary certitude and frantic aggressiveness. He insists that the world should recognise his uneasy conscience as the clearest conscience of all. He may no longer be concerned with any cause except one-self-justification.

Ambedkar is a figure who commands great respect from one end of the social spectrum. But he is also, among some non-Dalits, an object of great resentment, chiefly for his decision to carve out a political career independent of and sometimes in opposition to Gandhi's Congress. That is of course the burden of Shourie's critique but curiously, the very week his book was published, at a political rally in Lucknow the Samajvadi Party's Beni Prasad Verma likewise dismissed Ambedkar as one who "did nothing else except create trouble for Gandhiji". This line, that Ambedkar had no business to criticise, challenge or argue with Gandhi, was of course made with much vigour and malice during the national movement as well.

However, for Ambedkar to stand up to the uncrowned king and anointed Mahatma of the Indian people required extraordinary courage and willpower. Gandhi thought so too. Speaking at a meeting in Oxford in October 1931, Gandhi said he had "the highest regard for Dr. Ambedkar. He has every right to be bitter. That he does not break our heads is an act of self- restraint on his part." Writing to an English friend two years later, he said he found "nothing unnatural" in Ambedkar's hostility to the Congress and its supporters. "He has not only witnessed the inhuman wrongs done to the social pariahs of Hinduism", reflected this Hindu, "but in spite of all his culture, all the honours that he has received, he has, when he is in India, still to suffer many insults to which untouchables are exposed." In June 1936 Gandhi pointed out once again that Dr. Ambedkar "has had to suffer humiliations and insults which should make any one of us bitter and resentful." "Had I been in his place," he remarked, "I would have been as angry."

Gandhi's latter-day admirers might question Ambedkar's patriotism and probity, but the Mahatma had no such suspicions himself. Addressing a bunch of Karachi students in June 1934, he told them that "the magnitude of (Dr. Ambedkar's) sacrifice is great. He is absorbed in his own work. He leads a simple life. He is capable of earning one to two thousand rupees a month. He is also in a position to settle down in Europe if he so desires. But he does not want to stay there. He is only concerned about the welfare of the Harijians."

To Gandhi, Ambedkar's protest held out a lesson to the upper castes. In March 1936 he said that if Ambedkar and his followers were to embrace another religion, "We deserve such treatment and our task (now) is to wake up to the situation and purify ourselves." Not many heeded the warning, for towards the end of his life Gandhi spoke with some bitterness about the indifference to Harijan among his fellow Hindus: "The tragedy is that those who should have especially devoted themselves to the work of (caste) reform did not put their hearts into it. What wonder that Harijan brethren feel suspicious, and show opposition and bitterness."

The words quoted in the preceding paragraphs have been taken from that reliable and easily accessible source: the Collected Works of Mahatma Gandhi. Perhaps the most perverse aspect of an altogether perverse book is that Shourie does not once tell us what Gandhi said or wrote about his great adversary. A curious thing or, on reflection, a not-so-curious thing: for if that scholarly courtesy was restored to, the case that Ambedkar was an anti-national careerist would be blown sky-high.

One of the few Gandhians who understood the cogency of the Dalit critique of the Congress was C. Rajagopalachari. In the second half of 1932, Rajaji became involved in the campaign to allow the so-called untouchables to enter the Guruvayoor temple in Kerala. The campaign was led by that doughty fighter for the rights of the dispossessed, K. Kelappan Nair. In a speech at Guruvayoor on December 20, 1932, Rajaji told the high castes that it would certainly help us in the fight for Swaraj if we open the doors of the temple (to Harijans). One of the many causes that keeps Swaraj away from us is that we are divided among ourselves. Mahatmaji received many wounds in London (during the Second Round Table Conference of 1931). But Dr. Ambedkar's darts were the worst. Mahatmaji did not quake before the Churchills of England. But as repressing the nation he had to plead guilty to Dr. Ambedkar's charges.

As it was, the managers of temples across the land could count upon the support of many among their clientele, the suvarna Hindus who agreed with the Shankaracharyas that the Gandhians were dangerous revolutionaries who had to be kept out at the gate. Unhappily, while upper-caste Hindus thought that Gandhi moved too fast, Dalits today feel he was much too slow. The Dalit politician Mayawati has, more than once, spoken of the Mahatma as a shallow paternalist who sought only to smooth the path for more effective long-term domination by the suvarna. Likewise, in his book Why I am Not a Hindu Kancha Illiah writes of Gandhi as wanting to "build a modern consent system for the continued maintenance of brahminical hegemony".

Whereas in their lifetime Gandhi and Ambedkar were political rivals, now, decades after their death, it should be possible to see their contributions as complementing one another's. The Kannada critic D. R. Nagaraj once noted that in the narratives of Indian nationalism the "heroic stature of the caste-Hindu reformer", Gandhi, "further dwarfed the Harijan personality" of Ambedkar. In the Ramayana there is only one hero but, as Nagaraj points out, Ambedkar was too proud, intelligent and self- respecting a man to settle for the role of Hanuman or Sugreeva. By the same token, Dalit hagiographers and pamphleteers generally seek to elevate Ambedkar by diminishing Gandhi. For the scriptwriter and the mythmaker there can only be one hero. But the historian is bound by no such constraint. The history of Dalit emancipation is unfinished, and for the most part unwritten. It should, and will, find space for many heroes. Ambedkar and Gandhi will do nicerly for a short.

CONSTRUCTING NATION AS FAMILY

If Mahatma Gandhi is an emblem of India and its place in history, it is not primarily because he had a political program or theory of the citizen but because he helped shape an image of the Indian individual in everyday life. The figure of the family was a keystone of Gandhi's symbology. He saw it as an institution crucial to the individual's life, to his or her struggle for "self-rule," as well as a metaphor that could be deployed as a political analog in the struggle for independence from foreign (British) rule. But the metaphor of the family was also the most vulnerable "punctum" of Gandhi's symbology.

This essay focuses on this discursive punctum to develop a critical conflict between Gandhi and the Dalit ("Depressed Classes") leader, Dr. B.R. Ambedkar, and in the course of doing so turns briefly to an example of Dalit writing. Both Gandhi and Ambedkar had recourse to the metaphor of the family, in their different and even directly opposed ways. Ambedkar, and the Dalits for whom he was a figurehead and leader, exploited the figure of the family as the weak point in the dominant discourse of the nation since at least Gandhi's time, within which they, the Dalits, were objected and oppressed.

Gandhi's use of the family metaphor can be critiqued, and indeed, was criticised by Ambedkar and his followers as an ultimately oversimple concept that not only underestimated the asymmetries of political power in the public sphere but covered over its own effective exclusion of the Dalits from the national family even as it employed the troupe of inclusiveness. Certainly it would be misguiding to overemphasize the political perplexities of the Mahatma's ideology and undervalue his moral stature or his lasting influence on the domestic discourse of Indian leaders such as Jawaharlal Nehru as well as on that of leaders in other places and in other times, such as Martin Luther King Jr. and Nelson Mandela.

It would be equally absurd to make exaggerated claims about the potential or actual political influence of a minority group such as the Dalits even under the leadership of the intellectually powerful Ambedkar. Nevertheless, fifty years after the birth of independent India, Ambedkar's contribution, and that of his intellectual inheritors, is at least as notable a milestone in the history of the secularist experiment in the most populous democracy in the world, as Ambedkar and the Dalits were pointing the way to an emergent or embryonic counterdiscourse of post-nationality against the model of the national family. After all, in the light of contemporary debates about the nation-state, such counter-discourses can be an index of citizenship in modern India.

The family was a linchpin of Gandhi's conceptualization of Swaraj or "self-rule"-and it mediated both his progressive ideas about nation and his conservative and almost Luddite ideas about the home. Gandhi distinguished between the negative-merely political, from Gandhi's viewpoint-effort to oust the British and the positive struggle to preserve the integrity of the national family and the integrity of the family man-that is, "self-rule" must mean not only political self-governance but also and more importantly spiritual and personal self-government (and this often involved quite a struggle, as many real and apocryphal stories about Gandhi suggest). His politics should be understood against this nexus of national and personal agendas, but it was also influenced by a desire to defend a Hindu social hierarchy traceable at least to the Manusmrifi, the Laws of Manu. In his early career, before his return from South Africa to India in 1915, his use of the metaphor of "family" was central to his own measure of personal and communal success. Especially anxious about the border between the public and the private, Gandhi was given to Utopian pronouncements in reference to the society at large, such as "We are all one family."

The true India for Gandhi was to be found in the "motherland's villages" and within the Hinduized family. He valorized the day communal life of the villages, metaphorically as well as literally the family, still relatively untouched by Western civilization. He counselled those "who love the motherland to go to the interior that has yet been not polluted... and to live there for six months"; they might then "be patriotic and speak of Home Rule." He did try to practice what he preached. If the family was where the struggle for self-rule began, then, as Gandhi explained in the Autobiography, ironically enough, one of the key self-disciplines for himself was brahmacharya (continence), which meant "relinquishing the desire for children and wealth and living the life of a vanaprastha—of one retired from household cares," someone who had moved beyond, or effectively renounced, the literal family for a larger conceptualization of community.

The notion of brabmachatya was tied to his notion of the ideal man, although Gandhi expressed frustration at his own failures in practising the vow of brahmacharya with his Wife, but he did not usually mention her attitude to his efforts, for instance in the area of sexual abstinence. What is important is to recognize that his frustrated attempt to transcend the messiness of his immediate family life did not attenuate his enthusiasm for the metaphor of the family in the service of a larger philosophical belief in the good of community, fellowship, and the collectivity of nation under the sign of Hindu divine sanction.

It was this amplified conceptualization of family that would be brought to bear not only on key notions of his moral thought derived from the Bhagavad Gita such as aparigraha (non-possession), sambhava (equability), and sarpodaya (the uplift of all) but also on his conception of sayagraha, as well as brahmacbarya.

After his rise to political prominence, the figure of the family emerged in less innocuous aspect, as it applied to women and to minorities, and particularly the Untouchables; and it became increasingly crucial to his nationalist thinking. This development is critical to an understanding of the increasing dissatisfaction with the compulsory normativity of the national family on the part of the Untouchables and Ambedkar especially.

Within the Gandhian rhetoric of the national family the Untouchables were, constituted as at once necessary to the anti-imperialist cause and dispensable in the actual institution of instantiation of the nation. They were a supplement to the national family. It is this supplementarity that some more recent Dalit prose tries to problematize, just as Slavoj Zizek helps us to see that Judas is in some ways the hero of the New Testament narrative because he is called upon to endure the harder self-objection and self-sacrifice, the outcaste in India can be recognized as in some ways the Judas of the chaturvarnya (four castes) system. The Brahmin at least can improve himself, earn divine credit, by his generosity and magnanimity toward everyone below him in the caste hierarchy. But the outcaste can only perpetuate his own objection within the system, and he must understand the ambivalence of his interpellation and the potential for subversion, even as he is enjoined by Gandhian or Nehruvian nationalistic discourse to join in the struggle for Swaraj. For he is a "symptom" in Zizek's sense:

Marx "invented the symptom" (Lacan) by means of detecting a certain fissure, an asymmetry, a certain "pathological" imbalance which belies the universalism of the bourgeois "rights and duties." This imbalance, far from announcing the "imperfect realization" of these universal principles-that is, an insufficiency to be abolished by further development-functions as their constitutive moment-the "symptom" is, strictly speaking, a particular element which subverts its own universal foundation, a species subverting its own genus. In this sense, we can say that the elementary Marxian procedure of "criticism of ideology" is already "symptomatic": it consists in detecting a point of breakdown hetergeneous to a given ideological field and at the same time necessary for that field to achieve its closure, its accomplished form.

It is in this sense that the compulsory embrace of the Untouchables within the Gandhian "family" subverts that family.

This invocation of Zizek is intended to underscore that "theoretical," and in particular psychoanalytic, approaches-far from being merely extraneous, metropolitan forms grafted onto a heterogeneous discourse—offer extremely productive ways of understanding the complex, and sometimes probably unconscious, motivations of Gandhi's mobilization of the discourse of family, and their continuing interest and relevance for contemporary India. The attempt here is to try to locate the conflict between Gandhi and Ambedkar in the context of contemporary (and especially post-colonial) cultural critique.

The Gandhian Man and the Gandhian Woman: Gandhi's ideal national citizen, his ideal paterfamilias, was the "Sarvodaya" man. For him the ideal man is anything but idle, for idleness is a "disease"-but activity, and above all the activity of spinning yarn, is never so noble as when not self-directed, but in the interest of the rest of the human family, or at least the nation as family. Gandhi himself put it quite starkly, combining several of his favourite themes: "Idleness is the great disease of India and the spinning wheel is the sole remedy for it." Idleness is thus quite distinct from passive resistance.

In Hind Swaraj, Gandhi had written that passive resistance is "a method of securing rights by not obeying unjust laws. It is a refusal to do a thing that is repugnant to the conscience." As Ravinder Kumar points out, this notion was a "genuingly Indian ideal," rooted in and taking its meaning from an Indian social reality. That meant the social reality of a country that was predominantly agrarian, a country in which people experienced a scarcity of resources, but it was also a country in which religious sentiment defined to a great extent political identity and behaviour, in which communal factionalisms were endemic; in which there were "sophisticated enclaves of industry in the social matrix"; and of course in which the imprint of the colonial experience was indelible and deep. But it also meant, that the Sarvodaya man was a complete man.

Kumar notes that Gandhi was under no delusions about the perfection of the human animal in India, Gandhi felt that a truly religious individual would not insist on rigid distinctions between the secular and the transcendental, but would allow religion to guide him or her in everyday matters, in a way such that home life was on a continuum with public life. Thus, the "Sarvodaya" man 'looked upon his wealth and intellectual capacities as a reservoir of resources which belonged to the community as a whole, but could only be used virtuously on the condition of the moral integrity of the individual's private and public action. Further, whatever an individual possessed, existed only by virtue of the fact that he was part of a larger community; and it was therefore legitimate that the community should be free to partake of the goods, tangible or intangible, available with its individual members." This was, then, a communitarian expansion of the idea of a man not as a social atom or monad but as a member of an extended "family."

Naturally, Gandhi's connection of the public and the private had political implications, for it is on this basis that he conceived of independent India on the model of a traditional Hindu household, with caste determining who married whom, with men and women in clearly demarcated positions, and religion guiding every action. It is instructive to compare the point made by Partha Chatterjee regarding the subaltern groups that he studies in The Nation and its Fragments, he observes that the subaltern call to collective resistance was never made in terms of self-interest but in terms of collective identity, of brotherhood. This rhetoric, according to Chatterjee, was effectively a disillusioned, resistant rhetoric against the alliance of "Modern Indian nationalism" as well as against the colonial power.

For Gandhi the annihilation of any sharp distinction between the inner and the outer, self and other, mine and yours, and ultimately of private and public was equally significant as a philosophical perspective on the modern man, as a challenge to the Enlightenment conception of the autonomous bourgeois individual. This challenge was consistent with Gandhi's philosophy more over general disaffection with modernity and all its appurtenances, something made abundantly clear in Hind Swaraj. He would come to give up modern ("Western") clothing and to embrace the spinning wheel as powerful symbolic gestures, for instance.

In Hind Swaraj, Gandhi's opposition to modern civilization was vigorously expressed" and India's submission to British Ride itself is expressed as owing to the corrupt desire in Indians for the fruits of modern commerce, fruits that the British had come bearing, recognizing that they were more powerful than the sword. In his view, India's subjugation to colonialism resulted not from losing an external battle but from a loss sustained in an internal war. It was, one might say, a family affair. Gandhi's rejection of "modernity" is evident in his conflict with Nehru, on the National Planning Committee meeting in 1938, over the issue of modernization. Chatterjee observes that Gandhi's archaicism-his opposition to industrialization as the cause of India's deprivation-had to be embraced in the anti-imperialist phase, but as the new national state was in the process of being conceptualized in the light of a developmental ideology Gandhi's anti-industrialism seemed a dangerous anachronism to Nehru and his practical partisans.

Even if they appealed to the masses, Gandhi's ideas of worthwhile occupations (such as spinning your own cloth) might well seem retrograde in an internationalist perspective. The Gandhian program of a religiously-based Swaraj risked consigning the new India once more to a pre-modem space-time, lending itself to the troupe of colonial discourse Anne McClintock dubs "anachronistic space."

Gandhi's rhetorical image of the nation as family also had, the unfortunate consequence of consigning women to a complementary role, because in his metaphorization of family as a figure for social/political relationships, the literal family is hollowed out, so that the place of women becomes relatively insignificant in the larger discourse of family in which Gandhi was interested. In Gandhi's work, as in Ambedkar's and in Dalit writing in general, they are trapped in the discursive space of the family and denied any real role in political and economic decisions on the national and the domestic levels respectively. Gandhi's views on women were largely traditional, despite his many acknowledged efforts to uplift Indian women and give them political voice.

To the extent they were emancipated, his views remained part of emergent discourse in which women were recuperated and contained as mothers and custodians of the National Thing—within what scholars such as Partha Chatterjee and Kamala Visveswaran have identified as a restructured patriarchal family deriving its authority from a projective anteriority: "ancient India." As Forbes says, "[m]ale guardianship prevailed even though the Indian freedom movement was not characterized by 'patriarchal nationalism.' Women could 'come out' because the house was on fire.

Family and Community: In the Philosophy of Right, Hegel wrote that "in its character as universal family, civil society has the right and duty of superintending and influencing education, inasmuch as education bears upon the child's capacity to become a member of society." For Hegel the family is ethical mind in "its natural or immediate phase...[and] specifically characterized by love, which is mind's feeling of its own unity... One is in it not as an independent person by as a member." I want to rethink family in terms of membership in a community, and I do so bearing in mind Partha Chatterjee's citation of this passage precisely to point to Hegel's reduction of family to the "determinate form of the bourgeois nuclear family" even as he theorizes the "universal family's" role in civil society. Chatterjee maintains that an independent narrative of community has been suppressed in modern European social theory. A similar displacement of actual community is the ironic effect of the Gandhian moralized landscape of family as (national) community.

Community, for Gandhi, signified an ideal, more than it did a practical telos. It seemed to have been, for him, less important to actually organize community, to think through the difficult task of articulating discrete communities under the larger umbrella of nation, than to speak grandly about community as such. His popular image notwithstanding, Gandhi did not like hoipolloi, the jostling millions (who he thought, at least in his earlier years as Mahatma, were ruled by nothing more than what the great soul denigrated as "mobocracy'). But Gandhi was not alone in this condescension. In the 1920s and 1930s, as Omvedt reminds us,

while liberals and conservatives alike (Gandhians on one side and Arya Samajists and Hindu Mahasabhites on the other) were wooing dalits with temple entry programmes, organizational efforts and proclaimed reforms, they saw this as nothing but a dangerous diversion from the presumably central "anti-imperialist struggle." It was an attitude shared by all the Left, from Nehru and the Congress Socialists to the Communists.

Not to put too fine a point on it, social activism on behalf of the Untouchables, such as on the temple entry issue, was not the most pressing concern for Gandhi or other prominent leaders of the time, although it certainly played an important ideological role in Gandhi's public rhetoric.

Ambedkar himself had pointed out that the Temple Entry Bill of February 14, 1933, "does not regard Untouchability in temples as a sinful custom. It regards Untouchability merely as a social/evil not necessarily worse than social evils of other sorts....Its binding force is taken away, only, if a majority decides to do so." He noted that Gandhi had, before 1932, opposed allowing Untouchables to enter Hindu temples and that only when the Poona Pact of September 24, 1932 between caste Hindus and "Depressed Classes" was signed that Gandhi "took somersault," reversing his earlier position possibly because he sensed the occasion to add to his "name and fame, and rushed to make the most of it, as is his habit."

One can argue that in Gandhi's rhetoric as well as in contemporary elite nationalist discourse, it is primarily a sanitized notion of community that enters the discursive space nationalism wishes to occupy. Yet, at just this period, Chatterjee writes, "the possibilities of opposition as well as encapsulation arise because the concepts of the individual and the nation-state both become embedded in a new grand narrative: the narrative of capital. The narrative of capital seeks to suppress that other narrative of community and produce in the course of its Journey both the normalized individual and the modern regime of disciplinary power."

Chatterjee notes that the "destruction of community" and particularly pre-capitalist community was a premise for a global narrative of universal progress to take shape, which disguises or transforms the "violence of mercantilist trade, war, genocide, conquest and colonialism" into the story of civilization's progress." Capitalism feeds on "the reconstructed particularism of the nation." Anti-colonialist nationalist movements are a clear example of the contradictions between narratives of capital and community. One cannot underestimate the deliberateness with which Gandhi himself deployed the image of the nation-as-family as a keynote of his message, and he himself as its main support.

As a rhetorical strategy, and even as a policy of governmentality, it was not, however, unique to Gandhi. Chatterjee offers the example of Keshabchandra Sen (1838-84), who established a communal living arrangement he called "a modem apostolic organization." Here a number of Brahmo Samaj families were invited to share expenses and "the spiritual and educational advantages of the institution." At the foundation of this institution was Keshab's conviction that as a civilization India could learn much from the "ideas of neatness, order, punctuality and domestic devotions, which form such striking features in a well-regulated middle-class English home"-in other words, the basic metaphor for civilized national life in Keshab's model was already the idea of a well-organized family life, something very close to, though of course earlier than, Gandhi's own vision.

Gandhi, like Keshab, was trying to move the country toward what Chatterjee characterizes as "an authentic Indian religion of modernity" because of a shared belief that "far more than the strength of British arms" it was the alien ideals of reason and "rational religion" that engendered the "moral fôrce" responsible for holding India in the thrall of colonialism." He makes the important observation that recent Indian historiography has theorized the parliamentary and "public" as the domain of "elite" politics, and the communitarian and the private as the domain of "subaltern" politics. But each has "shaped the emergent form of the other." Developing this point, he writes that "the task is to trace in their mutually conditioned historicities the specific forms that have appeared, on the one hand, in the domain defined by the hegemonic project of nationalist modernity, and on the other, in the numerous fragmented resistances to that normalizing project.

Rama did not (as Gandhi saw it) give up his family ties. Rather, he showed how great a store he set by justice in leaving Sita-as a gesture of self-denial that only raises the worth of Sita and the family and attests the more powerfully to Rama's fidelity as a family man—As Gandhi goes on to say, "By his strict monogamy [Ramal showed that a life of perfect self-restraint could be led by a royal householder.... He lent splendour to his throne by his popular administration and proved that Ramarajya was the acme of Swaraj... Such Ramarajya is possible even today." Yet Gandhi's rather innocuous vision has lent itself to a much more sinister and exclusivist construction in present-day India, notably under the BJP's socialism, which has become an umbrella for a host of such reworkings of Gandhian nostrums-particularly, the question of untouchabilty and of caste in general.

Fondly and Tradition: It is hardly surprising that it is on the issue of how the issue of caste is thematized that Dalit groups have found it necessary to reject Hindutva. Walter Benjamin observed that a key feature of the nineteenth century's industrial capitalism was the access to "archaic images to identify what was new about the 'nature' of commodities." Several writers have picked up on this theme of the nation as Janus-faced, including Horni Bhabha who writes that nations "like narratives, lose their origins in the myths of time and only fully realize their horizons in the mind's eye.

But it is less frequently emphasized that the temporal contradiction is projected onto an axis of othering, be it gendered or classed, or in the Indian case, a function of caste. That is to say, if the past of the nation has to be constructed retrospectively to give historical depth to the claim of nationness, then that past is often embodied at aviastically in the contemporary body of the low classes or preferably the outcastes.

Today reference to the Indian past often bolsters immemorialist claims made on behalf of Hindutva to rationalize the rising communalist animus against Sikhs and Muslims, as if they were pariahs to the national family. But the outcastes, the Dalits, have experienced similar animosities. Leading up to and after the 1992 destruction of the Babri Masjid in Ayodhya, especially, a vicious rhetoric of the family has been deployed by Hindu extremists, but also by ordinary people, the media, and academics.' This rhetoric often sets in motion a vicious cycle of reciprocation. As Omvedt notes, the immemorialism of an ancient Hindu India undergirding Hindu majoritarianism has been countered by the Dalits with corresponding family mythologies of their own aboriginal identities-"adi" ideologies that construct the Dalits as the original inhabitants and the Brahmins as the interlopers."

As Chatterjee writes in Nationalist Thought and the Colonial World, the "unique achievement of Gandhism" was "its ability to open up the possibility for achieving perhaps the most important historical task for a successful national revolution in a country like India, *viz.*, the political appropriation of the subaltern classes by a bourgeoisie aspiring for hegemony in the new nation-state." This double-edge appropriation was at one level a political coup, a strategy deployed cynically by some leaders of the anti-inperialist opposition. If one takes Gandhi's position in the best possible light, it could be seen as a morally rationalized position rather than brazen exploitation, and Gandhi seemed to have understood and taken to heart a more general metaphor of the family, articulated powerfully by Hannah Arendt:

> *Mankind, for so long a time considered under the image of a family of nations, had reached the stage where whoever was thrown out of one of these tightly organized closed communities found himself thrown out of the family of nations altogether...the abstract nakedness of being nothing but human was their greatest danger.*

Indeed Gandhi acknowledged the even greater danger, namely the effective refusal of human status to some people such as the "harijans," whom only God and Gandhi seemed to be- willing to embrace.

But a less generous reading of Gandhi's motives was already being offered by his contemporary Ambedkar. He cited Gandhi's conflation of the moral and the political in a warning he published in Young India on December 29, 1920: "If Hindus do not remove the sin of untouchability, there will be no Swaraj.... Swaraj is unattainable without the removal of the sins of untouchability as it is without Hindu-Muslim unity."" Ambedkar glosses Gandhi's position in very disillusioned language, saying that Gandhi, who "had laid stress, ever since he entered Congress, upon the intimate relation between the winning of Swaraj and the abolition of Untouchability" had also regrettably 'learned to find unction in illusions" and suggests throughout that Gandhi's real aims were to secure his own individual stature and the Hindu nation's sovereignty."

For Nehru and other politicians of the time, in any case, Gandhi's was above all a rhetorical gesture that shared at best a fantasy connection with the realpolitik of nation-making, and did not require a material commitment to really include those subalterns. The inclusion of the Harijans into the "family" as metaphor for nation did not entail or result in political and social inclusion in institutional terms in the post-colonial period. Clearly, Gandhi recognized he needed Muslim and Depressed Classes' support in the noncooperative struggle for Swaraj.

But the Depressed Classes occupied a structurally different situation in the national family, and, given his understanding of the theory of caste and Untouchability, which leant heavily on the Gita, Gandhi could not extend equal and separate status to the Untouchables. Gandhi's invocation of the figure of the national family, even as it sympathetically embraced the Harijans, had a hard edge: "my intimate acquaintance with every shade of Untouchability,' he intoned, "convinces me that their lives, such as they are, are so intimately mixed with those of the caste Hindus in whose midst and for whom they live, that it is impossible to separate them. They are part of an indivisible family." This use of the family metaphor betrays all the anxiety of what in Lacanian language one might call extimite. They were for Gandhi "Just like us" (familiar) but could never be "completely like us" (familial, intimate).

In deploying this contradictory intimacy covering over radical difference, caste Hindus recognized that the outcastes were extrinsic to Varnashrama, the institution of caste, yet necessary to ensure its coherence. The Untouchables' intimate connection with themselves was a source of great anxiety This might partly explain Gandhi's sympathetic but anxiously doubled rhetoric decrying Untouchability but preserving the caste system (albeit by 1935 he distinguished caste from varna)." His cultivated attitude to Untouchability was a kind of fetish, necessary to maintain his foundational performative of "Bapu"—the "father" of the outcaste children of God, his "Harijans." Without the inferior castes, the superiority of the upper castes would become meaningless: it is instructive to recall analogously Slavoj Zizek's observation that it is the servant/ subject who legitimized or even constitutes the master.

In his study of the Poona Pact of 1932, Kumar writes that "Gandhi stressed that the upper caste and the Untouchable communities were tied to each other in such intimate social and economic bonds, that their severance would cause an upheaval of disastrous proportions within the macrocosm no less than the microcosm of Hinduism" (Masselos 98). Kumar's analysis suggests that the political is cast in terms of "intimate social and economic bonds." This humanization of the political is founded on a conception of the relationship of upper castes and Untouchables within the national family. This was not Just a vapid generalization but had material import. The Muslims during that time were not included in the metaphorical "family" in quite the same way by Gandhi-they were, as Kumar goes on to say, "the position of the Untouchables was radically different from that of the Muslims. Unlike the latter, the Untouchables constituted an organic part of Hindu society, howsoever lowly be the position which they occupied within it." The Minorities Pact of November 13, 1931 incensed Gandhi by recognizing the Untouchables as "a separate political entity-"

In short, it is in the light of the psychoanalytic frame one has to sketched above that we can best grasp why Gandhi—otherwise an exemplarily even-tempered and gentle apostle of peace-so vehemently rejected Ambedkar's demand for separate and equal status, for disavowal of the caste system to accompany the eradication of Untouchability. Gandhi's exclusion-and-inclusion of the Untouchables had a different psychic investment than did the official move of, for instance, providing Scheduled Caste members ministerial posts and preferential treatment as a matter of policy in schools and other institutions.

After all, it was not justa matter of political principle that made Gandhi so obdurate; it was nothing less than a deep psychical investment. Not surprisingly, however, the tension between Gandhi and Ambedkar manifested itself in the issue of political representation. As Teresa Hubel notes, Ambedkar equally vehemently rejected Gandhi's claim that he alone could represent the Untouchables. Particularly, Ambedkar objected strenuously to Gandhi's claim at the second session of the Round Table Conference of 1931 organized by the British." Mincing no words, he declared,

"A worse person could not have been chosen to guide India's destiny. As a unifying force he was a failure. Mr. Gandhi presents himself as a man full of humility. But his behaviour at the Round Table Conference [of November 12,1930] showed that. Mr. Gandhi can be very pettyminded.... He insulted [the non-Congress delegation whenever an occasion furnished him with an excuse by openly telling them that they were nobodies and that he alone, as the delegate of the Congress, represented the country."

Perhaps even more remarkable than the arrogation of leadership and presumption of being able to speak for his Harijans was the sense that in the "family" envisaged by Gandhi, in the passage quoted above, the Untouchables lived "for" the "caste Hindus," that their lives, "such as they are" were not for themselves but for other, superior people. This unidirectional dependency was understandably a major point of contention for the Untouchables- While "Bapu" proclaimed his desire to remove the stain of Untouchability from Hinduism, Ambedkar sensed that he could not countenance its literal dissolution. My interest is in the discursive manipulation of the sign of the fetishized Other as well as its occulted role in the performative of "Bapu" as (phallic) paterfamilias in the national family romance." As Gyanendra Pandey suggests, "Gandhi" along with "the people" became interchangeable "symbols of the nationalist essence, the Indian spirit."

In an argument that would have elicited the condemnation of the anti-arboreal philosophers Deleuze and Guattari, Gandhi endorsed the chaturvarnya as the grand trunk of the tree of Hindu India. Responding to an objection that "every attempt to remove Untouchability without ending the caste idea will prove as futile as attempting to cut off a tree at the top," Gandhi made it clear he had no intention of rooting out chaturvarnya, asserting its "universal application." The "fault" he said "does not... lie in recognizing the law of heredity and transmission of qualities from generation to generation, but it lies with the fault conception of inequality." This was his view even in the 1920s, precisely the turbulent postwar period, as Omvedt reminds us, of a "qualitative leap forward" in Dalit organization, spurred particularly by the Montagu-Chelmsford reforms of 1919. In this connection, another milestone in Dalit organization would be the Maoist Naxalite movement-and appositely, Omvedt diagnoses the Dalit project as aimed at felling the tree, citing an example from the Dalit-based Naxalite uprising that reinserts the Dalit body back into a revised and history, a man's body that dissents from the reigning national narrative of manhood and citizenship:

This man has risen from the grave: he seems to have gone berserk and is frensiedly chopping the branches of feudalism. His desire is to see that 2500-year old tree felled here and now. So far he has only been humiliated, whipped and slain, denied the status of a man; his wife treated as a prostitute. Then somebody brought him news of Naxalbari and things began to change. The Harijan died, the Koeri was burnt; the new man who rose from the flames felt that he was neither a Harijan not a Koeri but a man.

It need scarcely be insisted that the figure of the social order as a tree is homologous with the image of the family as tree.

Although anti-caste movements predated Naxalite and Marxist resistance in India, at the time of the Independence struggle, the Marxists regarded the Dalit resistance as a distraction. From Ambedkar's viewpoint the chief enemy had never been the British; in some ways the Europeans had shown it to be possible to resist the ossified regime of the upper castes and feudal powers of pre-colonial India." Besides, Ambedkar considered the "class" approach inadequate to the problem of caste," from which neither Nehruvian secularism nor Gandhian Ramarajya promised succour." So while he himself was anti-imperialist, he knew he risked the (groundless) charge of complicity or treason.

Of course some Dalit factions favoured Hinduistic integration. Scholars such as Omvedt have pointed to the examples of Kisan Faguji Bansode, G.A. Gaval, and their adherents. But most Dalits took Ambedkar, with his links to Phule's Satyashodak movement, as their leader. He pointed a way for Dalits, as ex-Untouchables, to refuse, as he put it, to die Hindu even if they were born Hindu, by renouncing Hinduism for Buddhism." In a 1927 speech at Mahad Ambedkar made an extended comparison of the Dalits' goals with those of the French National Assembly of 1789. For he wanted fraternity, not family, beyond the national he cited Paul and the Pilgrim Fathers as expressing the fraternal equality in "blood" and "body" of all people beyond national boundaries. He can therefore be regarded as an anarchist, pleading for an India that was not co-terminous with "Hindustan."

Ambedkar's own recourse to the figure of the family in his oppositional (anti-Gandhian) rhetoric was thus a kind of shared notion. He touched on the most problematic knot between the familial narratives of domestic and national spaces when he proposed the Occam's razor of intermarriage: "If we want to remove Untouchability in the home as well as outside, we must break down the prohibition against intermarriage. Nothing else will serve... we see that breaking down the bar against intermarriage is the way to establish real equality." He also developed the family metaphor in arguing that Untouchability is the "mother of all our poverty and lowliness," and recognized that since "the... nation is the mother source of sovereignty" and citizen rights "cannot be acknowledge as valid on any other ground," only a kind of anarchich postnationalist paradigm could enable independent self-determination for the Dalit family, for sublatern men and women. But Ambedkar could not bring himself to develop that option full and officially. It remained nascent or emergent, just as his struggle with the nation's "Father" and the family romance remained unresolvable.

The family romance is understandably ironized in Dalit writing A recent collection edited by Arjun Dangle is a good example' of the ironic imbrication of the discourses of family and nation. It evidences, first, a sense of betrayal of the Dalits, as sons of the soil, by their motherland, and, second, a disillusionment with the idea of the nation as a unitary family A primary goal of the Dalits was to reject the entire system in which they were only nominally "included" and domesticated (in every sense of the word) as instruments of other interests. There is a frequent expression of disenchantment with the dominant sign of the national. For instance, Bhimrao Shirwale's short story "Lively hood" in the collection dramatizes a character's disdain for the "speeches" of "national leaders" that only move them toward a radical amorality, a path "cut[ting] clean through good and bad, wicked and evil, right and wrong, ending in another world altogether." This character, one of the many in the story who move beyond good and evil, is ironically and allegorically named "Dharma"- roughly "Law" or "Righteousness"-and his wife is equally ironically named "Kashi,'" recalling Hinduism's holiest city, Benares." The story suggests that the Dalit body is subjected to police brutality, which stamps out any incentive for the subaltern to "live straight"; it is a world in which patriarchal convention can support a man's legal claims against those of a woman and mother, no matter how patently unjust those claims-an injustice that the story suggests is a redoubled burden on the already legally dispossessed subaltern woman."

What can appeals to family values and to allegorical motherhood mean to a subaltern beyond the pale of truly participatory citizenship? A third theme, imaginative separatism, is represented by Bapurao Jagtap's poem, "The Country Is Broken," in which the speaker exhorts his Dalit brothers, "Let us go to some country, brother /... where, when you die, there will at least be / a cemetery to receive you." Sharankumar Limbale's "White Paper" has a similarly post-national apocalyptic promise: "My rights," he proclaims, "are rising like the sun." Or consider Baburao Bagul's bitter "salute" to "Those who leave for foreign lands, / embrace other tongues, dress in alien grab / and forget this country"; he counsels the

Untouchables "who have made the mistake of being born in this country" to "either leave the country,/ or make War!

But most explicitly of all, the eponymous autobiography, Bandhumadhav's "The Poisoned Bread," reads like an anti-nationlist manifesto, against the whole social system. Bandhumadhav expresses the imperative that the Harijans "must free ourselves from... land-bondage and learn to live independently." That the word for the Dalits here is explicitly Gandhi's term, and that the villain of this vignette of a feudal society is called "Bapu" (like Gandhi himself) are features that emphasize the collection's ironic tone and point to its unifying theme of an internal deslabik. Zadon of the constitutive binaries of state and society: Hindu/ non-Hindu, us ("family") versus them ("aliens"). The Dalits occupy a necessary liminality, at once defining and disturbing the nation's space from within, in what remains an incomplete post-colonial and post-independence struggle for independence from the state." The collection reflects the Dalits' assertions of solidarity and readiness for even violent subversion, and the lived experience of what Prasenjit Duara calls the instability of national identities.'"

Samuel Weber writes of Walter Benjamin's valorization of the "extreme" as hermeneutically efficacious in reading the "empirical." Benjamin's insight may apply to the Dalits, whose "extremity" or subalternity is a wedge splitting, from within, the dominant rhetoric of citizenship and national life and bringing into crisis the question of subject constitution through the eruption of dissident subjectivity within the interstices of nation and family relatedly, Dipesh Chakrabarty usefully provides a general definition of the subaltern as that very figure who "fractures from with in the signs that tell of the insertion of the historian (as a speaking subject) into the global narratives of capital"; that is why it is important to insist on the proto-postnational impulse in Dalit writing.

Dalit writing properly is interested in rejecting, not merely adding to and refining, tradition. It thematizes the urgent "need for new myths" to counter the oppressive mythology of Ramarajya, where violence has frequently been elevated to nationally emblematic heroism. Thus Baburao Bagul mordantly remarks that "the hero who disgraced Sita and Shurpankha, who burnt down the Khandava-vana" has been "celebrated" in the holy scriptures and temples, and revered as a "mythical ideal." This call for a new, postnational mythology is echoed by A.N. Wankhade, president of the conference of Dalit writers represented in the Dangle collection: "There is an intimate relationship between literature and myth, and because the Dalit writer has rejected non-Dalit literature"-as well as having been de facto cast out of national citizenship, one could add-" the absence of myths and tradition has created a vacuum in his writing. It is necessary to create new myths to fill this vacuum."

If Wai-chee Dimock is right that the imperial self is an iteration of national culture, then the ontology of the self reiterates in a sense the ontology of the nation. For Dimock, the "Imperial self" in consciousness as well as in conduct is "once autonomous and impregnable... quite literally empire-like, his province akin to national polity."" To refract the metaphor, it follows too that the sovereignty of the self is constructed analogously with the sovereignty of the nation. And the crisis of the Dalit subject, insofar as it is a crisis of the meaning of the self as citizen, requires on the one hand a deconstruction of the dominant rhetorics of belonging, whether to nation or to nationally endorsed domestic and public life.

On the other hand, the crisis requires an affirmation of a different register of subjectivity, however, this is not just the eruption of the irrational and of affective subjectivity against the ratio of the nation, pace Veena Das's suggestion that affectivity is Imperative for the subaltern and pace Homi Bhabha's concurrence that this affectivity could enable subaltern consciousness to "emerge as relocation and reinscription" can be argue here as elsewhere that it is crucial to preserve the unpredictable and enigmatic possibilities of dissident subjectivity. But Dalits like other subalterns have often been constructed as merely visceral, incapable of rationality and intellect. This is confined by no less a student of subalternity than Ranajit Guha, in his magisterial argument in "The Prose of Counter-Insurgency." Writing about peasant insurgency in colonial India, Guha vigorously rejects the "myth, retailed so often by careless and irnpressionistic writing on the subject, of peasant insurrections being purely spontaneous and unpremeditated affairs."

This myth is part of a narrative that assimilates peasant revolts to natural phenomena: they break out like thunder storms, heave like earthquakes, spread like wildfires, infect like epidemics. In other words, when the proverbial clod of earth turns, this is a matter to be explained in terms of natural history. Even when this historiography is pushed to the point of producing an explanation in rather more human terms it will do so by assuming an identity of nature and culture, a hallmark, presumably, of a very low state of civilization.

Alternatively, rebellion is presented as a "sort of reflex action... as an instinctive and almost mindless response to physical suffering of one kind or another (*e.g.*, hunger, torture, forced labour, etc.) or as a passive reaction to some initiative of his superordinate enemy." An uncritical endorsement of affectivity could risk entrenching such stereotypes.

Omvedt rightly says that "the Dalit movement and the overall radical anti-caste movements were a crucial expression of the democratic revolution in India, more consistently democratic-and in the end more consistently 'nationalistic'-than the elite-controlled Indian National Congress." In the same vein Chatterjee notes that nationalism in India is not founded so much on sameness with the, modular" forms of European nationalism (according to Benedict Anderson, nationalists must look to European models to "Imagine" their "communities" in narrativizing their nationalisms. It is based rather on difference with modern Western nationalism. This is true a fortiori of subaltern forms of nationalism, sometimes dissenting from mainstream nationalism even in post-colonial history.

The Dalits' fragmentary and embryonic post-nationalism-not quite "micro-nationalism", promises different (and not just Western-derived) ways of accounting for subjectivity: diaspora, enigma, transnation, postnation—but also local anarchies. Ironically there were anarchic tendencies in both Gandhi and Ambedkar, but neither was able or willing fully to articulate these tendencies. Adjacent to the family metaphor, Gandhi's notion of Ramarajya retails an individualist ethos, rather than a model of social cohesion: a "state of enlightened anarchy in which each person will become his own ruler.

In an ideal State there will be no political institution and therefore no political power." Gandhi envisaged an ideal beyond a statist form, but this ideal turned out to be ultimately a moralized anarchy, not an open matrix of possibilities for all. Ambedkar for his part was explicit about his disillusionment with the dominant model of Indian citizenship-witness his 1931 remark to Gandhi: "Mahatmaji, I have no country." Ambedkar tries to describe the something else besides the national dominant, which he also attempts to dissolve. "For words such as society, nation and country," he writes, "are just amorphous if not ambiguous terms.

There is no gainsaying that 'nation' though one word means many classes. Philosophically, it may be possible to consider a nation as a unit but sociologically it cannot but be regarded as consisting of many classes and the freedom of the nation...must vouchsafe the freedom of the different classes comprised in it.... "Admitting that Ambedkar was much more radical in the 1930s than in the '40s and '50s, is it too much to suggest that his ideas hinted at a post-nationality avant la lettre?

Ambedkar felt a nation-state built upon the caste system would "crack and never be whole" and looked forward to a time when the very form of "the State" would "wither away." Paradoxically, such a post-statist anarchy was unrecognisable from his conceptual and discursive horizon, which remained circumscribed by the national paradigm as a demand for constitutional guarantees. Arguing for national unity, he could only tentatively and ambivalently allude to something he described as a truly "democratic" order but one in which the "exteriority" of the Untouchables is respected. Their exteriority is at once physical, social, and psychical: they "continue to live on the outskirts of the Hindu village, as an alien people." Stressing separateness to the late and crucial date of 1947 he voiced the Untouchable demand that they "be made separate geographically and territorially" with "safeguards."

What then was to be their citizen status? Could something benign take the place of the State-a Nehruvian secular industrialist Utopia? Anarchy? He settled for Buddhism as the best substitute for the State, with a mass conversion of 500,000 Dalits to Buddhism in 1956, just before his death. This was a disappointing half-measure of resistance, because the conversion was politically ineffectual.

Despite the Buddhist "revival" in India in the late nineteenth century, despite the organized strength of Buddhism as represented by the Maha Bodhi society based in Calcutta since 1892, despite the consolidation of the Buddhist constituency by the time of the 1956 World Fellowship of Buddhists Fourth Conference in Nepal, Buddha's birthplace, despite the Independent Indian government is official recognition of the Buddhist heritage through the publication of 2500 Years of Buddhism, and despite the exile of the Dalai Lama and the exodus of 80,000 Buddhist Tibetans into India, Buddhism had little impact on the political life of the Indian public sphere, and remained epiphenomenal to the national family.

Around the period of organized Indian nationalism, the complex history of shifting religious alliances—of massive attempts at conversion (such as Ambedkar's own efforts) and re-conversion-is a crucial context for the study of the micropolitics of power between and among minoritarian and majoritarian groups.

The argument is that a post-national Indian identity beyond the Hindu nation is already beginning to be articulated in Ambedkar's work, and recognized in more recent Dalit writing such as that collected in the Dangle collection, but while it suggestively anticipates post-national discourse, it appears in only emergent form, and is worth considering because it complicates the assumption that post-nationalism or even the discourse of micro-nationalism are strictly contemporary post-World War II notions developed in the West and only derivatively available to the rest.

The Dalits' impulses to imagine a way of belonging to community or family beyond the parameters of the British Raj and beyond the parameters that would emerge from Indian (Hindu) nationalism are significant not because they were politically effective alternative models of modern citizenship.

Emergent post-riationalisms are interesting in this connection because they counter the notion of subaltern groups being "incapable of acting on [their] own and impelled to rise, when [they did], only by economic motivation." They are interesting precisely because they are exorbitant, outside both the imperial and the dominant Indian narratives of the nation or national family or transitional phenomena, like Teilhard de Chardin's "peduncles."

Although they were emblematic in their emergent post-nationalist impulses, the Dalits were not alone in their dissidence. For instance, Tanika Sarkar has written about the attempts of the leader of another minority constituency, Jitu Santal, to register in 1932, fifteen years before Independence, a "tribal protest" against the status quo that was not subsumed into but was parallel to the dominant domestic resistance to the British Raj: "Jitu... called himself Gandhi declared the end of British Raj and proclaimed his own government." But Jitu's "association with a Hinduization movement and the Swarajists had created some sympathetic interest among—nationalistic Hindus."

Sarkar's analysis cautions that often the perspective of the participants themselves drops out of any external scrutiny of such dissident impulses. But an underlying principle is precisely why it is important to look at Ambedkar's own opinions as expressed in his writings as put in relief by their juxtaposition with the opinions and writings of the relatively far more prominent Mahatma Gandhi. It does not means that Ambedkar was more remarkable than, say, Muslim League leader Muhammad Ali jinnah or Subhas Chandra Bose in his dissidence, or more salient a figure than Nehru (who was at least as much a "frustrated visionary" as Gandhi himself, in his own secularist way, of the failed "tryst with destiny"-the failed vision of an egalitarian society).'" It is not to exaggerate neither Ambedkar's importance in the overall struggle for Independence nor to underestimate Gandhi's ethical force, political importance, or strategic brilliance as a nationalist leader who had some understanding of the geopolitics of the Indian struggle for self-rule. But to suggest that Ambedkar too had something to say about ethics, politics, and the national and the post-national-even if what he had to say was not disseminated as effectively as it might have been.

While Ambedkar drew on Western ideas, particularly the Marxist critics of colonialism," his arguments were peculiar to the Indian context, and rarely was he able consciously articulate an internationalist or pro to-post-nationalist view of the Dalit struggle (his comparison of the Dalit struggle with the struggle of American blacks is a notable exception). Besides, the models of post-nationalist discourse in the current sense, along with what Omvedt calls the tradition of decentralized socialism, were unavailable to him. So while he rejected the Hindu state, he was ultimately unable to move decisively beyond the dimly conceived hope for a regenerated and transfigured Indian nation, beyond a statist utopia.

Contemporary irredentist post-nationalist discourse cannot be understood outside the context of the world capitalist system, a system into which, as Omvedt points out, India was integrated along with the rest of Asia and Africa between 1750 and 1850, with the traditional landmark dates being 1757 (the battle of Plassey) and 1857 (when the East India Company gave way to the British imperial state and the first "war of independence" was fought)-and Ambedkar and the Dalit movement gesture toward this larger context.

As Chatterjee notes, "Contrary to the largely uninformed exoticization of nationalism" in popular Western media, nationalism in India meant self-assertion for a recently decolonized people. Yet the sign of the "nation" is not everywhere homogeneously a sign of empowerment. Rajni Kothari observes that if in post-Enlightenment futurist thinking it was believed that everyone could share in the fruits of (Western models of) national development, now it is clear that this optimism is not universal.'" And this is important to remember because the pattern is in fact a tradition of subaltern resistance that has informed more recent writing and other cultural work of those who are still excluded from full citizenship and from "unresented" access to Indian institutions and public office. (Note: Resentment has been expressed against "Scheduled Castes" being given the equivalent of a quota for access to educational institutions and for positions in government agencies and offices.)

The scheduled castes are no doubt given special consideration in college admissions and civil service jobs, but this "affirmative action" has been attacked more fiercely than affirmative action efforts in the United States. They would appear to fit Kothari's description of the "dispensability thesis"— that "certain States, communities and regions have become an unacceptable burden on the world economy" Ambedkar's intervention is a precedent for envisaging an exteriority beyond the ideological state apparatus of the family, and the Ambedkar-led Dalit revolution manque offers a less ambivalent though emergent sense of self-determination in a post-national, profane family contrasting with the moralized Gandhian nation-as-family. A space may be opened again between majoritarian, homely, "Heimlich" maneuvers, and the something else that the Dalits themselves could not fully conceive: an unheimlich or uncanny home in an increasingly globalized transnational or post-national future.'" Instead of a model of inclusion within or exclusion from a monolithic and normative national narrative, the Dalit dissenting voice speaks the "extreme," in the Benjaminian phrase, prior to and simultaneously beyond such a narrative.

Instead of a unified nationalist narrative of a heterosexual, Hindu, nation, the Dalit positionality invokes a model of a fragmented cultural economy in which geographical space is not confused with domestic or national space-the nation assimilated to a reconstructed familial narrative from the Mahabharata, say- is not unproblematically mapped onto the geographical subcontinent. The issue of the limits of the modern Indian nation has become, if anything, more salient in contemporary India. The history of the fragment can be honoured in the breach of the modern national narrative, but it promises a different account of the politics of rights and responsibilities that are not governed entirely by a centralized state. It also points to a kind of enlightened anarchism, where an ecologically sound lifestyle becomes definable according to local or minority agendas, and where an ethics of everyday life becomes possible—one that is respectful of the minority populations as well. It thus allows for the eruption of other, local systems, temporalities, or futures, so that, instead of the dream of a unitary nation in which differences and ironed out or ignored, contingent alliances and solidarities adequate for civic life become conceivable. Such an alternative to the conservative status quo was not always imaginable in India for even left-learning groups.

Dalits refuse the role they have been asked to occupy-at least since the time of Gandhi: the role of proletarians who accommodate themselves docilely into the "family"—doing the dirty domestic chores of the servant without demanding a place at the family table. In a literal and mundane sense, Ambedkar was agitating for simple privileges denied his people, such as "interdining" and intermarriage, privileges that are guaranteed by any true inclusion into a family, broadly understood. As he asked pointedly, "Who can say that the Untouchables have not sufficient justification for refusing to participate in the Congress' 'Fight for Freedom'?" Critical of Hindu responses throughout history to various invasions and foreign rule, Ambedkar notes that until the "advent of the British," the Untouchables too were "content to remain Untouchables"; under British rule it was British education in the army that awakened the Untouchables to the continuing political and social inequities they could look forward to as members of the great family of a Hindu-controlled India.

Ambedkar was obviously aware of some local models for Dalit autonomy short of another Partition, pre-eminently the autonomy enjoyed by the princely states in India under the provisions of the federal constitution of the 1935 Government of India Act. But the princely states had bargaining power whereas the Dalits did not. After Independence, Nehru fixed the nation-state, as Sunil Khilnani has written recently "at the core of India's society." The state "etched itself into the imagination of Indians in a way that no previous political agency had ever done." It is the post-national that points beyond the "misshapen muscularity of the state... strong in certain respects but feeble in others." Beyond the oppressively singularist national history of a consanguineous "family" shimmers the Foucauldian idea of emancipatory possibilities emerging from within discontinuties in the national narrative without actually forming new states, as in the Partition of 1947. Community may be fostered even in a plurarized sphere of local or Iobal kin ships, under the sign of an unthought-of "democracy."

Is this a future that can never arrive? Would it mean to imagine a future beyond the nation-state? Recently, there has been some provocative debate about this issue, perhaps nowhere more elegantly developed than in the work of Etienne Balibar.

Balibar, who, unlike Ambedkar, has access to recent theoretically sophisticated thinking on the nation form—such as that of Fernand Braudel and Immanuel Wallerstein-is able to speak of the "field of the reproduction of nations, of the deployment of the nation form" as having entered the "phase of the decomposition of national structures which were connected with the old forms of its domination...." Today, "it is the state which draws up and keeps the archives of Nadons and alkances" and "penetrate[s]" family relations so that resisting the ideological interpellation of the subject/citizen as a member of the national family has a special urgency for the minoritized or subaltern citizen. Moving beyond the nation state, through what psychoanalysis would call the imaginary into the symbolic register, can therefore be a promising goal:

Every "people," which is the product of a national process of ethnicization, is forced today to find its own means of going beyond exclusivism or identitarian ideology in the world of transnational communications and global relations of force. Or rather: every individual is compelled to find in the transformation of the imaginary of "his" or "her" people the means to leave it, in order to communicate with the individuals of other peoples with which he or she shares the same interests and, to some extent, the same future. This powerful vision of the future is something nationalist leaders in India could not conceptualize: this is why Ambedkar's thinking offers a fascinating glimpse of a precocious, emergent "transformation of the imaginary"-an emergent post-nationality, even if he did not grasp its contours fully.

Beyond the "national social state," says Balibar, citizenship can be refigured not just as cosmopolitan but "omnipolitan," just as the political too can be reconceived not merely as the politics of enlightenment modernity but in terms of the globalized and "more or less conflictual encounters between cultures and symbolic systems of communication", he stresses that we need to analyses that "take account of both impersonal economic processes and those of subjectivization-the 'scene' of the real and that of the imaginary even if these belong to different spheres altogether." Post-nationality implies a kind of "translation" between cultural spaces and times that leaves always a remnant" that becomes, in a hermeneutic circle, the spur of further, and endless, attempts at translation. The Post-nationality may be in the realm of the incommensurable-or in the imaginary-and perhaps even in the as-yet-unsymbolizable, the as-yet-unsayable. Its promise may lie in saying it again and again.

- In Hind Swaraj, Gandhi frequently depends on the analogy between the nation and the family, he presents some of the "editor's" core values in terms of the family. The troupe of brotherhood would become so important in Gandhi's own attempts to prevent Hindu-Muslim violence. The metaphor of brothers living together in a family was a primary image for the healthy state of nations: 'Two brothers quarrel'.
- One of them repents and reawakens the love that was lying dormant in him; the two again begin to live in peace.... And what is true of families and communities is true of nations. There is no reason to believe that there is one law for families and another for nations. History, then, is a record of an interruption in the course of nature. Soul-force, being natural, is not noted in history". But there were other familial troupes developed in this text, such as the editor's dictum, in reference to the reader's impatience with Gokhale's argument that the Indians had much to learn politically from the British, that those "who are discontented with the slowness of their parents and are angry because the parents would not run with their children, are considered disrespectful to their parents. Professor Gokhale occupies the place of a parent.... A nation that is desirous of securing Home Rule cannot afford to despise its ancestors". In another image dramatically counterposed to the founding notion of a healthy family, the editor likens the British Parliament to "a sterile woman and a prostitute".

- Geraldine Forbes notes the not atypical tale of the woman who was arrested in an anti-colonialist demonstration and jailed. Her husband sent word to the authorities that while "it was a great honour to have his wife arrested," he regretted that she had not asked his permission to leave the house." Forbes concludes that even though the gentleman eventually accepted his wife back, "the lesson was not lost on Congress workers: women's political work had to be conducted without a hint of social rebellion". In other words, the Indian family's patriarchal structure, whatever its structural parallels with the coloniser's infantilization and subordination of the colonized, could not be subverted. As Forbes says, when Gandhi exhorted upper-class women to educate themselves about their rural and poor sisters, "he cautioned them not to neglect their own families in the process". He was always mindful too of the symbolic significance of women's full participation in the public sphere and political struggle particularly. Gandhi invoked the Hindu female pantheon from the Ramayana of Sita, Damyanti, and Draupadi as icons of Indian womanhood. He characterized the British coloniser as Ravana, the abductor of Sita the virtuous; it was imperative on this model that the women assist the men in a moral struggle, where it was clear that the burden of morality itself rested primarily on the woman. Occasionally he would adapt this religiously.
- Rationalised appeal to Muslim audiences. Gandhi not only assigned a specific inferior role in the family. He also metaphorized "woman" as the very sign of inferiority: the weakness of Indian men was indexed in his mind as "effeminacy," as an overdetermined falling away from real, spiritualised manhood into dissolute self-indulgence. As he put it in Hind Swaraj, "A man who has realized his manhood.. fears only God,... no one else. If man will only realize that it is unmanly to obey laws that are unjust, no man's tyranny will enslave

him. This is the key to self-rule or home-rule". Notice here the conflation of the generic "man" with the gender-specific attribute "unmanly"-this conflation is a bridge between the figures of the weakened Indian family and the weakened Indian nation. The moralized family naturally would be the site of the reparation of India to a former glory, and women would have a specified role to play that did not complicate the requirements of masculine nationalism.

- Chatterjee notes the movement by which, at the end of the nineteenth century and at the beginning of the twentieth, the family became a zone of "protection" for Indian women and their literal domestication under the sign of the increasingly well-articulated discourses of anticolonialism and later nationalism. The Europeans held sway in the outer, material realm. But the Indian family was now a newly articulated inner sanctum, constructed ambivalently as a refuge from the secular public sphere but also as a miemcosm for the true, essentially Indian nation. It was a private sphere where the woman as such (beyond actual familial relationships) was preferentially identified and mobilized as mother even more than constructed as sister (behn, or behnji often being marked for use among Indians in public spaces), or even more than interpellated as wife. For one thing the mother is the source of the next generation-the continuation of the people is crucial. At the same time however, the mother is also desexualized, in part to preserve the aura of male self-sufficiency, in part to finesse the possible difficulty of having to deal with women as equal and independent controllers of their own desire, of their own reprôductive machinery and their own discretion in all matters domestic and public. Thus the site of the family is critical.
- When in March 1930 he undertook his 240-mile Salt March from Ahmedabad to Dandi in protest against the

British monopoly of salt, he denied women's participation because it would make men seem cowardly, indeed one reason why men were so willing to let their women take part in any activities organized by Gandhi was that they could be sure he would respect the patriarchal family values. When on April 6, 1919, he called for the participation of women in the satyagraha against the Rowlatt Acts outlawing public protest and denying civil liberties, he did so "to facilitate the total involvement of men". And it conveyed something of his attitude to women's place in the family and in the nation that Gandhi thought it necessary for a married satyagrhi to ask how "to carry one's wife with one, what are her rights, and other similar questions... those who wish to take part in a great work are bound to solve these puzzles".

- Self-directed humour, he described his early attitude to his wife: a "Hindu wife regards implicit obedience to her husband as the highest religion. A Hindu husband regards himself as lord and master of his wife who must ever dance attendance upon him"; he never entirely left behind his traditionalist view of women. Women were always in a secondary and complementary role. The real public agents were men. In this context, perhaps the most striking example of Gandhi's own reluctance to adopt any public position vis-i-vis women that might have rocked the established order was his failure to actively oppose the practice of sati, surely one of the most glaring of problems in a society facing the prospect of becoming "modern." See Lata Mani, "Contentious Traditions: The Debate on Sati in Colonial India," in Recasting Women: Essays in Indian Colonial History, ed. Kumkum Sangati and Sudesh Vaid.
- Even Latika Ghosh, the Oxford-educated leader of the Mahila Rashtriya Sangha (MRS), instituted in 1928 under the aegis of Congress, had to leaven the MRS's brave proto-feminist rhetoric with a ritualized deference

to hoary tradition. The MRS's carefully modulated position, as Forbes tells us, was that Swaraj could not be attained unless women were educated as to "their double oppression as colonial subject and inferior sex." But they "followed a mobilization strategy that constructed women as innate religious". Women who joined the revolutionary movements without regard to the homilies of the approved religious representation of Indian womanhood.

- He was quite conscious of being open to the charge of being a "traitor to the nationalist cause". But he also felt that he and his constituency had little stake in a Brahmin-dominated Hindustan. Ambedkar described members of the Indian communists as a "bunch of Brahmin boys" who had little incentive to investigate gender and caste bias. They had nothing to say about the twinned evils of Brahminism and capitalism, from his perspective. Besides, Ambedkar distanced himself from the communists' readiness to adopt violent means although he endorsed, especially in the 1930 address to the All-India Depressed Classes Conference in Nagpur, the goal of establishing a socialist society through class conflict and class struggle. Ambedkar was ambivalent about the radically separatist and post-nationalist potential of his argument, he may have been more conscious of the charge of being a "traitor". But in the 1930 address at the Round Table Conference in London, for instance, he was squarely and firmly critical of the British record, which was not more promising than the Indian record as far as Untouchables were concerned.
- Living up to his assertion-made 22 years before-that although born a Hindu he would not die one, Ambedkar in 1956, the very year of his death, organized a mass conversion of Dalits to Buddhism. A similar conversion to Islam of Dalits in Meenakshipuram in 1981 lent enough credence to the idea that Hindutva itself was

being challenged that the Vishwa Hindu Parishad (VHP) began to agitate for a reconversion of Muslims and Christians to Hinduism. What must be emphasized about Ambedkar's embrace of Buddhism was that it was not "just" a spiritual conviction that he wanted to share, but a persuasion marked by a declared allegiance to Communism, or to turn it around, he believed that the French Revolutionary ideals of "liberty, fraternity, and equality" and the Russian Revolutionary banner of "equality" had to be brought together on the "way of the Buddha".

- Ambedkar had consistently sought to link the caste system to a foundational hatred of miscegenation and argued in fact that "the superposition of endogamy over exogarny means the creation of Caste". He had made the same point in the first volume, too, to suggest that this was the cause of the formation of caste groups, Downwardly mobile intermarriage between castes has been seen as a degradation of the Indian family, in a Hindu- and Brahmin-dominated India in which the evidence suggested, he alleged, that Brahminism itself "had fallen to the utmost depth of moral degradation".
- It is important to complicate the picture, however, for it is not—as though Gandhi had not considered this solution. He wrote that since there were only four castes sanctioned by scripture, the "merger of sub-divisions in communities" (to be achieved through intermarriage, for instance) was something "to be actually welcomer since similar, social circles with rigid barriers have done great harm to Hinduism". But he did not here go so far as to endorse miscegenation or to suggest that it was all right for Muslims and Hindus to intermarry. That might well have been suicidal. It is well to bear in mind that as a young man in England Gandhi came perilously close to giving the impression to a young white British girl that he was courting her: he had not told her that he was already married until it became

clear that she and her parents were ready to negotiate their daughter's marriage to him.

- At the same time perhaps it is worth remarking on Ambedkar's position on women. He, like Gandhi, sometimes yoked gender and nationalism, but his rhetoric, while sexist, employed figures not so much anti-woman as formulaically and perhaps unconsciously masculinist, as when he argued that the protection of the Scheduled Castes from the oppression of Caste Hindus was a way of enabling the former "to develop to their manhood" or when he argued at some length that "Caste devitalizes a man. It is a process of sterilization". Recent Dalit writing is often more reflexive in its connection of the categories of gender, caste, race, and nation. Here the subduction of woman as subaltern is an important subtext or main idea. There are also parallels to be drawn between the subordination of women and that of the Dalits; Ambedkar exploited this analogy in his attacks on Manu's laws and Hinduism generally: he writes that "in pre-Mini, days a woman was a free and equal partner of man," and asks, "Why did Manu degrade her?' just as he had observed that while "in the time of Panini" those described as Magadha and Vaidehik (products of intercaste marriage) were not stigmatized, they became so in the writings of Manu, who lived around 200 B.C.. Indeed he suggested that Nietzsche's Zarathustra, the inspiration for the cult of the Superman "is anew name for Manu" and Thus Spake Zarathmstm "anew edition" of the Manusmriti with a few key differences and he implies that if the Nietzschean philosophy "stands in great odium" then so should Hinduism for failing the tests of both "social utility" and "individual justice".

2

UNTOUCHABILITY AND CASTE

INTRODUCTION

The notion of untouchability may have been present in the original *varna* system, though it is not clear precisely how it operated. Puranic texts mention untouchables, stating that they should be well-supported, but intimate connection with them avoided. They also state that those who fell from their status within the higher "twice-born" varnas were called *dvija-bandhu* (friends of the twice-born) and were accommodated within the *sudra* class. In actual practice, some who abandoned key rituals or moral standards were altogether ostracised. Additionally, jobs deemed to be particularly contaminating were held only by outcastes. These include sweepers, leather workers, and crematorium attendants. They were not allowed to live within the confines of regular village life, nor to share public facilities such as wells and temples.

A Western-born non-caste *Brahmana* performing a fire sacrifice. Many of the *bhakti* movements, have challenged rigid notions of caste and untouchability.

Organised opposition to rigid caste practices began with the medieval *bhakti* movements. Some of them rejected both caste and its precursor, *varnashrama-dharma*. Others considered the original *varnashrama-dharma* to be the genuine system, though it usually took second place to a revitalised spiritual egalitarianism. Some contemporary *bhakti* traditions continue to initiate non-caste *brahmanas* from amongst communities normally considered untouchable. This liberal practice has met opposition, particularly from caste-conscious *brahmanas*.

Gandhi called the outcastes Harijans – the children of God – and wanted to accommodate them within the fourth *varna*. Ranji Ambedkar, another important reformer, was a member of the untouchable caste who succeeded in attaining a scholarship to study law. He later disagreed with Gandhi over the future status of untouchables, and advocated instead a classless society. He was one of the main architects of the new Indian constitution of 1950, which outlawed untouchability and gave equal status to all citizens. In practice many rigid caste values continue, and former outcastes have organised themselves as Dalits (the oppressed), fighting for social and economic equality. The struggle continues today, and though "positive discrimination" is securing the outcastes equal opportunities, some claim that it is now displacing those who are actually more qualified.

Caste consciousness still continues, and is much debated amongst Hindu scholars and activists. Some advocate the mitigation of social injustice through the complete abolition of social divisions. Others attempt to redefine the ancient *varnashrama-dharma* in a way that is relevant to post-modern society. Although many other nations are characterized by social inequality, perhaps nowhere else in the world has inequality been so elaborately constructed as in the Indian institution of caste.

Caste has long existed in India, but in the modern period it has been severely criticized by both Indian and foreign observers. Although some educated Indians tell non-Indians that caste has been abolished or that "no one pays attention to caste anymore," such statements do not reflect reality. Caste has undergone significant change since independence, but it still involves hundreds of millions of people. In its preamble, India's constitution forbids negative public discrimination on the basis of caste. However, caste ranking and caste-based interaction have occurred for centuries and will continue to do so well into the foreseeable future, more in the countryside than in urban settings and more in the realms of kinship and marriage than in less personal interactions.

Castes are ranked, named, endogamous (in-marrying) groups, membership in which is achieved by birth. There are thousands of castes and subcastes in India, and these large kinship-based groups are fundamental to South Asian social structure. Each caste is part of a locally based system of interdependence with other groups, involving occupational specialization, and is linked in complex ways with networks that stretch across regions and throughout the nation.

The word *caste* derives from the Portuguese *casta*, meaning breed, race, or kind. Among the Indian terms that are sometimes translated as caste are *varna*, *jati*, *jat*, *biradri*, and *samaj*. All of these terms refer to ranked groups of various sizes and breadth. *Varna*, or colour, actually refers to large divisions that include various castes; the other terms include castes and subdivisions of castes sometimes called subcastes.

Many castes are traditionally associated with an occupation, such as high-ranking Brahmans; middle-ranking farmer and artisan groups, such as potters, barbers, and carpenters; and very low-ranking "Untouchable" leatherworkers, butchers, launderers, and latrine cleaners. There is some correlation between ritual rank on the caste hierarchy and economic prosperity. Members of higher-ranking castes tend, on the whole, to be more prosperous than members of lower-ranking castes. Many lower-caste people live in conditions of great poverty and social disadvantage.

According to the Rig Veda, sacred texts that date back to oral traditions of more than 3,000 years ago, progenitors of the four ranked *varna* groups sprang from various parts of the body of the primordial man, which Brahma created from clay (see The Vedas and Polytheism, ch. 3). Each group had a function in sustaining the life of society—the social body. Brahmans, or priests, were created from the mouth. They were to provide for the intellectual and spiritual needs of the community. Kshatriyas, warriors and rulers, were derived from the arms. Their role was to rule and to protect others. Vaishyas—landowners and merchants—sprang from the thighs, and were entrusted with the care of commerce and agriculture. Sudras—artisans and servants—came from the feet. Their task was to perform all manual labour.

Later conceptualized was a fifth category, "Untouchable" menials, relegated to carrying out very menial and polluting work related to bodily decay and dirt. Since 1935 "Untouchables" have been known as Scheduled Castes, referring to their listing on government rosters, or schedules. They are also often called by Mohandas Karamchand (Mahatma) Gandhi's term Harijans, or "Children of God." Although the term *Untouchable* appears in literature produced by these low-ranking castes, in the 1990s, many politically conscious members of these groups prefer to refer to themselves as Dalit, a Hindi word meaning oppressed or downtrodden. According to the 1991 census, there were 138 million Scheduled Caste members in India, approximately 16 percent of the total population.

The first four *varnas* apparently existed in the ancient Aryan society of northern India. Some historians say that these categories were originally somewhat fluid functional groups, not castes. A greater degree of fixity gradually developed, resulting in the complex ranking systems of medieval India that essentially continue in the late twentieth century.

Although a *varna* is not a caste, when directly asked for their caste affiliation, particularly when the questioner is a Westerner, many Indians will reply with a *varna* name. Pressed further, they may respond with a much more specific name of a caste, or *jati*, which falls within that *varna*. For example, a Brahman may specify that he is a member of a named caste group, such as a Jijotiya Brahman, or a Smartha Brahman, and so on. Within such castes, people may further belong to smaller subcaste categories and to specific clans and lineages. These finer designations are particularly relevant when marriages are being arranged and often appear in newspaper matrimonial advertisements.

Members of a caste are typically spread out over a region, with representatives living in hundreds of settlements. In any small village, there may be representatives of a few or even a score or more castes.

Numerous groups usually called tribes (often referred to as Scheduled Tribes) are also integrated into the caste system to varying degrees. Some tribes live separately from others—particularly in the far northeast and in the forested centre of the country, where tribes are more like ethnic groups than castes. Some tribes are themselves divided into groups similar to subcastes. In regions where members of tribes live in peasant villages with nontribal peoples, they are usually considered members of separate castes ranking low on the hierarchical scale.

Inequalities among castes are considered by the Hindu faithful to be part of the divinely ordained natural order and are expressed in terms of purity and pollution. Within a village, relative rank is most graphically expressed at a wedding or death feast, when all residents of the village are invited. At the home of a high-ranking caste member, food is prepared by a member of a caste from whom all can accept cooked food (usually by a Brahman).

Diners are seated in lines; members of a single caste sit next to each other in a row, and members of other castes sit in perpendicular or parallel rows at some distance. Members of Dalit castes, such as Leatherworkers and Sweepers, may be seated far from the other diners—even out in an alley. Farther away, at the edge of the feeding area, a Sweeper may wait with a large basket to receive discarded leavings tossed in by other diners. Eating food contaminated by contact with the saliva of others not of the same family is considered far too polluting to be practised by members of any other castes. Generally, feasts and ceremonies given by Dalits are not attended by higher-ranking castes.

Among Muslims, although status differences prevail, brotherhood may be stressed. A Muslim feast usually includes a cloth laid either on clean ground or on a table, with all Muslims, rich and poor, dining from plates placed on the same cloth. Muslims who wish to provide hospitality to observant Hindus, however, must make separate arrangements for a high-caste Hindu cook and ritually pure foods and dining area.

Castes that fall within the top four ranked *varnas* are sometimes referred to as the "clean castes," with Dalits considered "unclean." Castes of the top three ranked *varnas* are often designated "twice-born," in reference to the ritual initiation undergone by male members, in which investiture with the Hindu sacred thread constitutes a kind of ritual rebirth. Non-Hindu castelike groups generally fall outside these designations.

Each caste is believed by devout Hindus to have its own dharma, or divinely ordained code of proper conduct. Accordingly, there is often a high degree of tolerance for divergent lifestyles among different castes. Brahmans are usually expected to be nonviolent and spiritual, according with their traditional roles as vegetarian teetotaller priests. Kshatriyas are supposed to be strong, as fighters and rulers should be, with a taste for aggression, eating meat, and drinking alcohol. Vaishyas are stereotyped as adept businessmen, in accord with their traditional activities in commerce. Sudras are often described by others as tolerably pleasant but expectably somewhat base in behaviour, whereas Dalits—especially Sweepers—are often regarded by others as followers of vulgar life-styles. Conversely, lower-caste people often view people of high rank as haughty and unfeeling.

The chastity of women is strongly related to caste status. Generally, the higher ranking the caste, the more sexual control its women are expected to exhibit. Brahman brides should be virginal, faithful to one husband, and celibate in widowhood. By contrast, a Sweeper bride may or may not be a virgin, extramarital affairs may be tolerated, and, if widowed or divorced, the woman is encouraged to remarry. For the higher castes, such control of female sexuality helps ensure purity of lineage—of crucial importance to maintenance of high status. Among Muslims, too, high status is strongly correlated with female chastity.

Within castes explicit standards are maintained. Transgressions may be dealt with by a caste council (*panchayat*), meeting periodically to adjudicate issues relevant to the caste. Such councils are usually formed of groups of elders, almost always males. Punishments such as fines and outcasting, either temporary or permanent, can be enforced. In rare cases, a person is excommunicated from the caste for gross infractions of caste rules. An example of such an infraction might be marrying or openly cohabiting with a mate of a caste lower than one's own; such behaviour would usually result in the higher-caste person dropping to the status of the lower-caste person.

Activities such as farming or trading can be carried out by anyone, but usually only members of the appropriate castes act as priests, barbers, potters, weavers, and other skilled artisans, whose occupational skills are handed down in families from one generation to another. As with other key features of Indian social structure, occupational specialization is believed to be in accord with the divinely ordained order of the universe.

The existence of rigid ranking is supernaturally validated through the idea of rebirth according to a person's karma, the sum of an individual's deeds in this life and in past lives. After death, a person's life is judged by divine forces, and rebirth is assigned in a high or a low place, depending upon what is deserved. This supernatural sanction can never be neglected, because it brings a person to his or her position in the caste hierarchy, relevant to every transaction involving food or drink, speaking, or touching.

In past decades, Dalits in certain areas (especially in parts of the south) had to display extreme deference to high-status people, physically keeping their distance—lest their touch or even their shadow pollute others—wearing neither shoes nor any upper body covering (even for women) in the presence of the upper castes. The lowest-ranking had to jingle a little bell in warning of their polluting approach. In much of India, Dalits were prohibited from entering temples, using wells from which the "clean" castes drew their water, or even attending schools. In past centuries, dire punishments were prescribed for Dalits who read or even heard sacred texts.

Such degrading discrimination was made illegal under legislation passed during British rule and was protested against by pre-independence reform movements led by Mahatma Gandhi and Bhimrao Ramji (B.R.) Ambedkar, a Dalit leader. Dalits agitated for the right to enter Hindu temples and to use village wells and effectively pressed for the enactment of stronger laws opposing disabilities imposed on them. After independence, Ambedkar almost single-handedly wrote India's constitution, including key provisions barring caste-based discrimination. Nonetheless, discriminatory treatment of Dalits remains a factor in daily life, especially in villages.

In modern times, as in the past, it is virtually impossible for an individual to raise his own status by falsely claiming to be a member of a higher-ranked caste. Such a ruse might work for a time in a place where the person is unknown, but no one would dine with or intermarry with such a person or his offspring until the claim was validated through kinship networks. Rising on the ritual hierarchy can only be achieved by a caste as a group, over a long period of time, principally by adopting behaviour patterns of higher-ranked groups. This process, known as Sanskritization, has been described by M.N. Srinivas and others. An example of such behaviour is that of some Leatherworker castes adopting a policy of not eating beef, in the hope that abstaining from the defiling practice of consuming the flesh of sacred bovines would enhance their castes' status. Increased economic prosperity for much of a caste greatly aids in the process of improving rank.

India's caste system : India has a hierarchical caste system in the society. Within Indian culture, whether in the north or the south, Hindu or Muslim, urban or village, virtually all things, people, and groups of people are ranked according to various essential qualities. If one is attuned to the theme of hierarchy in India, one can discern it everywhere. Although India is a political democracy, in daily life there is little advocacy of or adherence to notions of equality.

Castes systems in India and caste like groups—those quintessential groups with which almost all Indians are associated—are ranked. Within most villages or towns, everyone knows the relative rankings of each locally represented caste, and people's behaviour toward one another is constantly shaped by this knowledge. Between the extremes of the very high and very low castes, however, there is sometimes disagreement on the exact relative ranking of castes clustered in the middle.

Castes system in India are primarily associated with Hinduism but also exist among other Indian religious groups. Muslims sometimes expressly deny that they have castes—they state that all Muslims are brothers under God—but observation of Muslim life in various parts of India reveals the existence of castelike groups and clear concern with social hierarchy. Among Indian Christians, too, differences in caste are acknowledged and maintained.

Throughout India, individuals are also ranked according to their wealth and power. For example, there are "big men" (*bare admi*, in Hindi) and "little men" (*chhote admi*) everywhere. "Big men" sit confidently on chairs, while "little men" come before them to make requests, either standing or crouching down on their haunches, certainly not presuming to sit beside a man of high status as an equal. Even men of nearly equal status who might share a string cot to sit on take their places carefully—the higher-ranking man at the head of the cot, the lower-ranking man at the foot.

Within families and kinship groupings, there are many distinctions of hierarchy. Men outrank women of the same or similar age, and senior relatives outrank junior relatives. Several other kinship relations involve formal respect. For example, in northern India, a daughter-in-law of a household shows deference to a daughter of a household. Even among young siblings in a household, there is constant acknowledgment of age differences: younger siblings never address an older sibling by name, but rather by respectful terms for elder brother or elder sister.

Even in a business or academic setting, where colleagues may not openly espouse traditional observance of caste or class ranking behaviour, they may set up fictive kinship relations, addressing one another by kinship terms reflecting family or village-style hierarchy. For example, a younger colleague might respectfully address an older colleague as *chachaji* (respected father's younger brother), gracefully acknowledging the superior position of the older colleague. Untouchability has played an important role in Indian history and still affects many millions of Indians. *The Untouchables* focuses on its connections with poverty and state politics, with a primarily political and historical focus, but also looks at its social construction and effects on the lives of individuals. With a broad approach not burdened with too much theory, it will interest scholars, students, and lay readers of history, politics, religion, economics, sociology, and other disciplines.

Mendelsohn and Vicziany begin with the vexed question of the identity of "the Untouchables" and an explanation for their choice of that term for their title, over *Harijan*, *Dalit*, or Scheduled Caste. (They use all these terms and others in the text.) There has been a long-running debate over the nature of Untouchable identity and its relationship with Hindu culture. For Mendelsohn and Vicziany the key issue is

"whether the Untouchables share a social situation that is sufficiently common to be the basis or potential basis for their mobilisation as a distinct unit for some important purposes.... There is indeed something of a `hard bar' separating Untouchables from the rest of Indian society, and Untouchables themselves have come to see that bar as the basis for a certain amount of common consciousness and action."

The category as it exists now may be a recent construction, a response to British actions and Muslim/Hindu rivalry, but it was constructed on long-standing foundations: evidence from the *bhakti* literary tradition shows that Untouchable ritual subordination existed in medieval times.

Recent violence against Untouchables—the so-called "Harijan atrocities"—has brought the issue of Untouchability to prominence. Mendelsohn and Vicziany argue "that the incidence of violence involving Untouchables has increased significantly over the post-Independence period". The violence can be divided into "traditional" forms and others that are responses to Untouchable resistance to ritual subordination, often taking the form of organised retaliatory violence by caste Hindus, sometimes abetted by the police and state apparatus. There are marked regional variations in such violence and it is often tied up with broader political violence, associated with mainstream electoral contests as well as with class conflict and Naxalite revolutionaries.

Early Untouchable politics involved Hindu reform movements, often motivated by the threat, however nugatory, of Untouchable conversion to Christianity or Islam. Early organisation by Untouchables themselves was on a caste and regional basis, and relationships between different Untouchable castes were often difficult. The 1930s saw key struggles between Gandhi and Ambedkar, most notably over whether Untouchables would have separate electorates or joint electorates with reserved seats. Congress was the only national organisation with a large Untouchable following, but Gandhi failed to gain their commitment. Ambedkar, an Untouchable himself, developed a deeper analysis of Untouchability, but lacked a workable political strategy: his conversion to Buddhism in 1956, along with millions of followers, highlighted the failure of his political endeavours.

In the years since 1956 Ambedkarite political organisations have been riven by internal conflicts, notably between young, modernist, and urban elements and older, rural, and often

Buddhist ones. But Ambedkar's legacy remains fruitful. Maharashtra and Karnataka have produced a Dalit literary movement, while there have been political success in northern India. In Uttar Pradesh, the Bahujana Samaj party lead by Kanshi Ram has, through alliances of convenience with other parties, attained minority government, installing Mayawati as Chief Minister. Though their achievements in power were limited, this illustrates how Dalits are now using their voting power directly rather than as simple vote banks at the service of mainstream parties.

Public policy on Untouchability has been "abstract and unrealistic" but not completely ineffective. One strand has been action against adverse discrimination. Discrimination against Untouchables is still widespread in rural areas in the private sphere, in ritual matters such as access to eating places and water sources.

It has largely disappeared, however, in urban areas and in the public sphere, in rights of movement and access to schools. Mendelsohn and Vicziany argue, however, that this has been part of a broader movement towards a new civic culture rather than the result of legislative action: "court enforcement of the anti-disabilities legislation has not been a powerful force in bringing about an abatement of the practice of Untouchability".

Compensatory discrimination has been more controversial. One success of Ambedkar's was the creation of quotas within public service for Scheduled Castes, though targets set after Independence are only being attained now. Complaints about this system are that it benefits an elite group of well-off Untouchables, that particular castes or regions benefit more, and that those in office do little to help their fellows.

Compensatory discrimination in education, through scholarships and reserved places, has had some effects but has generally been poorly implemented. Despite this, basic literacy amongst Untouchables is gradually catching up to that of the broader population.

Brief biographies of some Scheduled Caste politicians, national and state, show that they have indeed come from the better off among their communities. But their advantages have often been very slight: family ownership of a cow, for example, or a small plot of land — just enough to alleviate the desperation of poverty and allow an opportunity for education. Along with public service reservations, scholarships (however small and corruptly administered) and the "Harijan hostels" associated with colleges have helped them overcome the barriers of poverty and Untouchability. While Scheduled Caste politicians have not been effective in representing Untouchables generally, Mendelsohn and Vicziany find little evidence of a "Harijan elite".

Other public policy initiatives of key importance to the Untouchables have been the anti-poverty programs: famine prevention, land reform, food-for-work schemes, and the Integrated Rural Development Program, among others. Apart from the first, these have had limited success. There has been considerable regional variation in alleviation of Untouchable poverty.

Along with the population generally, Untouchables in Kerala score extremely well on social indicators such as literacy, education, health, and fertility, but they face high unemployment and lack of opportunity. For contrast Mendelsohn and Vicziany look in detail at the village of Behror, located in a relatively affluent "Green Revolution" area midway between Delhi and Jaipur. Different Untouchable communities here exhibit great variation in their employment patterns and economic success.

The Faisalabad stone quarries, just outside Delhi, provide an example of the new Untouchable proletariat being created through urbanisation and migration: eight out of ten workers there are Untouchable and most of the rest are tribals. A case to have welfare legislation enforced and end-bonded labour was taken to the Supreme Court by activist Swami Agnivesh, but ostensible success was vitiated by the failure of governments and employers to implement court directives and by an excessive focus on bonded labour. And union organisation amongst Untouchables faces many obstacles.

The negotiations between Gandhi, Ambedkar, and the British in the late 20s and early 30s had a key role in shaping subsequent Untouchable history. But the greatest changes have been gradual, brought about by improvements in education and possession of the franchise. Mendelsohn and Vicziany foresee no end to Untouchable poverty: with the decline of ritual discrimination, "Untouchables will become decreasingly differentiated from other Indians" in their poverty.

Purity and Pollution: Many status differences in Indian society are expressed in terms of ritual purity and pollution. Notions of purity and pollution are extremely complex and vary greatly among different castes, religious groups, and regions. However, broadly speaking, high status is associated with purity and low status with pollution.

Some kinds of purity are inherent, or inborn; for example, gold is purer than copper by its very nature, and, similarly, a member of a high-ranking Brahman, or priestly, caste is born with more inherent purity than a member of a low-ranking Sweeper (Mehtar, in Hindi) caste. Unless the Brahman defiles himself in some extraordinary way, throughout his life he will always be purer than a Sweeper.

Other kinds of purity are more transitory—a Brahman who has just taken a bath is more ritually pure than a Brahman who has not bathed for a day. This situation could easily reverse itself temporarily, depending on bath schedules, participation in polluting activities, or contact with temporarily polluting substances.

Purity is associated with ritual cleanliness—daily bathing in flowing water, dressing in properly laundered clothes of approved materials, eating only the foods appropriate for one's caste, refraining from physical contact with people of lower rank, and avoiding involvement with ritually impure substances. The latter include body wastes and execrations, most especially those of another adult person. Contact with the products of death or violence are typically polluting and threatening to ritual purity.

During her menstrual period, a woman is considered polluted and refrains from cooking, worshipping, or touching anyone older than an infant. In much of the south, a woman spends this time "sitting outside," resting in an isolated room or shed. During her period, a Muslim woman does not touch the Quran. At the end of the period, purity is restored with a complete bath. Pollution also attaches to birth, both for the mother and the infant's close kin, and to death, for close relatives of the deceased (see The Ceremonies of Hinduism; Islam.

Members of the highest priestly castes, the Brahmans, are generally vegetarians (although some Bengali and Maharashtrian Brahmans eat fish) and avoid eating meat, the product of violence and death. High-ranking Warrior castes (Kshatriyas), however, typically consume nonvegetarian diets, considered appropriate for their traditions of valour and physical strength.

A Brahman born of proper Brahman parents retains his inherent purity if he bathes and dresses himself properly, adheres to a vegetarian diet, eats meals prepared only by persons of appropriate rank, and keeps his person away from the bodily exuviae of others (except for necessary contact with the secretions of family infants and small children).

If a Brahman happens to come into bodily contact with a polluting substance, he can remove this pollution by bathing and changing his clothing. However, if he were to eat meat or commit other transgressions of the rigid dietary codes of his particular caste, he would be considered more deeply polluted and would have to undergo various purifying rites and payment of fines imposed by his caste council in order to restore his inherent purity.

In sharp contrast to the purity of a Brahman, a Sweeper born of Sweeper parents is considered to be born inherently polluted. The touch of his body is polluting to those higher on the caste hierarchy than he, and they will shrink from his touch, whether or not he has bathed recently. Sweepers are associated with the traditional occupation of cleaning human feces from latrines and sweeping public lanes of all kinds of dirt. Traditionally, Sweepers remove these polluting materials in baskets carried atop the head and dumped out in a garbage pile at the edge of the village or neighbourhood. The involvement of Sweepers with such filth accords with their low-status position at the bottom of the Hindu caste hierarchy, even as their services allow high-status people, such as Brahmans, to maintain their ritual purity.

Members of the Leatherworker (Chamar) caste are ascribed a very low status consonant with their association with the caste occupation of skinning dead animals and tanning the leather. Butchers (Khatiks, in Hindi), who kill and cut up the bodies of animals, also rank low on the caste hierarchy because of their association with violence and death.

However, castes associated with ruling and warfare—and the killing and deaths of human beings—are typically accorded high rank on the caste hierarchy. In these instances, political power and wealth outrank association with violence as the key determinant of caste rank.

Maintenance of purity is associated with the intake of food and drink, not only in terms of the nature of the food itself, but also in terms of who has prepared it or touched it. This requirement is especially true for Hindus, but other religious groups hold to these principles to varying degrees. Generally, a person risks pollution—and lowering his own status—if he accepts beverages or cooked foods from the hands of people of lower caste status than his own. His status will remain intact if he accepts food or beverages from people of higher caste rank. Usually, for an observant Hindu of any but the very lowest castes to accept cooked food from a Muslim or Christian is regarded as highly polluting.

In a clear example of pollution associated with dining, a Brahman who consumed a drink of water and a meal of wheat bread with boiled vegetables from the hands of a Sweeper would immediately become polluted and could expect social rejection by his caste fellows. From that moment, fellow Brahmans following traditional pollution rules would refuse food touched by him and would abstain from the usual social interaction with him. He would not be welcome inside Brahman homes—most especially in the ritually pure kitchens—nor would he or his close relatives be considered eligible marriage partners for other Brahmans.

Generally, the acceptance of water and ordinary foods cooked in water from members of lower-ranking castes incurs the greatest pollution. In North India, such foods are known as *kaccha khana*, as contrasted with fine foods cooked in butter or oils, which are known as *pakka khana*. Fine foods can be accepted from members of a few castes slightly lower than one's own. Local hierarchies differ on the specific details of these rules. Completely raw foods, such as uncooked grains, fresh unpeeled bananas, mangoes, and uncooked vegetables can be accepted by anyone from anyone else, regardless of relative status. Toasted or parched foods, such as roasted peanuts, can also be accepted from anyone without ritual or social repercussions. (Thus, a Brahman may accept gifts of grain from lower-caste patrons for eventual preparation by members of his own caste, or he may purchase and consume roasted peanuts or tangerines from street vendors of unknown caste without worry.)

Water served from an earthen pot may be accepted only from the hands of someone of higher or equal caste ranking, but water served from a brass pot may be accepted even from someone slightly lower on the caste scale. Exceptions to this rule are members of the Waterbearer (Bhoi, in Hindi) caste, who are employed to carry water from wells to the homes of the prosperous and from whose hands members of all castes may drink water without becoming polluted, even though Waterbearers are not ranked high on the caste scale.

These and a great many other traditional rules pertaining to purity and pollution constantly impinge upon interaction between people of different castes and ranks in India. Although to the non-Indian these rules may seem irrational and bizarre, to most of the people of India they are a ubiquitous and accepted part of life. Thinking about and following purity and pollution rules make it necessary for people to be constantly aware of differences in status. With every drink of water, with every meal, and with every contact with another person, people must ratify the social hierarchy of which they are a part and within which their every act is carried out. The fact that expressions of social status are intricately bound up with events that happen to everyone every day—eating, drinking, bathing, touching, talking—and that transgressions of these rules, whether deliberate or accidental, are seen as having immediately polluting effects on the person of the transgressor, means that every ordinary act of human life serves as a constant reminder of the importance of hierarchy in Indian society.

There are many Indians, particularly among the educated urban elite, who do not follow traditional purity and pollution practices. Dining in each others' homes and in restaurants is common among well-educated people of diverse backgrounds, particularly when they belong to the same economic class. For these people, guarding the family's earthen water pot from inadvertent touch by a low-ranking servant is not the concern it is for a more traditional villager. However, even among those people whose words and actions denigrate traditional purity rules, there is often a reluctance to completely abolish consciousness of purity and pollution from their thinking. It is surely rare for a Sweeper, however well-educated, to invite a Brahman to dinner in his home and have his invitation unselfconsciously accepted. It is less rare, however, for educated urban colleagues of vastly different caste and religious heritage to enjoy a cup of tea together. Some high-caste liberals pride themselves on being free of "casteism" and seek to accept food from the hands of very low-caste people, or even deliberately set out to marry someone from a significantly lower caste or a different religion. Thus, even as they deny it, these progressives affirm the continuing significance of traditional rules of purity, pollution, and hierarchy in Indian caste system.. 1995 data. India's caste system. Courtesy Library of Congress.

Dalit: In the Indian caste system, a Dalit, often called an untouchable, is a person who does not have any varnas. Varna refers to the Hindu belief that most humans were created from different parts of the body of the divinity Purusha and according to which part they were created from it defines their social standing for issues such as who they can marry and what jobs they can do. Dalits fall outside varnas system and have historically been prevented from doing any but the most menial jobs. They are also known as outcastes. Included are leather-workers (called chamar), poor farmers and landless labourers, scavengers (called bhangi or chura), street handicrafters, folk artists, clothes washers dhobi etc.

The name Dalit means the oppressed. It is a term used by the Dalits themselves to denote their protest. This was a quite a new term as it has come into use only after the 1950's. The movements that fought for the rights of the untouchables achieved much during the twentieth century, though the fundamental place for Dalits as a whole has not yet significantly changed. The struggle however has intensified and has been contested severely. The Dalits are today a formidable force. The resolving of this problem by a final and complete abandonment of the caste ideal of society is very much on the agenda. It can easily be said that the greatest enduring achievement of India in the twentieth century is the progress, though small, that has been made in liberating the Dalits. The primary contributors to this process are the Dalits themselves. It is beyond dispute that Ambedkar had contributed more than any other single individual to bring about this situation. It is quite obvious that Dalits have selected him as their symbol.

Ambedkar's Annihilation Of Caste (AOC). This was a speech that Ambedkar had prepared when asked to preside over the Jat Pat Todak Mandal conference. Even though the conference was cancelled, for reasons he has mentioned in the preface, Ambedkar published the speech.

Following are the salient feature of this speech AOC:

- Ambedkar has the deepest and the most correct understanding of the subject and he has presented the evils of the caste system very well.
- He has correctly diagnosed the problem that the Hindu society faces because of the caste system.
- His solution to the problem *i.e.* Annihilation of the Caste can not be more correct. He understands that no matter how many programmes you run for the upliftment of the backward caste, true equality will not be achieved as long as the caste system lives. A contention that one cannot agree more with.
- However it is difficult to agree with the manner in which he has presented the solution. Even though he has explained in detail what he means by the different terms *e.g.* "destruction of religion", these are so powerful words that can cause most logical men to close their eyes to reasoning. Choosing a language as strong as this he gave an easy tool to the detractors to put his entire speech in bad light and that is exactly what Mahatma Gandhi did when he reviewed the speech in his periodical, "Harijan". Because of this it was easy for the Mahatma to overlook the entire content of the speech and focus on this aspect that asked for the destruction of religion. Even though Ambedkar wrote a reply to Mahatma but till that point it had become just a play of words.

While both Gandhi and Ambedkar had the interest of the BC in mind their approach to the problem and solution was different.

GANDHI'S VIEW POINT

1. Abolish Untouchability
2. Maintain Varna vyavastha which he argued was different than caste system. A difference so subtle and difficult to comprehend.

3. He believed that the hearts of the upper castes could be changed to treat the lower castes equally and his entire struggle was directed towards bringing that change of heart.

AMBEDKAR'S VIEW POINT

1. Abolish the Caste System.
2. Ambedkar believed that the caste system derived its strength from the Vedas and Shashtras and hence asked for the destruction of the shashtras. A proposition so strong and it provided the ammunition to the detractors.
3. He wanted a strict legislation in place to make sure that caste could not be misused again.

What Ambedkar sought was a legal remedy to a social problem. In his proposal to seek the remedy he went too far in asking for the destruction of the hindu religion, which sounds strong but in essence what he wanted was to change the laws that governed the hindu society for ages. He wanted to take out the religious sanctity of the caste system by rejecting the shashtras. What he meant was to change the shashtras to remcve the support for the caste system that it provides. In essence he wanted a religious reform as well. Ambedkar's understanding of the system was very profound and in his zeal to make others understand the depth of his solution *i.e.* Annihilation of Caste, he went too far in explaining the consequences which unnecessary and he extrapolated too much. Or maybe he didn't. Maybe the times in which he was living such a change would have caused exactly what he feared.

Had the Mahatma agreed to the abolishing of caste system then, we would have seen the end of it by now. Mahatma Gandhi has done a lot of great things but also like humans he has committed some mistakes and this was one of the more serious ones.

Today the social condition is different if not much better. There are a lot more educated elite that would agree to abolish the caste system rather than maintain it in some other form.

The reasons for this agreement maybe different. Whatever their reasons but one strongly feel it is time to start a social movement against caste system that aims for nothing less than the complete "Annihilation Of Castes".

Terms Associated with the Dalit Caste: Dalit is the latest and currently most politically correct of many terms used for the caste. Offensive terms used mostly in the past include chura, bhangi, neech, kanjjar, and mirasi. Whereas the terms chura and bhangi are profession-based terms for scavengers, they can serve as general terms for the low-born; others are actual names of the caste. Harijan was a term for untouchable, coined by Mahatma Gandhi, which means Children of God—Hari is another name for the god Vishnu. It is now considered patronizing.

The term can also be attributed to Dalit castes of Pakistan called the haris, who are a group of mud-hut builders. Neo-Buddhist Dalits try to make 'Harijan' appear as a disgrace to all Dalits as it comes from a Hindu name. This term had already been used, in a different form, by the medieval philosopher Ramanuja who uplifted many backward caste peoples: as Thirukulattar, or People of Holy Clan. (He was probably the first to allow the untouchables into temples, albeit for limited periods.)

The word 'Dalit' comes from the Marathi root dal, and means 'held under check', 'suppressed', or 'crushed', or, in a looser sense, 'oppressed'. Maharashtrian Dalit Activist and poet Namdeo Dhasal made it a symbol of pride to fight against social injustice. He said:

> *"Yes, I do feel that the fight to eradicate caste has to be fought by Dalits and caste Hindus together carrying forward the tradition of Adi Shankara, which got broken somewhere in between. It is possible that Dr. Ambedkar borrowed this term from Swami Vivekananda from his quote, "Deena-Dalita-Dukhi Devo Bhava!"*

Another term used for the Dalits was Matanga named after Maharshi Matanga, a Matanga Bhil and guru of Bhakta Shabari.

In fact, Dalits are often addressed as 'Matanga 'in passages like Varaha Purana.

Dr. B. R. Ambedkar, a Dalit, and one of the leaders of the Indian independence movement, is considered the chief architect of the Indian Constitution, in which Article 17 abolishes untouchability. Ever since, under the aegis of the Constitution of India, a 'Reservation System' (privilege in education and other services given only to the Dalits) has been implemented for the benefit of the 'Dalits' which is a step towards affirmative action. The terms scheduled castes/scheduled tribes (SC/ST) and non-caste tribes are also used in the Indian legal system to refer to this social group in India.

The Untouchables: This period of Buddhism in India, which was also one of the richest in India and in world history, came to an end with the collapse of Buddhism in India and the rebuilding of Hinduism. The reason for the collapse Ambedkar says was the Mohammedan invasions and the killing of Buddhist monks by the Mohammedans.

The period of revivalism of Hinduism was marked by great tensions between the low castes and Bhrahmins. The Bhrahmins tried to establish their hegemony as the superior caste and to have their position accepted by all. The Low Castes rejected this. This internal struggle had determined the characterisation of untouchables even by the colonial officers of the British Empire. The distinguishing features of untouchables, according to a census circular issued by Census Commissioner in 1911, are these: "they deny the supremacy of Bhramins, do not receive Mantra from a Bhramin or otherwise recognise Hindu Guru, deny the authority of Vedas, do not worship Hindu Gods, are not served by good Bhrahmins as family priests, have no Bhrahmin priests at all, are denied access to interior of Hindu temples, cause pollution (a) by touch, or (b) within a certain distance, bury their dead and eat beef and not reverence the cow."

Thus while the Sudras period was marked by the imposition of Veda's doctrine and at least considering Sudras as lower in the ladder of Hindu caste structure, the untouchability resulted in creating the total outcasts. Physically this meant ousting the untouchables even from their habitats and pushing them into a ghetto. Ambedkar called them, people of the Indian ghetto. All forms of contact were forbidden by the use of rules of untouchability.

The Untouchables movement best described by the use of the name of its current mythic leader, the late Dr. B.R. Ambedkar (1891-1956), has recently experienced an enlargement to the international scene. We confine here with the religious aspect of that movement toward internationalism in India itself in a historical perspective. Four stages in the attitude toward religion can be noted, three of them best seen by three specific incidents which stand for a larger set of changes. A review of the impact of foreign Buddhist organizations in India, the international Vipassana Meditation phenomenon, and Sakyadhita, the international women's Buddhist organization, completes the paper

The first incident is the 1894 poem which accompanied the petition of Gopal Baba Walankar (incidentlly one of Dr. Ambedkar's relatives) requesting readmission to the army; the second the 1935 statement of Ambedkar that he would not die a Hindu; next, the sense of Buddhists in 1969 that they wanted a Buddhism of their own, not a foreign one; and the current varied response to the work of English, Japanese, and Taiwanese Buddhists in India as well as the international scene. The term globalization may not be liked, but in many ways, this new phase of the Buddhist movement as well as the Dalit diaspora and its international consequences gives a global dimension to what has been until recently a totally Indian movement.

Consciousness and "Sanskritization": The late 19th poem by "Pandit Kondiram", a Mahar name, accompanied a petition by an ex-army man, Gopal Baba Walankar, for re-admission into the British army of all avarna (those without varna) after the caste based reorganization prevented recruitment of Untouchables. The petition is quite modern in its demands, but the poem is a long one to the sorrows of Untouchables, and includes this complaint:

In the name of religion we know Satvai, Jokhai, Mesai
Vetal, Mhasba, Bahiri, Badvi, Mariai.
We never meet Brahma, Vishnu, Mahesh, Krishna, Rukmai,
Rama, Sita, Lakshman.
Even in dreams we don't see the Arya gods.

The total document exhibits two characteristics of the early movement. Enough change had come through British induced opportunities for Untouchables to begin to demand recognition of their abilities, if not their rights, and, secondly, there was a great consciousness of the miserable condition of the ordinary Untouchable, and his distance from the traditions of the dominant Hindu.

This phase, which lasted in Maharashtra up to 1935, attempted to "see the Arya gods" in various ways. There were some early efforts to conduct sacred thread ceremonies. There were three temple satyagrahas in the 1927-35 period (the Gandhian word satyagraha was used although Gandhi remained aloof and Congress was critical of these efforts). There was an effort to claim religious worth through pride in Cokhamela and his family, the Mahar saint of the 14th century.

However, Dr. Ambedkar, who imprinted the movement from 1920 on, gave more attention to gaining political representation and to taking water from a public source in the Mahad Satyagraha of 1927. A suggestion of future rejection of Hinduism came later that same year in the burning of sections of the Manusmriti, the classical Brahmin text which decreed the low status of the Sudra and the punishment for any effort at religious rights or economic gain.

Social Background and Origins: In the context of traditional Hindu society, Dalit status has often been historically associated with occupations regarded as ritually impure: namely, any occupation involving killing, handling of animal cadavers or night soil. Engaging in these activities was considered to be polluting to the individual who performed them, and this pollution was considered to be 'contagious'. As a result, Dalits were commonly banned and segregated from full participation in Hindu social life (they could not enter the premises of a temple), while elaborate precautions were sometimes observed to prevent incidental contact between Dalits and other Hindus.

Historically, there may not have been clear demarcation between Dalit castes and the Sudra castes. Dalits are not a single identifiable race or caste. Instead, like the rest of the Hindu society, they are divided into various subcastes known as 'jatis' found some association between caste status and genetic markers seeming to indicate a more European lineage.

Dalit diversity may be due to newly outcaste individuals or communities over the years. It is note worthy that sometimes, regional tribes that are considered Dalits are seen by Indians as racially distinct. In both northern and southern India it is different. For example, in North India, in places such as Rajasthan they are usually lighter because Rajasthan was invaded several times by white tribes. In addition they also have different colour of eyes and sometimes hair. As a result in superstition, it is said to never trust a cat-eyed person. Then, in South India, they are often regarded as more closely related to Tibetans, Burmese, Khmers, Thais, and other Southeast and East Asians.

Many Dalits who have converted to other religions in the past few centuries continue to retain their Dalit heritage. In the 1991 census, Dalits numbered just over 130 million and constituted more than 16% of India's population,.

Discrimination against Dalits is not limited to the Hindu community. This situation is exacerbated by the fact that non-Hindu Dalit groups have traditionally not been recognized as Scheduled Castes under hiring quota laws. The Dalit Muslims or "Arzal" (also called Mojahir in Pakistan), as well as Dalit Christians form an integral part of the caste system in South Asia among Muslims and Christians. Many Dalit Muslims are discriminated against by the upper-caste "Ashraf" Muslims, and Dalit Christians discriminated against by upper caste Christian priests and Nuns.

Some Dalits have successfully integrated into urban Indian society, where caste origins are less obvious and less important in public life. In rural India, caste origins are more readily apparent and Dalits remain excluded from local religious life, though this exclusion in its severity is in fact fast diminishing due to changing social norms of acceptable behaviour. Dalits and similar groups are also found in Nepal, Pakistan and Bangladesh.

Dalits and Indian Politics: Mahatma Gandhi made it part of the Indian National Congress's mission to eradicate untouchability. For this reason, untouchability has been officially abolished in India, although the social practice still exists today, particularly in rural villages.

In these villages, Dalits are still not allowed to let their shadows fall upon a non-Dalit caste member (particularly a Brahmin, for fear of contaminating them), and they are still required to sweep the ground where they walk to remove the 'contamination' of their footfalls. In some of these villages, rural Dalits are forbidden to worship in temples or draw water from the same wells as caste Hindus, and they usually live in segregated neighbourhoods outside the main village.

In urban areas and most villages the old concepts of a rigid caste system and untouchability usually no longer exist, though most Indians still voluntarily hold on to their caste origins, which is intended to reflect that their ancestors belonged to their castes with a sense of pride in the duties and responsibilities as required by the caste rules. In matrimonial matters, whether the wed couple is Dalit or non-Dalit, caste identity is a practical near-must. This is, however, ignored by inter-caste couples, who marry ignoring castes but due to an attraction on the basis of education or economic status, of either or both members of the couple.

While the Indian Constitution has duly made special provisions for the social and economic uplift of the Dalits, comprising the so-called scheduled castes and tribes in order to enable them to achieve upward social mobility, these concessions are limited to only those Dalits who remain Hindu. There is a demand among the Dalits who have converted to other religions that the statutory benefits should be extended to them as well as social relief to "overcome" historical injustices.

Another major politically charged issue with the rise of Hindutva's role in Indian politics is that of religious conversion. This political movement alleges that conversions of Dalits are due not to any social or theological motivation but to allurements like education and jobs. Critics argue that the inverse is true with laws banning conversion, and the limiting of social relief for these backward sections of Indian society being revoked for those who convert. Bangaru Laxman, a Dalit politician, was a prominent member of the Hindutva movement.

Another political issue is over the affirmative measures taken by the government towards the uplift of the Dalits by implementation of quotas in government jobs and university admissions aimed at improving Dalit representation. About 8% of the seats in the National and State Parliaments are reserved for Scheduled Caste and Tribe candidates, a measure sought by B.R. Ambedkar and other Dalit activists in order to ensure that Dalits would obtain a proportionate political voice.

THE SUDRAS

This category comes from the Vedas, the sacred texts of the Hindus. This word "Hindu" also needs an explanation. "The name Hindu is itself a foreign name. It was given by the Mohammedans to the natives for the purpose of distinguishing themselves. It does not occur in any Sanskrit work prior to the Mohammedan invasion. They did not feel the necessity of a common name because they had no conception of their having constituted a community. Hindu society as such does not exist. It is only a collection of castes. Each caste is conscious of its existence. Its survival is the be all and end all of its existence. Castes do not even form a federation. A caste has no feeling that it is affiliated to other castes except when there is a Hindu-

Muslim riot. On all other occasions each caste endeavours to segregate itself and to distinguish itself from other castes. Each caste not only dines among itself and marries among itself but each caste prescribes its own distinctive dress."

The Vedas classified every one into four castes. Ambedkar explained this thus

1. According to the Brahmins, the Vedas have defined what is an ideal society and the Vedas being infallible, that is the only ideal society which man can accept.
2. The ideal society prescribed by the Vedas is known by the name Chaturvarna.
3. Such a society, according to the Vedas, must satisfy three conditions.
4. It must be composed of four classes, Brahmins, Kshatriyas, Vaishyas and Sudras.
5. The interrelations of these classes must be regulated by the principle of graded inequality. In other words, all these classes are not to be on equal level but to be one above the other, in point of status, rights and privileges.
6. The Brahmins were placed at the top; the Kshatriyas were placed below the Brahmins but above the Vaishyas; the Vaishyas were placed below the Kshatriyas but above the Sudras and the Sudras were placed the lowest of all
7. The third feature of Chaturvarna was that each class must engage itself in an occupation assigned to it. The Brahmins' occupation was to learn, teach and officiate at religious ceremonies. The Kshatriyas' occupation was to bear arms and to fight. The occupation of the Vaishyas was trade and business. The Sudras' occupation was to do menial service for all the three superior classes.
8. No class is to transgress and trench upon the occupation of the other classes.

At this stage Sudras still enjoyed some rights. The right to collect food from villagers, the right to collect corn from each villager at the harvest seasons and the right to appropriate the dead animals belonging to the villagers.

The Buddha's Challenge to Caste: This period of Sudras came to a serious crisis, when Buddha began to reject the entire doctrine of the Veda's and preached equality as against caste. It is one of the great events of human history when the people of most parts of India were converted to the preaching of Buddha, in his own lifetime. Later his teaching spread to most other neighbouring countries.

Ambedkar gives the following as a summary of Buddha's teachings on caste:

> *"The Buddha opposed it root and branch. He was strongest opponent of caste and the earliest and staunchest upholder of equality. There is no argument in favour of caste and inequality which he did not refute. There were many Brahmins who challenged Buddha on this issue. But he silenced them completely. The story is told in the Assalayana-Sutta that once the Brahmins persuaded one of them, by name Assalayana, to go to the Buddha and controvert his views against caste and inequality. Assalayana went to the Buddha and placed before him the case in favour of the superiority of the Brahmins.*
>
> *He said, "Brahmins maintain, Gautama, that only Brahmins form the superior class, all other classes being inferior; that only Brahmins form the white class, all other classes being black fellows; that purity resides in Brahmins alone and not in non Brahmins; and that only Brahmins are Brahma's legitimate sons, born from his mouth, offspring of his, creations of his, and his heirs. What does Gautama say hereon?" The Buddha's answer simply pulverised Assalayana. The Buddha said: "Assalayana, are not the Brahmin wives of Brahmins known to have their periods, and to conceive, and to lie and give birth? Notwithstanding this do Brahmins really maintain all what you have said though they are themselves born of women like everybody else?" Assalayangave no answer.*

The Buddha went further and asked Assalayana another question. "Suppose, Assalayana, a young noble consorts with a Brahmin maiden, what would be the issue? Will it be an animal or human being?" Again Assalayana gave no answer. "As to the possibility of moral development, is it only a Brahmin and not a man of the other three classes, who in this country, can develop in his heart the love that knows no hate or ill-will?" "No. All four classes can do it," replied Assalayana. "Assalayana! Have you ever heard," asked the Buddha, "that in the Yona and Kamboja countries and in other adjacent countries, there are only two classes, namely, masters and slaves, and that a master can become a slave and vice versa?" "Yes, I have heard so," replied Assalayana. "If your Chaturvarna is an ideal society, why is it not universal?" On none of these points was Assalayana able to defend his theory of caste and inequality. He was completely silenced. He ended by becoming a disciple of the Buddha. A Brahmin by name Vasettha had embraced the religion of the Blessed Lord. The Brahmins used to abuse him for his conversion. One day he went to Buddha and disclosed to him what the Brahmins said of him. Then Vasettha said: "The Brahmins, Lord, say thus: 'Only a Brahmin is of the best social grade; other grades are low. Only a Brahmin is of a clear complexion; other complexions are swarthy. Only Brahmins are of pure breed; not they that are not of the Brahmins. Only Brahmins are genuine children of Brahma, born of his mouth, offspring of Brahma, created by Brahma, heirs of Brahma. As for you, you have renounced the best rank and have gone over to that low class, to the shaven recluses, to vulgar rich, to them of swarthy skins, to the foot-born descendants.

Such a course is not good, such a course is not proper, even this, that you, having forsaken that upper class, should associate with an inferior class, to wit, with shovelling, fair folks, menials, swarthy of skin, the offspring of our kinsmen's heels. In these terms, Lord, do the Brahmins blame and revile me with characteristic abuse, copious, not at all stinted." "Surely, Vasettha," said the Buddha, "the Brahmins have quite forgotten the ancient lore when they say so. On the contrary, the wives of Brahmins, like all women of other classes, are seen to be with child, bringing forth and nursing children. And yet it is these very womb-born Brahmins who say that Brahmins are genuine children of Brahma, born from his mouth; his offspring; his creation; and his heirs! By this they make a travesty of the nature of Brahma." Once the Brahmin Esukari went to the Buddha to argue with him three questions. The first question he raised related to the permanent division of occupations.

In defence of the system he began by saying: "I have come to ask you a question. The Brahmins say they shall serve nobody because they stand above all. Everyone else is born to serve them. "Service, Gautama, is divided into four—service of Brahmin, service of noble, service of a middle-class man, or by a peasant; while a peasant may be served only by a peasant,—for who else could?" What does the reverend Gautama say hereon?" The Buddha answered him by asking a question: "Is the whole world in accord with Brahmins in their fourfold division of service?" asked the Lord. "For myself, I neither assert that all service is to be rendered nor that all service is to be refused. If the service makes a man bad and not good, it should not be rendered; but if it makes him better and not bad, then it should be rendered.

This is the guiding consideration which should decide the conduct alike of nobbles, of Brahmins, of middle-class men and of peasants; each individual should refuse service which makes him bad and should accept only the service which makes him a better man." The next question raised was by Esukari. "Why should ancestry and lineage not have a place in determining the status of a man?" To this question the Buddha replied thus: "As against pride of ancestry, the station into which a man happens to be born determines only his designation be it noble or Brahmin or middle-class or peasant.

Even as a fire is called after the material out of which it is kindled, and may thus be called either a wood-fire, or a chip-fire, or a bracken-fire, or a cow dung fire, just in the same way the noble, transcendent doctrine, I aver, is the source of true wealth for every man, birth merely determining his designation in one of the four classes. Lineage does not enter into a man's being either good or bad: nor do good looks or wealth. For, you will find a man of noble birth who is a murderer, a thief, a fornicator, a liar, a slanderer, a man of bitter tongue, a tattler, a covetous person, a man of rancour or of wrong views, and therefore I assert that noble birth does not make a good man. Or again you will find a man of noble birth who is innocent of all these vices; and, therefore, I assert that it is not lineage which makes a man bad." The third question which Esukari raised was with regard to the ways of earning a living assigned to each class.

The Brahmin Esukari said to the Lord: "Brahmins give a fourfold assignment of income, from alms, for Brahmins; from his bow and arrows, for the noble; from ploughing and tending cattle, for the middle-class man; and for the peasant, by the carriage of crops on the pole slung over his shoulder. If anyone of these deserts his vocation for something else, he does what he should not do, not less than a guardian who appropriates what is not his. What does the reverend Gautama say on this?" "Is the whole world in accord with this Brahmin classification?" asked the Lord. "No," replied Esukari. To Vasettha he said: "What is important is high ideals and not noble birth. "No caste; no inequality; no superiority; no inferiority; all are equal.

Dr. Ambedkar's analysis and formulations on the ruling classes, Congress and Gandhism were quite different from the official Ambedkarite perceptions. Moreover, "his evaluation about the western parliamentary system and approving references to the Paris Commune and the soviet system exploded all theories that Ambedkar was anti-communist".

> *As it comes out, Gandhian approach was basically to undertake some reforms within Hinduism through what is called "constructive work" to secure the support of untouchables behind the savarna leadership of Congress in the freedom struggle. Ambedkar, on the other hand, strove*

> *for a radical restructuring of Hinduism to do away with caste system itself and to provide a political platform to the rising Dalit aspirations. These two contradictory approaches of Gandhi and Ambedkar defined their relationship with each other, with other communities like Muslims and with the British Government.*

Commenting on Gandhi's economic philosophy Ambedkar wrote, "there was nothing new in the Gandhian analysis of economic ills as attributable to machinery and the civilisation built upon it. These were old and worn out arguments, a repetition of Rousseau, Pushkin and Tolstoy. His economics was hopelessly fallacious because the evils produced by the mechanised production system and civilisation are not due to machinery as such... They are due to the wrong social organisation which has made private property and pursuit of personal gain a matter of absolute sanctity... The remedy therefore is not to condemn machinery and civilisation but to alter the organisation of society so that the benefits will not be usurped by the few but accrue to all."

In his conflict with Gandhi, Ambedkar undoubtedly emerges as the foremost exponent of a radical socioeconomic programme in the freedom struggle:

> *From Harijans to dalits—there lies the whole course of transformation in the self-perception of untouchables and none but Ambedkar had been the moving spirit behind this transformation. He was perhaps the first Dalit leader, who combined with a fair degree of success the social awakening of dalits with their political assertion.*

Ambedkar's other major contribution was drafting the Constitution of independent India. He shared Nehru's vision of a modern India and in a certain sense exhibited a greater insight than Nehru. In contrast to Nehru's emphasis on discovery of India, he declared, "In believing that we are a nation we are chasing a great delusion. We can only attempt to become a nation-in the-making."

He opted for a constitutional state socialism, stood for a strong centre, and advocated an economic programme comprising nationalisation of land and its distribution among peasants for collective cultivation and nationalisation of key industries. He believed that such an economic programme backed by state welfare measures positively discriminated in favour of depressed classes will lead to the 'annihilation of caste', his ultimate goal.

His crusade for social liberation of dalits remained central to him and he parted company with Nehru when Nehru gave in to the conservative pressure on Hindu Code Bill. This further convinced Ambedkar that casteism was basic to Hinduism and dalits have no option but to break out of its fold.

And thus he embraced Buddhism which he interpreted in a modernistic sense hoping to herald a new sociocultural awakening among dalits. In the realm of political action he envisaged the formation of the Republican Party as an independent democratic party of the oppressed classes.

Thus, Ambedkar's crusade reached its crescendo. Unfortunately for him only his community of Mahars joined him in conversion to Buddhism and after his death his political movement represented by the Republican Party of India got splintered and appropriated by the Congress.

In class terms Ambedkar represented the petty bourgeois stratum of dalits that included the small-medium peasantry. Their particular socioeconomic conditions were the basic roots of Ambedkar's radicalism and also the source of his limitations. In given conditions he could only strive for a full-scale development of capitalism and a strong capitalist welfare state which shall be instrumental in breaking the age-old social immobility and inertia. His approving references to some aspects of communist practice and invoking socialist jargons only reveal his radical bourgeois democratic essence.

This is not an indictment of Ambedkar. On the contrary, it places him high above many historical figures of his times who stood for a conservative path of capitalist development preserving the "Brahminical-Bania alliances" to use Ambedkar's own phrase.

Ambedkar's vacillations, compromises and ultimate recourse to a religious praxis too emanate from the same socioeconomic conditions of his existence. The inherent limitations of a Dalit petty bourgeois to chart out an alternative strategy of freedom movement forced him sometimes to enter into compromises with Gandhi and Congress and at other times to pin hopes on British. The alternative strategy could have been chalked out only by communists who represented the Indian urban and rural proletariat — a good majority of whom came from dalits. A close political alliance with radical bourgeois democrats of all hues must have been an inalienable part of the alternative strategy. Communist Party of India failed to undertake this responsibility. But that is another story.

"It was the sincerity of purpose, the human weakness and 'forget and forgive' characteristic of the dalits, the oppressed, as opposed to the cunning and calculating nature of the Brahminical classes" that made Ambedkar adjust with Congress over and over again. "Ambedkarism remained within the confines of bourgeois democratic consciousness" for 'it could not transcend the limit set by its peasant roots".

To transcend the limits which Ambedkar failed to do, is fascination to analyse.

"Ambedkarism was not rooted in a class with total upward mobility permitting complete merger of the class or even individuals and small groups within the bourgeois system. It representcd a peasant society in the process of partial proletarianisation and partial dispossession with an upper crust eagerness for upward mobility being frustrated. It was this phenomenon which destroyed all the efforts at alignment between the untouchables and the ruling bourgeoisie. This was why Dr. Ambedkar was repulsed from the ruling classes after each and every encounter with them. It provides the great potential of Ambedkarism to grow out of limits of bourgeois society."

Ambedkar's certain approving references on Marx, Paris Commune and Soviet system. Combined with Ambedkar's denunciation of twin enemies of Brahminism and capitalism and his advocacy of "Socialist programme", all this is taken to symbolise Ambedkar's journey towards communism.

Even conversion to Buddhism is interpreted as an answer to the problems raised by Marxism in general and by its concrete application in India in particular. His religio-political praxis becomes a precursor to the Cultural Revolution and democratic resurgence within Marxist ideology and movement. "In some sense Ambedkar's Buddhist resurrection presaged Mao's Cultural Revolution".

Untouchables would often do work considered too dirty by members of regular caste society. The caste system has been mainly criticised for its treatment of outcastes or untouchables. This group has been termed the *panchama* (the fifth *varna*), collectively designating all who fall outside the regular four classes.

DALITS AND RELIGION

Hindu Dalits (Harijans): Many Dalits continue to debate whether they are 'Hindu' or 'non-Hindu'. Missionaries have initiated several Dalit organizations. In some regions of India and Nepal, missionaries have been successful among the Dalits. Both in Eastern India and Nepal, many Dalits have come under the combined influence of Maoists and the missionaries, even attacking and murdering Hindus.

Traditionally, Hindu Dalits or Harijans have been barred from many activities that were seen as central to Vedic religion and Hindu practices of orthodox sects. Among Hindus each community has followed its own variation of Hinduism. The wide variety of practices and beliefs observed in Hinduism makes any clear assessment difficult.

Some of the movements in Hinduism have welcomed Dalits into their fold. The Satnami movement was founded by Guru Ghasidas a Dalit himself. In addition, other Hindu groups have reached out to the Dalit community in an effort to reconcile with them, with productive results. On August 2006, Dalit activist Namdeo Dhasal engaged in dialogue with the Rashtriya Swayamsevak Sangh in an attempt to "bury the hatchet".

In addition, the "Pandaram" are an order of Dalit Hindu priests (a task traditionally reserved for the Brahmins) based largely in Nepal and parts of South India. These Pandaram priests maintain the same tradition as the Brahmin priests, including using Sanskrit for the rituals (a language traditionally reserved for the Brahmins). They perform religious ceremonies from weddings to death rituals. They are not generally as well trained as the Brahmin priests, but are highly respected within their community and are addressed reverentially.

Another popular Harijan includes Babaji Palwankar Baloo, who joined the Hindu Mahasabha and was both a politician and a cricketer. He was an independence fighter.

However, extremist far-right militia groups such as the Ranvir Sena, largely run by upper-caste landlords in backward areas of the Indian state of Bihar, oppose equal treatment of Dalits and have resorted to violent means to suppress them. The Ranvir Sena is considered a terrorist organization. On the other side, extremist groups run by small minority of Dalits such as the "Dalit Panthers Movement" have committed violent acts against Brahmins and middle-caste people.

In Pakistan, a predominantly Muslim nation, more than 60% of the 1.4 million Hindu minority are Dalits.

Muslim Dalits (Arzal/Muhajir): Muslim society in India can also be separated into several caste-like groups. Descendants of indigenous lower-caste converts are discriminated against by "noble", or "ashraf", Muslims who can trace their descent to Arab, Iranian, or Central-Asian ancestors. There are several groups in India working to emancipate them from upper-caste

Muslim discrimination. The Dalit Muslims are referred to by the Ashraf and Ajlaf Muslims as Arzal or "ritually degraded". They are also referred to as "Mujahir" in Pakistan and euphemistically called "Bhaiya". They were first recorded in the 1901 census as those "with whom no other Muhammadan would associate, and who are forbidden to enter the mosque or to use the public burial ground". They are relegated to "menial" professions such as scavenging and carrying night soil. Baba Saheb Ambedkar, a reknowned Dalit activist and the framer of the Constitution of India, wrote about the Dalit Muslims and was extremely critical of their mistreatment by upper-caste Muslims quoting that "Within these groups there are castes with social precedence of exactly the same nature as one finds among the Hindus".

In Pakistan, a predominantly Muslim nation, 80% of the Muslim farmers of Sindh or 24% of the total population are Mojahir. There are estimated to be 6.8 million Mayazurs (bonded labourers) in Punjab and another 7.5 million in Sindh. Although the Pakistani Supreme Court has ruled bonded labour unconstitutional and the National Assembly has passed laws prohibiting it, these laws remain largely unenforced due to the influence of large landlords.

Sikh Dalits: Master Tara Singh himself helped uplift the Sikh Dalits. KP Singh a Dalit activist in UP was himself a Sikh. Kanshi Ram himself was of Sikh background although converted because he found that Sikh society did not respect Dalits and so became a neo-Buddhist. The Mazhabi are one Dalit of the Punjabi Dalits that are treated as outcastes from mainstream Sikh society and not allowed to enter Sikh temples. Jivan Singh, a friend of Guru Gobind Singh was a Dalit.

Christian Dalits: Converts to Christianity (facilitated by the influence of missionaries) have retained the caste system in their communities. The Dalit Christians are at the lowest rung of that hierarchy.

A 1992 study of Catholics in Tamil Nadu showed that Dalit Christians face segregated churches, cemeteries, services and processions. They also face economic and social hardships due to the discrimination by upper-caste priests and nuns. One famous Dalit activist with the nom-de-plume of Bama Faustina has written books that provide a first-hand account of the discrimination against them by nuns and priests in South India.

Dalits and Neo-Buddhism: In Maharashtra and a few other regions, Dalits have come under the influence of the neo-Buddhist movement initiated by Ambedkar. Some of them have come under the influence of the Neo-Buddhist and Christian Missionaries and have converted away from Hinduism into religions such as Christianity and Buddhism in what they have been told is an "attempt to eliminate the prejudice they face". Activists such as Udit Raj have claimed that such conversion will solve all discrimination problems faced by Dalits. Such claims have been criticized as "fragile at best".

The conversion attempts have also been criticized by Hindu advocacy groups as "unhelpful" as Casteism is a complex dynamic that extends across all religions in India. However, the Constitution of India guarantees religious freedom and their right to choose their religion, although controversies related to mass-conversions have led to laws being passed against them in some states in India. Since then, several Christian converts have reconverted back into Hinduism as the conversions did not award them the financial rewards that the missionaries lured them with.

3

CONVERSION BY OPERATION OF THE LAW

There is only one case in which conversion takes place by operation of the Law. That case is the case of Partners. Under the Partnership Act of 1890, Section 39, every partner has a right to require, that the property belonging to the Partnership shall be sold and the proceeds, after the discharge of all debts and liabilities, shall be divided among the partners according to their shares in the capital. As a result, land which is partnership property is treated as Personality and not as Realty:

- It is treated as Personality, not only as between Partners themselves and their representatives after death, for the purposes of distribution of the partnership assets, but it is also treated as personality for purposes of inheritance as between the persons entitled to the property of a deceased partner.
- The conversion of Realty into Personality under the Partnership Act takes place not on the date of the dissolution of the Partnership or the death of a partner but at the moment when it became Partnership Property.
- The doctrine of conversion applies to Partnership Realty unless the contrary intention appears. The reason why partnership agreements convert Realty into Personality is, because a partner ordinarily is not entitled on dissolution to any specific part of the partnership property. But there may be a proviso in the partnership agreement permitting a partner to have specific

property, in which case conversion will not apply, there being intention to the contrary.

CONVERSION BY ORDER OF THE COURT

- Where an order is made by the Court for the sale of Realty, the Realty is treated as being converted into Personality for purposes of succession to the estate of the person whose property was ordered to be sold. The Court orders the sale of the Realty. This order has the effect of converting their shares in Realty into Personality, so that the persons entitled to succeed would be the next of kin and not the heir:
- The following points must be:
  - — The order for sale must be within the jurisdiction of the Court
  - — It is immaterial whether the purpose for which it is sold will or will not exhaust the sale proceeds. The sale may be merely to pay cost. All the same, if the order is for sale, within the jurisdiction, it will effect conversion
  - — It is immaterial whether it is actually sold or is merely ordered to be sold. Order for sale is enough to effect conversion.
  - — Conversion takes place from the date of the order and not from the date of the sale.
- There are two cases in which the order of the Court will not effect conversion for the purpose of inheritance:
  - — Where the Court itself makes an order that such change in the nature of the property shall not affect its devolution on death, in which case the sale proceeds will go to the heir and not to the next-of-kin.
  - — Where the provision of some statute prohibits a change in the nature of the property from affecting its devolution *e.g.* Section 123 of the Lunacy Act, 1890, which provides that if the property of a

lunatic is sold, the proceeds will go to persons entitled to them as though it was not sold.

CASES OF PARTIAL FAILURE

- Where the purposes have only partially failed, then conversion is necessary to carry out such purposes as have not failed. Consequently the doctrine of conversion would operate and the representative entitled to take the property in the form in which it is directed to be converted.
- It will be carried out to the extent necessary.

RECONVERSION

- Reconversion means annulment or cancellation of prior conversion. It is a reversion or restoration of the notional state of the property to its actual state. Reconversion can take place in two ways :
  - (i) By act of parties.
  - (ii) By operation of law.

BY ACT OF PARTIES

- This occurs where a person has the right to choose between taking the property in its converted State or in its actual state.
- Persons who have a right to make such an election and thereby reconvert property are:
  - — An absolute owner.
  - — A owner of an undivided share—without the concurrence of the co-owner in the case of money to be converted into land but not in the case of land to be converted into money. This is because money is capable of apportionment while land is not.

Infants and Lunatics are persons under disability and cannot, therefore, reconvert. But the Court may direct reconversion on their behalf if it is beneficial to them.

Married woman can reconvert if the property belongs to her for her separate use. If it is not her separate property, then she can do so only with the consent of her husband. (4) Evidence of election to reconvert:

(i) express declaration of intention in that behalf;

(ii) conduct amounting to election.

Reconversion by Law: Where a person, who is under an obligation to convert property, is in possession of and absolutely entitled to the property after the obligation has ceased/the property is at home and reconverted without any act on his part. Thus—

A converts within 3 years after his marriage with B to invest £ 1,000 in the purchase of lands and settle them upon his wife *B*. B dies within a year of the marriage. Since the obligation to invest money in land and the right to require its investment are both vested in A, the obligation is discharged by operation of law and the money which was converted into land by the covenant is reconverted and passes to the next-of-kin.

NECESSITY FOR THE DOCTRINE OF CONVERSION

- The English Law had prescribed a different mode of devolution of the Realty and Personality of the owner, if he died intestate. His Realty went to his heir and Personality went to his next-of-kin.
- That being so, whether the property will go to the heir or to the next of kin must depend upon the state of the property on the date on which the succession opens.
- Ordinarily there is no difficulty. The actual state in which the property will be found on the material date will determine its devolution. But suppose, circumstances are such that on the date on which the succession opens, land is to be sold for money but is not sold, or money is to be invested in the purchase of land but is not so invested, how is the devolution of the

property to be determined? If the land is to be treated as land, until it is actually sold, then it will go to the heir. On the other hand, if it is to be treated as money, because it was intended to be sold for money, then although it is land, it will go to the next-of-kin. In other words, the question was whether property was to devolve according to the actual state in which it is found to exist or according to the form in which it was intended to be converted. The answer given by equity was, that property was to devolve, not according to the actual state in which it exists, but according to the form in which it was intended to be converted.

- This is what is called the doctrine of conversion. There would have been no necessity for the doctrine, had there been no difference in the rules of inheritance for Real and Personal Property. This difference is now abolished by Sections 33,45 and therefore, conversion has lost all its importance.
- In India there is no such distinction in the inheritance of property—Realty to heir and Personality to next-of-kin.

FOUR CASES WHICH GIVE RISE TO CONVERSION.

- By operation of the law.
- By operation of the order of the Court.
- By operation of a Contract.
- By operation of a direction in a deed or a will.

CONVERSION BY OPERATION OF A CONTRACT

- When there is a binding contract to sell Realty, the Realty is treated as part of vendors Personality. Conversely, the interest of the purchaser is treated as Realty, even if he dies before completion.
- This is, however, subject to one condition. That is, the contract must be one of which specific performance would be ordered by the Court.

Mere notice to treat does not suffice to bring into operation the doctrine of conversion. There will be no conversion if the contract is abortive or unenforceable.

CONVERSION UNDER A CONTRACT TO LEASE WITH AN OPTION TO PURCHASE

A leases certain property *to B* for seven years, giving him by the lease an option to purchase the property at a certain price during the term. *B* exercises his option. Three questions arise:

- Does the exercise of the option effect a conversion?
- Does it effect a conversion even if the option is exercised after the death of the Lessor?
- From what date does such conversion begin to operate?

Does the Exercise of the Option Effect a Conversion?: In law, the option given is an offer to sell. The exercise of the option is an acceptance of the offer and when there is an acceptance of the offer, there is a contract. The exercise of the option by respecting in a contract effects a conversion. The answer to the first question is therefore in the affirmative.

EXERCISE OF THE OPTION BEFORE THE DEATH OF THE LESSEE AND AFTER THE DEATH OF THE LESSOR

- If the Lessee exercises his option *before* the death of the Lessor, *i.e.*, while he is alive, then there is conversion, because the offer conveyed by the option can be legally accepted and a binding contract can arise.
- If the lessee exercises the option *after* the death, then, on principle, there ought not to be conversion, because there cannot be a contract. An offer cannot be accepted after the person, who make the offer, is dead.
- The rule in *Lawes vs. Benett* being anomalous, is confined in its operation. It is applied as between persons claiming under the lessor. But it is not made applicable as between lessor and lessee.

FROM WHAT DATE DOES CONVERSION BY CONTRACT BEGIN TO OPERATE.

- Conversion becomes operative from the moment when the contract is made.
- In the case of option to purchase, conversion takes place as from the execution of the lease.
- For the purposes of profits etc., the property remains real estate until the option is exercised, so that the rents and profits are taken by the heir entitled to Realty.
- For the purposes of devolution, it is personality.

CONVERSION BY DIRECTION OF THE OWNER— WHETHER CONTAINED IN A DEED OR A WILL

- Two things are necessary for conversion by deed or will : (i) There must be a direction to sell or purchase Realty. (ii) There must be some person in existence who can be said to have the right to insist upon the direction being carried out. Conversion is always for the benefit of some person. If there is no person to claim the benefit, then there need be no conversion.
- In order to effect a conversion, the direction must be imperative. If direction is only *optional*, there will be no conversion and property will be treated as real or personal, according as to the actual condition in which it is found.
- Distinction must be made between direction to sell or purchase Realty and discretion as to the time at which sale or purchase shall be made:
  - — If the direction is imperative, mere fact that it is accompanied by discretion, will not prevent conversion having its effect.
  - — If the direction is imperative, the fact that those to whom the direction was given have failed to carry it out, will not prevent conversion having its effect.

- Distinction must be made between a simple direction to sell or purchase and a direction, the execution of which, is made dependent *on the request* or *consent* of some other person. In such a case, whether there will be conversion or not, rests upon the construction of the document :
  — If the intention of the clause is to enable the person named to *enforce the obligation to convert,* then there will be conversion.
  — If the intention of the clause is *to control the operation of the direction* by making it subject to application, then there will be no conversion until such application is made.
- Distinction must be made between the power to convert and direction to convert.

TIME FROM WHICH CONVERSION BY DIRECTION TAKES

- This varies according as the direction is contained in a will or in a deed.
- If the direction is contained in a will, conversion will take place as from the death of the testator.
- If the direction is contained in a deed, conversion will take place as from the date of the execution of the deed—not withstanding that the trust to sell or purchase is not to arise until after the, settlor's death.

EFFECT OF THE FAILURE OF OBJECTS FOR WHICH CONVERSION WAS DIRECTED IN A WILL OR DEED

Two cases must be distinguished:

(i) Cases of total failure.

(ii) Cases of partial failure.

CASES OF TOTAL FAILURE

- Where there is a *total* failure of the objects *before* or *at the time* when the deed or will came into operation, or before the time at which the duty to convert is to arise, no conversion will take place at all and the property will remain as it was.

The reason is that, there is no one who can insist upon the character of the property being altered.

- The failure must *beprior* failure and not *subsequent* failure.
- The rule regarding conversion is uniform in the case of total failure and there is no difference between the effects of a direction in a deed and a direction in a will.

4

MARXISM, COMMUNISM AND AMBEDKAR

INTRODUCTION

Marx has given scientific explanation of religion, and that it is "Religion is the Opium of the people". But "it can not lead people who suffer difficulties to overcome the difficulties. It only allows them to anaesthetize themselves, thereby, Religion changes material struggle into a kind of spiritual comfort. It transforms real needs to hopes of an illusory world." It apparently equate religion with God, and as Science has disproved the existence of God, and as so called religious ethics comes from the will of God, it has no meaning.

Secondly, only Marxism holds that, ultimately, rooting out private ownership will remove all evil. Though Socialism has brought liberation of masses, still people believe in religion. This is because of legacy of feudalism, influence of capitalism, imperialism, beurocratism.

Lastly it outline the line of action not only for their own country but for the whole world. It appears, as if, the Communist party of China thinks it necessary to form a united front with "patriotic religious believers to oppose the reactionary forces at home and abroad and to carry out socialist revolution and modernization". These are bound to expound Marxism through "research into religion and into its history, doctrine and present circumstances." This propaganda one wishes to do with "unhurried discussion to reason things out" by criticizing religion but not the people who follow or preach it, except the "criminals". Of course they do not forget to assign the power of final judgment to a few persons as they say that all this must be according to the "theories, plans and policies of Party Central".

They, however, admit that there were "religious wrongs", but blame the "Gang of four" with their "ultra leftist" attitude for these religious wrongs. Further claiming that State is not controlling Religion.

There is such a vast literature by Dr. Ambedkar in favour of Buddhism and against Communism, that only quoting from Ambedkar, who has already thought over Communism for years before giving Buddhism to the multitudes of Indian masses, will answer all points raised before. One thing needs to be remembered is that Ambedkar's views are nearly fifty years old, and are still valid. They do not mention Mao, as his theories had not then come into prominence, but what he says about communism in general should also apply to Maoism too.

The very fact that "The Gang of Four" can become successful in capturing power and do the things, against the "real" Marxism, proves the fact that there is some inherent weaknesses in Marxism.

PREREQUISITES OF COMMUNISM

Dr. Ambedkar avers that there are certain prerequisites for the Marxism to succeed. These are the society should be a "Free society", meaning it should give importance to an Individual over the society and that it should be based on equality, fraternity and liberty. [Ambedkar, "India and the Prerequisites of Communism", (W&S vol. 3,), p. 95]

These have been brought to China by Buddhism and to Russia by Christianity. The absence of these factors in caste ridden Indian society could not foster the growth of Marxism in India, and that is why Marx failed in Hindu India. Marx could not properly evaluate the importance of caste or its influence on Indian masses. Because, Marx failed here, his followers in India talk of "Class" and not of "Caste". That is the reason, the movement of Marx in India was and still is in the hands of oppressor class.

RESIDUE OF MARXISM

Marx expounded his theories about 150 years ago. Most of Marxism is demolished during these years. But what remains of the Karl Marx, Dr. Ambedkar feels, is a residue of fire, small but still very important. The residue in his opinion, consists of four items:

1. The function of philosophy is to reconstruct the world and not to waste its time in explaining the origin of the world.
2. That there is a conflict of interest between class and class.
3. That private ownership of property brings power to one class and sorrow to another through exploitation.
4. That it is necessary for the good of society that the sorrow be removed by the abolition of private property.

COMPARISON BETWEEN BUDDHA AND KARL MARX

Taking the points form the Marxian Creed which have survived Dr. Ambedkar compares the Buddha and Karl Marx. He feels that, on the first point there is complete agreement between the Buddha and Karl Marx. That language is different but the meaning is the same. If for misery one reads exploitation Buddha is not away form Marx.

On the question of private property, Dr. Ambedkar quotes the illuminating extract from a dialogue between Buddha and Ananda, Buddha saying avarice is because of possession, which in turn is because of tenacity. Not only Buddha prohibited private property in Sangha, he put more restrictions and "rules are far more rigorous than are to be found in Communism in Russia".

MEANS TO ACHIEVE GOALS

Dr. Ambedkar, then, examines the means to achieve the goals. Having summarized Buddha's tenets, he feels that, it is clear that the means adopted by the Buddha were to convert a man by changing his moral disposition to follow the path voluntarily. The means adopted by the Communists are equally clear, short and swift. They are (1) Violence and (2) Dictatorship of the Proletariat.

The Communists say that there are the only two means of establishing Communism. The first is violence. Nothing short of it will be suffice to break up the existing system. The other is Dictatorship of the Proletariat. Nothing short of it will be suffice to continue the new system. It is now clear what are the similarities and differences between Buddha and Karl Marx. The differences are about the means. The end is common to both.

The Bhikshu Sangha had the most democratic constitution. The Buddha was only one of the Bhikkus. At the most he was like a Prime Minister among members of the Cabinet. He was never a dictator. Twice before his death be was asked to appoint some one as the head of the Sangha to control it. But each time he refused saying that the Dhamma is the Supreme Commander of the Sangha. He refused to be a dictator and refused to appoint a dictator. Can the Communists say that in achieving their valuable they have not destroyed other valuable ends? They have destroyed private property. Assuming that this is a valuable end can the Communists say that they have not destroyed other valuable end in the process of achieving it? How many people have they killed for achieving their end. Has human life no value? Could they not have taken property without taking the life of the owner?

Dictatorship is often defined as absence of liberty or absence of Parliamentary Government. Both interpretations are not quite clear. There is no liberty even when there is Parliamentary Government. For law means want of liberty. The difference between Dictatorship and Parliamentary Government lies in this. In Parliamentary Government every citizen has a right to criticize the restraint on liberty imposed by the Government. In Parliamentary Government you have a duty and a right; the duty to obey the law and right to criticize it. In Dictatorship you have only duty to obey but no right to criticize it.

We must now consider whose means are more lasting. One has to chose between Government by force and Government by moral disposition. As Burke has said force cannot be a lasting means. In his speech on conciliation with America he uttered this memorable warning:

> *"First, Sir, permit me to observe, that the use of force alone is but temporary. It may subdue for a moment: But it does not remove the necessity of subduing again; and a nation is not governed which is perpetually to be conquered."*

"The next objection is its uncertainty. Terror is not always the effect of force, and an armament is not a victory. If you do not succeed, you are without resource, for, conciliation failing, force remains; but force failing, no further hope of reconciliation is left. Power and authority are sometimes bought by kindness; but they can never be begged as alms by an impoverished and defeated violence.

A further objection to force is, that you impair the object by your very endeavours to preserve it. The thing you fought for is the thing which you recover, but depreciated, sunk, wasted and consumed in the contest."

WITHERING AWAY OF STATE

Dr. Ambedkar also discusses the Communist theory of "withering away of the state". He says, The Communists themselves admit that their theory of the State as a permanent dictatorship is a weakness in their political philosophy. They take shelter under the plea that the State will ultimately wither away. There are two questions which they have to answer. (1) When will it wither away? (2) What will take the place of the State when it withers away? To the first question they can give no definite time.

Though the second question is more important than the first, Dr. Ambedkar feels, the Communists have no satisfactory answer to the question what would take the place of the State when it withers away. Will it be succeed by Anarchy? If so, he feels, the building up of the Communist State is an useless effort. If it cannot be sustained except by force and if it results in anarchy when the force holding it together is withdrawn what good is the Communist State.

He therefore avers that, the only thing which could sustain it after force is withdrawn is Religion. He observes:

> *"But to the Communists, Religion is anathema. Their hatred to Religion is so deep seated that they will not even discriminate between religions which are helpful to Communism and religions which are not. The Communists have carried their hatred of Christianity to Buddhism without waiting to examine the difference between the two."*

CHARGES AGAINST CHRISTIANITY

Dr. Ambedkar discusses two charges against Christianity levelled by the Communists. Surprisingly, the same charges are levelled by Chinese Research Scholars in the same terminology. Ambedkar answers these charges as he observes:

> *"Their first charge against Christianity was that they made people worship other worldliness and made them suffer poverty in this world. As can be seen from quotations from Buddhism in the earlier part of this tract such a charge cannot be levelled against Buddhism."*

Dr. Ambedkar then answers the second charge as follows:

> *"The second charge levelled by the Communists against Christianity cannot be levelled against Buddhism. This charge is summed up in the statement that Religion is the opium of the people. This charge is based upon the Sermon on the Mount which is to be found in the Bible. The Sermon on the Mount sublimates poverty and weakness. It promises heaven to the poor and the weak. There is no Sermon on*

the Mount to be found in the Buddha's teachings. His teaching is to acquire wealth." [Ibid. p.460]

He then gives the Buddha's Sermon on the subject to Anathapindika one of his disciples, wherein Buddha describes how wealth should be acquired justly and legitimately.

Dr. Ambedkar concludes the discussion by observing:

The Russians are proud of their communism. But they forget that the wonder of all wonders is that the Buddha established Communism so far as the Sangha was concerned without dictatorship. It may be that it was a communism on a very small scale but it was communism without dictatorship, a miracle which Lenin failed to do.

The Buddha's method was different. His method was to change the mind of man: to alter his disposition: so that whatever man does, he does it voluntarily without the use of force or compulsion. His main means to alter the disposition of men was his Dhamma and the constant preaching of his Dhamma. The Buddha's way not to force people to do what they did not like to do although it was good for them. His way was to alter the disposition of men so that they would do voluntarily what they would not otherwise to do.

"It has been claimed that the Communist Dictatorship in Russia has wonderful achievements to its credit. There can be no denial of it. That is why I say that a Russian Dictatorship would be good for all backward countries. But this his no argument for permanent Dictatorships. Humanity does not only want economic values, it also wants spiritual values to be retained. Permanent Dictatorship has paid no attention to spiritual values and does not seem to intend to. Carlyle called Political Economy a Pig Philosophy. Carlyle was of course wrong. For man needs material comforts. But the Communist Philosophy seems to be equally wrong for the aim of their philosophy seems to be fatten pigs as though men are no better than pigs. Man must grow materially as well as spiritually. Society has been aiming to lay a new foundation was summarized by the French Revolution in three words. Fraternity, Liberty and Equality. The French Revolution was welcomed because of this slogan. It failed to produce equality. We welcome the Russian Revolution because it aims to produce equality. But it cannot be too much emphasized that in producing equality society cannot afford to sacrifice fraternity or liberty.

Equality will be of no value without fraternity or liberty. It seems that the three can coexist only if one follows the way of the Buddha. Communism can give one but not all.

TESTS OF RELIGION

In his memorable treatise, "Buddha and future of His Religion", after comparing Buddhism with Hinduism, while comparing Buddhism with other non-hindu religions, Dr. Ambedkar concludes by enumerating the tests a religion must pass:

1. That society must have either the sanction of law or the sanction of morality to hold it together. Without either society is sure to go pieces. In all societies law plays a very small part. It is intended to keep the minority within the range of social discipline. The majority is left and has to be left to sustain its social life by the postulates and sanction of morality. Religion in the sense of morality, must therefore, remain the governing principle in every society.
2. That religion as defined in the first proposition must be in accord with science. Religion is bound to lose it respect and therefore become the subject of ridicule and thereby not merely lose its force as a governing principle of life but might in course of time disintegrated and lapse if it is not in accordance with science. In other words, religion if it is to function, must be in accordance with reason which is merely another name for science.
3. That religion as a code of social morality, must recognize the fundamental tenets of liberty, equality and fraternity.

Unless a religion recognizes these three fundamental principles of social life religion will be doomed.

4. That religion must not sanctify or ennoble poverty. Renunciation of riches by those who have it may be a blessed state. But poverty can never be. To declare poverty to be a blessed state is to pervert religion, to perpetuate vice crime, to consent to make earth a living hell."

Dr. Ambedkar asks, which religion fulfils these requirements today, reminding that the days of the Mahatmas are gone and the world cannot have a new Religion. It will have to make its choice from existing religions. Some of the religions might satisfy one or two tests but Buddhism is the only religion satisfying all tests. He observes:

"So far as I know the only religion which satisfies all these tests is Buddhism. In other words Buddhism is the only religion which the world can have. If the new world—which be it realized is very different from the old—must have a religion—and the new world needs religion for more than the old world did—then it can only be religion of the Buddha."

"COULD THE BUDDHA ANSWER KARL MARX?"

Admitting that all this may sound very strange, because most of writers on Buddha have propagated the idea that the only thing Buddha taught was Ahimsa. It is true Buddha taught Ahimsa, he says, he does not want to minimize its importance, because it is a great doctrine and the world can not be saved without it. He further observes:

"What I wish to emphasize is that Buddha taught many other things besides Ahimsa. He taught as a part of religion, social freedom, intellectual freedom, economic freedom and political freedom. He taught equality, equality not between man and man only but between man and woman. It would be difficult to find a religious teacher to compare with Buddha whose teachings embrace so many aspects of the

social life of a people whose doctrines are so modern and whose main concern was to give salvation to man in his life on earth and not to promise it to him in heaven after he is dead." [Buddha and future of his religion", p. 10]

Dr. Ambedkar says many divergent views expressed about Buddha's teachings, including Samadhi, Vippasana, Esoterism etc. are because the authors are not students of Buddhism, but of history or anthropology. He asks "Did the Buddha have no social message?" If pressed for an answer, the Buddhist scholars admit that Buddha taught:

Ahimsa and Peace. But the real questions are seldom asked and replied. These are: Did the Buddha teach: Justice, Love, Liberty, Equality, Fraternity, and "Could the Buddha answer Karl Marx?" He further avers that "My answer is that the Buddha has a social message. He answers all these questions. But they have been buried by modern authors."

COMMANDMENTS OF BABA SAHEB AMBEDKAR

Achievements: Nothing valuable in this world is achieved except by great efforts. All great things in the world were achieved by patient industry and by undergoing toil and tribulations.

Ahimsa: Ahimsa Permo Dharma is an extreme Doctrine. It is a Jaina Doctrine. It is not Buddhist Doctrine. Buddha meant to make a distinction between 'will to kill' and 'need to kill'. What he banned was killing where there was nothing but the will to kill. Buddha made a distinction between principle and Rule. He did not make Ahimsa a matter of Rule. He enunciated it as a matter of \Principle or way of life. A Principle leaves you freedom to act. A rule does not. Rule either breaks you or you break the rule.

Ambition: One should always cherish some ambition to do something in the world. They alone rise who strive.

Anarchy: In anarchy and dictatorship, liberty is lost.

Appeasement: Appeasement means buying off the aggressor by conniving at his acts of murder, arson and loot against innocent victims of his displeasure.

Appeasement sets no limits to the demands and aspirations of the aggressor.

Army: The ultimate guarantee of the independence of a country is a safe army—an army on which you can rely to fight for the country at all times and in any eventuality. A safe army is better than a safe border.

Back to Nature: The call of back to nature means back to nakedness, back to squalor, back to poverty and back to ignorance for the vast mass of people.

Buddhism: I prefer Buddhism because it gives three principles in combination, which no other religion does. Buddhism teaches Prajna (understanding as against superstition and supernaturalism), Karuna (love), and Samata (equality). This is what man wants for a good and happy life.

Buddhist Culture: Even though Buddhism is almost extinct in India, yet it has given birth to a culture, which is far better and richer than the Brahminic culture. When the question of the National Flag and the National Emblem was being considered by the Constituent Assembly we could not find any suitable symbol from the Brahminic culture. Ultimately, the Buddhist culture came to our rescue and we accepted the Wheel of Law (Dhamma-Chakra) as the National Symbol.

Caste and Class: Caste System is not merely a division of labour. It is also a division of labourers. It is an hierarchy in which the divisions of labourers are graded one above the other.

Caste has killed public spirit. Caste has destroyed the sense of public charity. Caste has made public opinion impossible. Virtue has become caste ridden and morality has become caste bound. There is no sympathy to the deserving. There is no appreciation of the meritorious.

There cannot be a more degrading system of social organisation than the Chaturvarna. It is the system which deadens, paralyses and cripples the people from helpful activity.

Caste in the hands of the orthodox has been a powerful weapon for persecuting the reforms and for killing all reform.

These castes are anti-national. In the first place because they bring about separation in social life. They are anti-national also because they generate jealousy and antipathy between caste and caste.

The Caste system is a system which is infested with the spirit of isolation and in fact it makes isolation of one Caste from another a virtue. There is isolation in the class system. But it does not make isolation virtue nor does it prohibit social intercourse. The class system, it is true produces groups, but they are not akin to Caste groups. The groups in the class system are only non-social while the Castes in the Castes system are in their mutual relations definitively and positively antisocial.

Practically speaking, in a class structure, there is on the one hand, tyranny, vanity, pride, arrogance, greed selfishness and on the other insecurity, poverty, degradation, loss of liberty, self reliance, independence dignity and self-respect. The group setup prevents an individual from acquiring consistency of mind, which is possible only when society has common ideals, common models. The group setup leads to stratification of classes. Those who are masters remain masters and those who are born in slavery remain slaves. Owners remain owners and workers remain workers. The privileged remain privileged and the serfs remain serfs.

Constitution: I feel that the Constitution is workable; it is flexible and it is strong enough to hold the country together both in peacetime and in wartime. Indeed, if I may say so, if things go wrong under the new constitution the reason will not be that we had a bad Constitution. What we will have to say is that Man was vile.

Courage: The secret of freedom is courage and courage is born in combination of individuals into a party.

Culture: It is true that man shares the constitution and functions of animals, nutritive, reproductive etc. But these are not distinctively human functions. The distinctively human function is reason, the purpose of which is to enable man to observe, meditate, cogitate, study and discover the beauties of the universe and enrich his life and control the animal elements in his life.

What divides the brute from man is culture. Culture is not possible for the brute but it is essential for man.

The aim of human society must be to enable every person to lead a life of culture which means the cultivation of the mind as distinguished from the satisfaction of mere physical wants.

While the ultimate goal of a brute's life is reached once his physical appetites are satisfied, the ultimate goal of a man's existence is not reached unless and until he has fully cultivated his mind.

Democracy: Political Democracy rests on four premises, which may be set out in the following terms: (i) The individual is an end in himself. (ii) That the individual has certain inalienable rights, which must be guaranteed to him by the Constitution. (iii) That the individual shall not be required to relinquish any of his constitutional rights as a precondition precedent to the receipt of a privilege. (iv) That the State shall not delegate powers to private persons to govern others.

The soul of Democracy is the doctrine of one man, one value. Democracy is a form and method of government whereby revolutionary changes in the economic and social life of the people are brought about without bloodshed. Democracy is not merely a form of Government. It is primarily a mode of associated living of conjoined communicated experience. It is essentially an attitude of respect and reverence towards fellowmen.

Democracy is incompatible and inconsistent with isolation and exclusiveness, resulting in the distinction between the privileged and the unprivileged. Democracy cannot work without friction unless there is fellow feeling among those who constitute the State. The first thing required for the successful working of democracy is that there must be no glaring inequalities and there must be neither an oppressed class nor a suppressed class. The second thing required is the existence of opposition to show whether the Govt. is going wrong. The third thing is equality before law and in administration.

The fourth is the observance of constitutional morality. The fifth point is the functioning of moral order in society, for moral is taken for granted in the democracy. The sixth thing is the requirement of public conscience. A democratic Government can remain democratic only if it is worked by two parties? a party in power and a party in opposition.

Despotism: To have popular government run by a single party is to let democracy become a mere form for despotism to play its part from behind it. Despotism does not cease to be despotism because it is elective. Nor does despotism become agreeable because despots belong to our own kindred.

Dhamma: According to the Buddha, Dhamma consists of Prajna and Karuna. Prajna is understanding. The Buddha made Prajna one of the two comer stones of His Dhamma because he did not wish to leave any room for superstition. Karuna is love.

Because, without it society can neither live nor grow, that is why the Buddha made it the second cornerstone of his Dhamma. A unique amalgam of Prajna and Karuna is the Dhamma of the Buddha. In Dhamma there is no place for prayers, pilgrimages, rituals, ceremonies or sacrifices. Dhamma is righteousness, which means right relations between man and man in all sphere of life.

Duty: Blessed are those who are awakened to their duty to those among whom they are born. The duty must be performed; let the efforts be successful or not; let the work be appreciated or not. When a man's sincerity of purpose and capacity are proved even his enemies come to respect him.

Education: Give up the idea that parents give 'Janma' to the child and not destiny (karma). They can mould the destiny of their children by giving them education. Knowledge is the foundation of a man's life. Education is as necessary for females as it is for males. If one's education is detrimental to the welfare of the poor, the educated man is a curse to the society. Character is more important than education.

Ethics and Economics: History shows that where ethics and economics come in conflict, victory is always with economics. Vested interests have never been known to have willingly divested themselves unless there was sufficient force to compel them.

Equality: Equality may be a fiction but nonetheless one must accept it as a governing principle.

Fate: Do not believe in fate. Believe in your strength.

Force: Force, it cannot be denied, is the medicine of the body politic and must be administered when the body politic becomes sick. But just because force is the medicine of the body politic, it cannot be allowed to become its daily bread.

Fraternity: Fraternity is the name for the disposition of an individual to treat men as the object of reverence and love and the desire to be in unity with his fellow beings.

Freedom: Freedom of the nation, if it is to be a reality, must vouchsafe the freedom of the different classes comprised in it, particularly of those who are treated as the servile classes.

Glory: Glory to those who devote their time, talents and their all to the annihilation of slavery. Glory to those who would keep on their struggle for the liberation of the enslaved in spite of heavy odds, carping humiliations, storms and dangers till the down trodden secure their human rights.

Great Man: A great man must be motivated by the dynamics of a social purpose and must act as the scourge and the scavenger of the society.

Happiness: Poverty gives rise to sorrow. But removal of poverty does not necessarily give rise to happiness. Not high standard of living but a standard of culture is what gives happiness.

Hero-worship: Bhakti (hero-worship) in religion may be a road to salvation of the self. But in politics, bhakti or hero-worship is a sure road to degradation and to eventual dictatorship. Hero-worship in the sense of expressing our unbounded admiration is one thing. To obey the hero is a totally different kind of hero worship. There is nothing wrong in the former while the latter is no doubt a most pernicious thing. The former is only man's respect for everything which is noble and of which the Great Man is only an embodiment. The former is consistent with respect, but the latter is a sign of debasement.

Hinduism: Inequality is the soul of Hinduism. To the Untouchables, Hinduism is a veritable chamber of horrors. The iron law of caste, the heartless law of karma and the senseless law of status by birth are veritable instruments of torture, which Hinduism has forged against the Untouchables.

Hinduism and Buddhism: There is a great difference between Buddhism and Hinduism. Buddhism means casteless society based on equal rights. Hinduism on the other hand is primarily based on caste system; a system which encourages aloofness, inequality and exploitation.

Unlike Hinduism, Buddhism lays no emphasis on the attainment of heaven. Nor it is necessary. To be happy in the present life, one should practice the ethics of morality, non violence (ahimsa), equality and universal brotherhood. This is an eternal truth taught by the Buddha.

It is quite wrong to hold that man is not a factor in the making of history. Man is necessary to rub two pieces of flint to make fire. Man is a factor in the making of history and the environmental forces, whether impersonal or social, if they are, they are the first and not the last things.

5

PRINCIPLES UNDERLYING THE ENGLISH CONSTITUTION

INTRODUCTION

According to Dicey there are three principles which distinguish the English Constitution from the Constitution of other countries. These principles are:

(1) The legislative supremacy of Parliament.

(2) The prevalence of the rule of law.

(3) The dependence of the Constitution on the conventions.

Two comments may be legitimately made on the assertion that these principles form distinguishing characteristics of the English Constitution. In the sense that they are not to be found in other Constitutions. One is this. That some of these characteristics have ceased to be true at any rate, to the extent they were true when Dicey wrote. For instance the legislative supremacy of Parliament is to some extent modified and circumscribed by the Statute of Westminster passed in the year 1930. The second comment that must be made that these characteristics, especially the prevalence of the rule of law and the dependence of the Constitution on conventions are not special to the English Constitution. Conventions are a feature of all Constitutions and the rule of law, in one of its senses at any rate, obtains in the United States. All the same it is Constitution in principles form a feature of the English Constitution in a manner and to an extent unknown in other Constitutions. And understood in that sense they no doubt serve to distinguish the English Constitution from other Constitutions.

LEGISLATIVE SUPREMACY OF PARLIAMENT

One of the first and foremost of foreign Commentators on the English Constitution Hontessquie came to the conclusion as a result of his study that the English Constitution exhibited a feature which was absent from the Constitution of France as it existed at the time when he wrote. He found that under the English Constitution the three organs of the State, namely, the legislative, the executive and the judiciary were distinct and were separated from one another in their composition as well as their functions. Each was limited to its own sphere of activity and was not permitted to invade the dominion of another. Whatever liberty the Englishman had in the days when he was writing and which his countrymen did not possess, was attributed by him to this feature of the English Constitution. So convinced was he of the virtue of this principle of the English Constitution that he propounded it as a vital principle of political Organisation and recommended it to his countrymen for adoption in their own Constitution.

This doctrine of separation of powers of Hontessquie has been laid at the base of every new Constitution made thereafter. This is an interesting illustration of how countries have been misled by the wrong conclusions of a student of politics, for there is no doubt about it that Hontessquie misunderstood the English Constitution. The English Constitution certainly does not recognise the principle of the separation of powers. The King is a part of the legislature, the head of the judiciary and the supreme executive authority in the land. The Ministry which carries on the executive Government of the country in the name of the King are members of Parliament. There is, therefore, no separation between the executive and the legislature.

The Lord Chancellor is the working head of the Judicature. He is also a member of the Cabinet. There is, therefore, no separation between the executive and the judiciary. Not only is there no separation between the three organs of the State, but there is no foundation for the statement that their authority is limited by the Constitution for the simple fact that there is no Constitution in the American sense of the word which allocates the functions of the different organs of the State and delimits their authority. Under the English Constitution there is one supreme authority under the law, and that is Parliament. If the functions of the executive and the judiciary are limited, it does not follow that the functions of Parliament are limited. It only means that Parliament has for the time being allotted certain functions to be discharged by certain bodies, in a certain manner. The limitations of the judiciary and the executive do not result in putting consequential limitation. On the other hand as the limitations proceed from the authority of Parliament, Parliament retains the authority to widen them or to curtail them.

MEANING OF THE LEGISLATIVE SUPREMACY OF PARLIAMENT

A complete idea of the legislative supremacy of Parliament must involve a grasp of the two parts which it must include. The first is that Parliament has, under the English Constitution, the right to make or unmake any law whatsoever. Secondly, no person or a body of persons is recognised by the law of England as having a right to override or set aside the law made by Parliament. It is unnecessary to recall that the words Parliament and law must be understood in their strictly legal sense. Parliament means as has been already explained, the King, the Lords and the Commons, and that none of them individually exercised the authority, belonged to them jointly so as to make it an Act of Parliament.

The term law again must be understood in the strictly legal sense. It means only such rules as are enforced by the Courts. Having stated what is involved in the notion of the legislative supremacy of Parliament, we may next ask what is the proof of this legislative supremacy of Parliament?

The doctrine of legislative supremacy is accepted by all the lawyers who have written about the English Constitution. Sir Edward Coke, speaking of the power and jurisdiction of Parliament, agreed that it was so transcendent and absolute that it cannot be confined either for causes or persons, within any bounds.

Blackstone the author of the celebrated commentaries agrees that, "Parliament has sovereign and uncontrollable authority in the making, confirming, enlarging, restraining, abrogating, repealing, reviving and expounding of laws concerning matters of all possible denominations ecclesiastical or temporal, civil, military, maritime or criminal. This being the place where that absolute despotic power, which must in all Governments must reside somewhere, is entrusted by the Constitution of those Kingdoms. All mischiefs and grievances, operations and remedies that transcend the ordinary course of laws are within the reach of this extraordinarily tribunal. It can regulate the succession to the crown, as was done in the reign of Henry VIII and William III. It can alter the established religion of the land, as was done in a variety of instances in the reigns of Henry VIII and his three children. True it is that "what the Parliament doth no authority upon earth can do."

Delome, a French lawyer agrees with Coke and with Blackstone. He observes, "that Parliament can do everything but make a woman a man and a man a woman ". a woman a man and a man a woman".

This legislative supremacy of Parliament which is acknowledged by all lawyers can be proved by reference to a large number of instances drawn from the history of the British Parliament. But the following may suffice.

Parliamentary Sovereignty and the Acts of Union: The Acts of Union with Scotland and Ireland are in the nature of treaties and contain certain clauses which were then regarded as fundamental and essential conditions of Union and which were understood as not being liable to abrogation by the Parliament of Great Britain. The Act of Union with Scotland stipulated that every professor of a Scotch University shall acknowledge and confess and subscribe the confession of faith as his profession of faith. This was regarded as a fundamental condition of the treaty of Union with Scotland. But this very provision has been repeated by the Universities Scotland Act, 1853, which relieves most professors in Scotch Universities from the necessity of subscribing the confession of faith. The Act of Union with Ireland stipulated "that the Churches of England and Ireland as now by law established, be united into one Protestant Episcopal Church, to be called the United Church of England and Ireland, and that the doctrine, worship, discipline and the Government of the said United Church shall be and shall remain in full force forever as the same are now by law established for the Church of England and that the continuance and preservation of the said United Church, as the established Church of England and Ireland shall be deemed and be taken to be an essential and fundamental part of the Union". There is no doubt that from the language of the clause that it was intended to limit the legislative supremacy of Parliament and yet Parliament by the Irish Church Act of 1869 disestablished the Church in Ireland and its legislative competency to enact such a measure was not questioned.

The Septenial Act of 1707 is another illustration of the legislative supremacy of Parliament. Under the Act of 1694, the duration of Parliament was limited to 3 years. In the year 1716 a new election was due. But both the King and the Ministry were convinced that under the political circumstances of the day, a new election would be disastrous to the ministry and to the state and ministry of the day persuaded Parliament to pass an Act extending the duration of Parliament from 3 years to 7 years. The House of Commons was accused by the critics of a breach of trust, as representatives of the electors and even the peers joined in the protest on the ground that this Act deprived the people of their remedy against their M.P's, who had failed to do their duty. In the wake of political criticism against the Act, the legal connotation was missed altogether. Whether such an Act was proper or improper was one thing.

Whether Parliament could alter the law governing its life was another question. It should be noted that while the Act was attacked from the first point of view it was never questioned from the second. Indeed it was taken for granted that the Septenial Act was within the legislative competence of Parliament.

There is another feature of the Septennial Act which should be noted because it helps to explain the extent of the legislative supremacy of Parliament. Parliament could have passed a law extending the life of Parliament and probably no question would have been raised if the Act was made applicable to future Parliaments. But the Septennial Act not only extended the life of all future Parliaments, but it also enlarged the terms of the very Parliament which passed the Act. It was undoubtedly an Act of usurpation of political power not contemplated and not given by law to the Parliament which passed the Act and yet such an Act of usurpation was a legal Act. It is unnecessary to go back so far in the past to cite an authority of the Legislative supremacy of Parliament, as the Septennial Act. A similar exercise of the legislative supremacy was resorted to by Parliament during the late war when the sitting Parliament in 1914 instead of dissolving itself passed an Act extending its own life.

Acts of Indemnity are examples which constantly occur and which serve as sharp reminders of the legislative supremacy of Parliament An Act of Indemnity is a statute the object of which is to free individuals from penalties imposed upon them by law. This is the highest proof of the legislative supremacy of Parliament, for it imports the legalisation of an illegality legalisation of an illegality.

INTERFERENCE WITH PRIVATE RIGHTS

Most legislative assemblies confine their legislative powers to the regulation of the rights of the public in general. Private rights and domestic rights are deemed either to be too particular and too sacred to be interfered with by Parliament. But the

British Parliament has never accepted these limitations upon its legislative authority. In the case of the lives of the Duke of Clearance and Clocester, Parliament passed an Act declaring that their daughters and wives should inherit their property although they were alive. In the case of the Duke of Buckingham, he was an infant but Parliament passed an Act declaring that he should be treated as a major for all legal purposes.

Sir Robert Playfinston was dead yet long after his death. Parliament passed an Act holding him guilty of treason. The case of the Marquis of Winchester is an illustration in which Parliament by law declared a legitimate child to be illegitimate. A contrary illustration in which illegitimate children born before marriage were declared legitimate, is supplied by the law passed by Parliament in respect of the issues born to Catherine Swinfoid by John of Gaunt, the Duke of Lancaster. Catherine had, before marriage from the Duke four illegitimate children, Henry, John, Thomas and a daughter, Joan. The King by an Act of Parliament in the form of charter legitimised these children. These illustrations that Parliament cannot only regulate by law the affairs of a single individual but it may also alter the course of general law.

WHAT IS PARLIAMENT?

With a large, mass of the people Parliament in these days means the House of Commons. It does not include in it the House of Lords, and certainly not the King. This popular notion is due largely to the fact that the House of Commons has become the most dominant element in the working of the English Constitution. But however justifiable such a notion may be, speaking in terms of law it is a wrong notion. Legally Parliament consists of three constituent elements, the King, the House of Lords and the House of Commons. All legislative power belongs to the King, the House of Lords and the House of Commons jointly. It is vested in the King in Parliament, *i.e.,* in the King acting in consent with the two Houses of Parliament. Legally, every Act before it can become the law of the land, requires the King's assent. How important element the King is in the Constitution of Parliament will be evident, if it is borne in mind that the two Houses of Parliament can transact their business only if they are summoned by the King.

They cannot meet on their own initiative and authority and transact business. How important place the King occupies will also be obvious if it is remembered that the power to summon, prorogue and to dissolve the Houses of Parliament vests in the King and is exercisable at any time according to his pleasure. On the other hand, it is usually true that without the consent of the two Houses of Parliament, the King has no inherent power of legislation whatever within the United Kingdom. Every act of the King to be law must have the assent of the House of Commons and the House of Lords, unless it is otherwise provided by Statute.

The proposition, that all legislative power is vested in the King in Parliament and that no law could be passed without the concurrence of the King, the House of Lords and the House of Commons's subject to two qualifications.

The King's Veto: Although in law the King's assent is necessary to every measure before it can become law, his power to refuse assent, *i.e.*, his power to veto has become absolute by misuse. The right of veto has not been exercised since the days of Queen Anne, who refused her assent to the Scotch Militia Bill of 1707. The impairment of this power of veto by the King is not a legal impairment. In law his power of veto exists in all its amplitude without any qualifications. This is due to forbearance founded on a convention whereby it is settled that when the two Houses agree, the King should not refuse his assent. It's disuse does not mean that it is buried beyond revival. Suppose a ministry resigns after a bill is passed by the House of Commons. The House of Lords insists upon passing the bill in spite of the opposition of the new ministry. It would be rash to assert that in such a case the Royal assent would not be withheld even though both the Houses have concurred in the legislation.

The Veto of the House of Lords: The House of Lord was once a coordinate and coequal branch of the legislation, and every measure before it could become an Act of Parliament depended upon it's assent, as much as upon that of the House of Commons. Although this was the position in law, the House of Commons had claimed in practice exclusive authority for themselves in finance and an overriding authority in other legislation.

In 1671, the House of Commons passed the following resolution: "That in all aids given to the King by the Commons, the rate of tax ought not to be altered by the Lords."

In 1676, the Commons adapted another resolution as follows: "That all bills granting supplies ought to begin with the Commons, and it is the undoubted and the sole right of the Commons, to direct limit and appoint in such bills the ends, purposes, considerations, conditions, limitations and qualifications of such grants which ought not to be changed or altered by the House of Lords."

In ordinary legislation of a non-fiscal character, the Commons claimed that although the House of Lords might differ from the House of Commons, yet when a conflict arose between the two Houses the Lords should at some stage wield to the views of the Houses, the Lords should, at some stage, wield to the views of the claim. Ever since the Lords had never expressly admitted them, although in practice the Lords conformed to them, the practice was a mere matter of political understanding, a convention and was not reduced to law. The House of Lords was possessed in law of the power of veto, *i.e.*, the right to refuse assent to any measure fiscal or non-fiscal. Here again the case was not one of legal impairment of power. It was a case of forbearance in the exercise of it. In 1910, the House of Lords, contrary to established practice, insisted in asserting their right to refuse assent to the financial proposals in the budget of Mr. Lloyd George. A conflict between the House of Commons and the House of Lords arose. It was settled by the Parliament Act of 1911. The Act is a most important piece of legislation relating to the English Constitution inasmuch as it has affected the veto power of the House of Lords in certain matters in a vital manner.

The Parliament Act of 1911 applies to Public Bills only. It does not apply to Private Bills. In regard to Private Bills, the veto power of the House of Lords remains in tact. Even though this applies to Public Bills it does not apply to all of them. It does not apply to a Public Bill which affects the duration or life of Parliament. Under the Parliament Act the House of Commons retains the power of veto in respect of such bills. In the case of these Public Bills to which it does apply, its effect on the veto power of the House of Lords is not the same. It varies. The Parliament Act divides Public Bills into two classes. (1) Public Bills which are money bills and (2) Public Bills which are not money bills. A money bill is defined as a Public Bill which in the opinion of the Speaker of the House of Commons contains only provisions dealing with all or any of the following subjects, namely; imposition, repeal, remission, alteration or regulation of taxation, the imposition for the payment of debt or other financial purposes of charges on the Consolidated Fund or on money provided by Parliament or the variation or repeal of any such charges, supply, the appropriation, receipt, custody, issue or audit of accounts of public money, the raising or guarantee of any loan or repayment thereof or subordinate matters incidental to those subjects of any of them.

The Act lays down that if a Money Bill having been passed by the House of Commons and sent up to the House of Lords at least one month before the end of the Session, is not passed by the House of Lords without amendment within one month after it is so sent up to that House, the bill shall, unless the House of Commons direct to the contrary, be presented to His Majesty and become an Act of Parliament on the Royal assent being signified, notwithstanding that the House of Lords have not consented to the Bill.

With regard to other Public Bills, the Parliament Act of 1911 provides that if it is passed by the House of Commons in three successive sessions (whether of the same Parliament or not) and having been sent up to the House of Lords at least one month before the end of the session, is rejected by the House of Lords in each of these sessions, that bill shall, on its rejection for the third time by the House of Lords, unless the House of Commons direct to the contrary, be presented to His Majesty and become an Act of Parliament on the Royal assent being signified thereto, notwithstanding that the House of Lords have not consented to the Bill, provided that this provision shall not take effect unless two years have elapsed between the date of the second reading in the first of these Sessions of the Bill in the House of Commons and the date on which it is passed by the House of Commons in the third of those Sessions. House of Commons in the third of those sessions.

These are the main provisions of the Parliament Act of 1911. It has altered the character of that veto with regard to a Public Bill other than a money bill by making it a merely suspensory veto which has the effect of merely holding up the legislation passed by the House of Commons during the prescribed period. The power to block legislation, which the House of Lords once possessed as a coequal member of Parliament, has now been taken away by the Act.

Subject to these deductions, conventional and legal, regarding the authority of the King and the Lords, the proposition that Parliament consists of King, Lords and the Commons and that without their consent a bill cannot become law, remains as true today as it was before the Act of 1911.

THE CROWN

The King's Title to the Crown: Before the Resolution of 1688 when James II fled from the country, it was not certain by what right the King claimed the Crown, whether it was hereditary or elective. But there can be no doubt that thereafter the title to the Crown has become a Parliamentary title, in the sense that Parliament can alter the succession to the Crown. The title to the Crown is at present regulated by the provisions of the Act of Settlement passed in the year 1701. By that Act, the title to the Crown was conferred upon William and Mary and the heirs of their body. The title stipulates two conditions: One, the Successor must be an heir, male or female and two, the Successor must be a Protestant Christian by faith.

Rights and Duties of the Crown: The rights of the King are either Statutory or Prerogative. Statutory rights are those which are conferred upon the King by an Act of Parliament. The prerogative rights are the Customary or Common Law Rights of the King which he has been exercising and which have not been taken away by law. It is unnecessary... with those rights and duties of the King which are statutory because they are capable of exact definition and ascertainment by reference to the Statute from which they are derived. The prerogative rights on the other hand are not capable of such ascertainment by reference to any statute because it is of the essence of a prerogative right that is not derived from Statute. Prerogative rights of the King are customary rights and are independent of Statute, and like all customary rights the nature and extent have to be investigated by a Court of Law whenever they are asserted. The King's prerogatives may be conveniently discussed under the following heads:

PERSONAL PREROGATIVES

The King can do no Wrong: All acts are done in the name of the King, but by virtue of this Prerogative, the King is not responsible for any of his acts. The person responsible for his royal acts are his Ministers. The King, therefore, cannot be sued or otherwise held responsible for his executive acts. When a subject is aggrieved by a breach of contract, he cannot sue the King, nor can he sue the King in respect of a tort.

A special provision is made to soften the rigour of the rule which is known as *the Petition of Right procedure.* Under it, a subject aggrieved may petition the Crown for redress and that petition will become justiciable only if the Attorney-General, who is the Law-Officer of the Crown, issues his fiat permitting justice to be done in which case alone, the Courts can proceed with the petition as though it was a plaint in a suit.

Even then there are certain rules which though they are binding between private parties, would not be binding upon the Crown, for instance it is a rule that the Crown cannot by contract hamper its future executive actions. As a result, the Crown can always dismiss a servant of the Crown at any time, no matter what the period of contract was, because such a contract would hamper the future executive action of the Crown. Consequently a servant of the Crown cannot sue the Crown for damages for wrongful dismissal even by a Petition of Rights.

The King never Dies: The King has the attributing immortality. A particular person wearing the Crown may die. But the King survives. Immediately upon the decease of a reigning King, his Kingship, without any interregnum or interval, vests in his heirs. That is the law, and the popular cry—The King is dead; Long live the King—is in conformity with the Law. The Coronation ceremony is not necessary to invest the King with Kingly power. A King can act as a King although he has not been coronated, provided he is the next heir of the last King. The Coronation ceremony has no other effect than to proclaim to the subjects and to the world at large, who the King is.

Lapse of Time will not as a Rule Bar the Right of the Crown to sue or to Prosecute: To put it in a different way, the law of limitation does not apply to the Crown, as it does to a private individual. The private individual must sue or prosecute within a stated period fixed by the law of limitation. The Crown is free from the time-bar. The statement of this prerogative right must now be qualified so far as the right to sue is concerned. The law of limitation has made the time-bar applicable to the Crown although the period of limitation is sixty years. The Prerogative of the Crown's right to prosecute remains in tact.

When the right of the King and the right of the subject come in conflict, a subject's right must give way to the King's.

The King is not bound by statutes unless expressly named in it.

POLITICAL PREROGATIVES

Now these may be divided into two categories into which they naturally fall '.those which relate to the internal Government of the country and those which relate to foreign affairs. As to the King's Political Prerogatives which relate to the internal Government of the country, they may be considered in relation to the three divisions of State activity, *e.g.*, the executive, the judicial and the legislative. According to the English Constitutional law, the executive Government vests in the King. It is his Prerogative to be the supreme head of the executive. As such, he has the authority to appoint Ministers and other officers of the state, political as well as permanent. It is his prerogative to dismiss them. He is also the head of the Army, the Navy, the Air-force and the Civil Service. Every one appointed to discharge the service of the State, no matter how he is appointed, is in law the servant of the Crown.

Turning to his Judicial Prerogative, the King at one time actually sat in Court to dispense justice but this Prerogative the King has now lost. The King at one time could create any Court and invest it with jurisdiction to try any matter or any cause he chose to prescribe. The establishment of the Star Chamber and the Court of High Commission by Charles I is an illustration of how wide was the King's judicial Prerogative. But this Prerogative also, the King has now lost. The King can now only create by Prerogative, *i.e.,* without the Sanction of Parliament, Court to administer the Common law. Even this remnant of a Prerogative he cannot exercise, because of the necessity of financial legislation which such a course would involve, which would make it necessary for him to obtain the sanction of Parliament. Only four bits of his Judicial Prerogatives now remain. (1) He can grant leave to appeal to the Privy Council. (2) He can appoint judges. (3) He can pardon a criminal. (4) He can stifle the prosecution of a criminal, either by declining to offer evidence or by entering a formal *Grote Praseu.*

Coming to the legislative Prerogatives of the King, they extended at one time to vast proportions. The King at one time claimed the power to make laws independently of Parliament, to suspend laws in particular cases and to dispense with them generally. All this has now been altered. The right to suspend and dispense with laws made by Parliament is now completely lost. The right to legislate is also lost, except in so far as it relates to Crown Colonies. The only legislative Prerogatives that remains to the King are the Prerogatives right (1) to summon Parliament, (2) to prorogue Parliament, (3) to dissolve Parliament.

There are two other classes of Prerogatives which relate to the internal administration of the Country which must be referred to before considering the other classes of Prerogatives which relate to foreign affairs. They are Ecclesiastical Prerogatives and Revenue Prerogatives.

Ecclesiastical Prerogatives: The King is the supreme head of the Church of England as established by law. As the head of the Church, he appoints on the recommendation of the Prime Minister, Archbishops, Bishops and certain other dignitaries of the Church. In his Prerogative right, the King convokes, prorogues and dissolves two Houses of the convocation and it is in his Prerogative right that the King can grant leave of appeal to the Privy Council from the decisions of the ecclesiastical Courts.

Revenue Prerogatives: The revenues of the British Government fall into two classes, (1) the ordinary revenues and (2) the extraordinary revenues. The ordinary revenues are called the Prerogative revenues and they are derived from the following sources, (1) The custody of a Bishop's temporalities, *i.e.,* the right of the King to take the profits which the episcopal sea is vacant, though these are held in trust for his successor. (2) The rights to annates and tenths. Annates were the first year's profits of church's benefits formerly paid to the Pope and afterwards to the Crown. Tenths were the tenth part of the annual profits of a church's benefit formerly paid to the Pope.

These are now paid to the Governor of the Queen Anne's Bounty. (3) Profits derived from the Crown lands. (4) The right to Royal fish wreck, treasure-trove, waifs and cotrays, royal mines and escheats.

The foregoing items constituting the ordinary revenues of the Crown were collected by Prerogative and paid to the King until 1715 when the first Civil Lists Act was passed whereby an arrangement was made between the King and Parliament whereby the King surrendered his Prerogative revenues to the state which are since then paid into the Consolidated Fund and Parliament in consideration of this assignment granted to the Royal family for its maintenance a fixed sum, which is made an annual charge upon the Consolidated Fund and is called the Civil List. The Civil List is not a permanent arrangement but is a temporary agreement made between the reigning King and the Parliament and lasts during the lifetime of that King. When a new King succeeds, a new agreement is made with him which again is to last during his lifetime. If no agreement is made, the Prerogative of the King in respect of the ordinary revenue will revive. The Civil List arrangement does not abrogate it in any way. It merely affects the appropriation of the revenue. It does not affect the right to raise that revenue.

The King's Prerogatives in relation to the foreign relations of the Country. The King possesses the right and the power to receive Ambassadors of foreign Countries and to send his Ambassadors to them. This is his Prerogative right. The right is important because of the immunity from Civil and Criminal process which Ambassadors, who are recognised as such by the King, enjoy. What those immunities are will be discussed at a later stage. It is enough here to note that they depend upon the recognition by the King of a person as an Ambassador and that recognition is a Prerogative Right of the King.

The King has also the right to make war and peace whenever he thinks fit to do so. This also is his Prerogative right. The King possesses the power to make a treaty with any foreign nation. The treaty may be a political treaty or a commercial treaty. It is his Prerogative. The only limitation upon the King's Prerogative to make a treaty is that he must not in any manner affect the rights of his subjects given to them by law.

There are some questions that arise in connection with the question of the King's Prerogatives and which it would not be desirable to pass over without some consideration being bestowed upon them. The first question is this. What is the exact relation of the King's Prerogative to the authority of Parliament? The second question is what happens if the King becomes incapable of exercising his Prerogative or other Statutory rights?

Taking the first inquiry for consideration it is necessary to get a clear idea of what is exactly meant when it is said that it is the King's Prerogative to do this, that or other act. What is meant by this expression, that when the King acts on the authority of his Prerogative, he does not need the sanction of Parliament. His authority is inherent in him and is independent of Parliament. But while it is true that the Prerogative power of the King is inherent and independent of Parliament, it must not be supposed that it is on that account beyond the control of Parliament. On the other hand the Prerogative power of the King can be regulated, amended or abrogated by Parliament, so that the correct position would be that the King possesses Prerogative power so long as Parliament has not by law trenched upon it. A matter which was once a matter of Prerogative if subsequently regulated by law made by Parliament, then the King cannot resort to his Prerogative power, but must act within the law which has superseded the Prerogative. Therefore, so far as the first inquiry is concerned, the conclusion is that the King's Prerogative is a source of independent power to him so long as Parliament has not interfered with its existence.

What happens if the King becomes incapable of exercising his Prerogative and other Statutory rights. Now this is no idle inquiry because there are certain important duties which are attached to the Kingly office and the King may become incapable of discharging them. Four contingencies of incapacity may be visualised. (1) The King may be absent from his Kingdom. (2) The King may be a minor. (3) The King may be insane. (4) The King may be morally incapable.

The absence of the King from the Kingdom cannot raise any very great difficulty. Modern means of communication have annihilated distance and have facilitated quick dispatch. The King, therefore, could discharge his Kingly duties from a distance with expedition at any rate without delay. There is also the other possibility of the King delegating his powers to somebody who could exercise them on his behalf when he is away.

Minority of the King cannot create any difficulty so far as the law is concerned. The law holds that the King is never an infant and is capable of transacting business even though he is a minor. A minor King, therefore, can exercise all his powers and discharge all his duties lawfully. Ordinarily if the reigning King is expected to die leaving an infant as his heir, Parliament always takes the precaution of appointing by law a regent. But this is by way of prudence and not by way of any requirement by law.

Insanity makes a hard case. The King cannot delegate his powers if he is insane. Parliament cannot pass a law, appointing a regent because the King being insane cannot give his assent to the Bill. There are two cases of English Monarchs having gone insane, while on the throne, Henry VI (1454) and George 111(1788). The procedure then adopted was a very crude one and certainly could be deemed to be strictly in conformity with the law of the Constitution, which requires the assent of all three elements which constitute Parliament.

The moral incapacity of the King is another hard case. Can the King resign supposing people do not want him? Can the King be deposed if he does not resign? There is no legal provision regulating the insanity or the moral incapacity of the King. Question of moral incapacity may not perhaps arise under the English Constitution owing to the development of responsible Government. But the question of insanity might.

EFFECT OF THE DEATH OF THE KING

On Parliament

The original rule was that Parliament was automatically dissolved by the death of the King. The Constitution and theory of which this was a consequence regarded members of Parliament as councillors of the King who summoned them. The tie of summons was regarded as a personal tie between the King who summoned and the members who assembled in return and that tie was broken by the death of the King. The members called by deceased King could not be on this account be called the councillors of the new King, and the King was entitled to call new councillors, which could happen only when the old Parliament was dissolved and the new King obtained an opportunity to call a new Parliament. This rule was first amended in by 7-8 William III Chapter XV whereby it was provided that the existing Parliament was to work for six months after the death of the King if not sooner dissolved by his successor. Subsequently in the year 1867, (30, 31 Victoria, Chapter II 102), the rule was altogether abrogated and the life of Parliament was made independent of the death of the king.

ON THE TENURE OF OFFICE

The original rule was that all executive officers were to vacate their offices on the death of the King, and for the same reasons whereby the death of the King resulted in the dissolution of Parliament. Here again the law has gradually altered the theory. The Succession to the Crown Act of 1707 extended the tenure of executive Officers to six months after the death of the King. By another Act passed in the year the period was again extended and finally the Demise of the Crown Act of 1901 made the tenure of office independent of the death of the King.

THE HOUSE OF LORDS

The House of Lords consists of three different classes of Peers. (1) Hereditary Peers of England and United Kingdom, (2) Representative Peers and (3) Peers by virtue of Office.

The first question that must be raised and answered in order to understand the Constitution of the House of Lords is this. What is the title of the Peers to sit in the House of Lords?

PEERS OF ENGLAND AND THE UNITED KINGDOM

The title of the English Peers and the Peers of the United Kingdom is founded on the King's writ of summons addressed to each Peer individually to come and to attend Parliament. The English Peerage is created by the King by Letters Patent. No difficulty arises, therefore, with regard to persons holding Peerage by Letters Patent. The only question that arises is whether the King could create a Peerage for life. This was at one time a matter of controversy and the controversy was whether a life-Peer created by the King entitles the Peer to sit in the House of Lords. But the issue was decided finally in the Weynesdale Peerage case in 1856 in which two things were decided. (1) That the King had the right to create any class of life-peer or hereditary but (2) the life-Peer cannot sit as a member of the House of the Lords and the King could not send such a Peer a writ of summons. The reason assigned was that the hereditary character of the Peerage was by custom, if not by law, an integral feature of the Peerage and the King while entitled to exercise his right to create a Peerage was not entitled to abrogate the custom.

What about the right of the Peers whose Peerage was not created by Letters Patent? Their right also was founded upon the King's writ of summons.

Two questions, however, were long agitated with regard to the writ of summons to such Peers. Could every Peer claim the writ of Summons? Was the King free to address or not to address the summons to any Peer? On behalf of the Peers it was contended that only Peers who held their Peerage by what is called tenure by Barony were entitled to summons and that no other Peer was entitled to summons, nor was the King free to address the summons to a Peer who fell outside that class. On the other hand it was contended on behalf of the King that the writ was not a special privilege confined to Peers by Barony nor was there any limitation upon the King's right to address the summons to the Peers. The controversy was in the long run settled and two rules can now be laid down as rules governing the right to writ by Peers whose Peerage is not evidenced by Letters Patent:

(1) Tenure by Barony is no ground for a claim to a writ from the King.

(2) The King was bound to summon by a writ to sit in the House of Lords a descendant of a person, who had received a writ and taken his seat in that House in accordance therewith. In other words the descendant of a person, however distant and whatever the break in the interval, who can be proved to have received a writ from the King can claim a similar writ by a hereditary right. The English Peerage, therefore, is a hereditary Peerage and all hereditary English Peers are, therefore, entitled by their hereditary right to a writ of summons from the king and be members of the House of Lords.

(3) Although the right is a hereditary right it is subject to two rules, (1) The rule of Primogeniture and (2) The rule of male descendant.

REPRESENTATIVE PEERS

The representative peers fall into two classes. Representative Peers of Scotland and representative Peers of Ireland. The title of the representative Peers of Scotland is founded on the treaty of Union between England and Scotland which took place in 1707 and which made them into a Common Kingdom under a Common King and was called the United Kingdom of Great Britain. Prior to its Union with England, Scotland had its own Peerage with its hereditary right to sit. The Union of Ireland with Great Britain took place in 1800. As in the case of Scotland, Ireland has also its own Peerage with hereditary right to sit in the old Irish Parliament. On the amalgamation of Ireland and Scotland by their respective treaties of Union with England, the question arose as to how much representation was to be allowed to the old Scottish and Irish Peers in the new Parliament of Great Britain and Ireland. The English Peers claimed for every one of themselves the right to sit in the new Parliament. The Scottish and the Irish Peers claimed similar right for every member of their own class.

In the settlement that was arrived at, it was agreed (1) that the English Peers should be allowed each to sit in the new Parliament. (2) The Scottish Peers were allowed to elect sixteen (16) out of their number as their representatives in the new Parliament. (3) The Irish Peers were allowed to elect 28 out of their number. The Scottish Peers are elected for the duration of a single Parliament., When Parliament is dissolved, there takes place a new election of the 16 representative Scottish Peers by the Peers of Scotland. The Irish representative Peers on the other hand are elected for their lives, and there is no new election of Irish Peers when Parliament is dissolved. A new election takes place only when a vacancy takes place in the representative Irish Peers by death or by any other disqualifying cause.

In addition to these three ancient territorial Peerages existing from before the time of the Union, there has been created a fourth category of Peerage known as the Peers of the United Kingdom with a right to sit in the House of Lords. Such a Peerage could be conferred by the King even on a Scottish Peer or an Irish Peer in which case if the Peerage is hereditary, the holder would be entitled to sit in the House of Lords notwithstanding of the treaties of Union with Ireland and Scotland.

PEERS BY VIRTUE OF OFFICE

The Peers who sit in the House of Lords by virtue of office fell into two divisions (1) The Lords spiritual and (2) the Lords of appeal in ordinary. By law twenty-six, officials of the Church are entitled to sit in the house of Lords. Of these, the Archbishops of Canterbury and York and the Bishops of London, Durham and Winchester have the right to sit in the House of Lords as Lords Spiritual. Of the remaining 21 spiritual Peers, 21 diocesan Bishops in order of seniority of appointment have a right to sit in the House of Lords. So when one of the 21 Bishops dies or resigns, his place in the House of Lords is taken not by his successor but by the next senior diocesan Bishop.

THE LORDS OF APPEAL IN ORDINARY

The House of Lords, besides being a Legislative Assembly, is also a Court of Judicature. It is for most purposes, the final and the highest Court of Appeal from the King's Courts in England, Scotland and Ireland. This judicial function being the function of the House of Lords as such, there is nothing to prevent any Peer of Parliament from taking part in the decisions of any appeal that would be brought before the House in its judicial capacity. The House of Lords in the main is a body of lay Peers not versed in the intricacies of law and not possessing any legal training.

To allow such a body to permit to discharge the functions of the highest Judiciary involved a great danger to the cause of justice. It was, however, not possible to take away this jurisdiction from the House of Lords altogether. As a compromise, the Act of 1876 called the Appellate Jurisdiction Act was passed. It retained the Jurisdiction of the House of Lords as the final Court of Appeal but provided that no appeal should be heard and determined by the House of Lords unless there were present at such hearing and determination at least three Lords of Appeal. The Lords of Appeal consist of (1) The Lord Chancellor for the time being, (2) such sitting Lords in the House as have held high judicial office and (3) the Lords of Appeal inordinacy, appointed by the King.

The Appellate Jurisdiction Act of 1876 which gave the power to the Crown to appoint Lords of Appeal inordinacy to sit in the House of Lords, made the tenure of those Lords of

Appeal as Peers dependent on the continuance of his discharge of his judicial functions as a Lord of Appeal. In 1887, however, this was altered and the tenure of a Lord of Appeal in ordinary is now a life tenure.

Having stated the composition of the House of Lords, we may next proceed to consider certain questions that arrive in connection therewith. The first is this. What is the title of the Peers to sit in the House of Lords? The title of the Peers to sit in the House of Lords is not founded upon election by a Constituency as is the case with the members of the House of Commons. Their title is founded by a writ of summons addressed to each Peer individually to come and attend Parliament. It is a kind of nomination by the King although the power to nominate is strictly regulated and does not leave any discretion in the King to revoke and alter the course of nominations from Parliament to Parliament

While the right of the Peer is founded on the writ of summons issued by the King, there are certain restrictions on the King's right to summon Peers. An Alien Peer that is a Peer who is not a British subject cannot be summoned to sit in Parliament.

A second question that must also be considered relates to the admissibility and divesting by the Peer of his title. A Peerage is a non-transferrable dignity and the title to it cannot be transferred by sale or by gift to another. It can be claimed by another only by inheritance in accordance with the rules of heritage. Similarly a Peer cannot surrender his title and cease to be a Peer. The principle which govern the Peerage is, once a Peer always a Peer.

A third question must relate to the difference between Peerage and the House of Lords. Popularly the expression Peers of the Realm and the House of Lords are used synonymously. Legally speaking there is a difference between the two. A person may be a Peer of the Realm and yet not be a member of the House of Lords. The case of a life-Peer is an illustration in point. A life-Peer is a Peer of the Realm and yet he cannot be a member of the House of Lords, because of the rule that the Peer who is a Peer otherwise than by virtue of office must be a hereditary Peer in order that he may get a right to sit in the House of Lords. Contrariwise, a person may be a member of the House of Lords, although he is not a hereditary Peer. The case of the spiritual Lords and the Lords of Appeal inordinacy is an illustration in point. The Archbishops and Bishops as also the Lords of Appeal inordinary are entitled to writ of summons from the King to the House of Lords, the former while they hold their offices and the latter during their lifetime. Yet they are not Peers in the legal sense of the term inasmuch as Peerage connotes a hereditary right.

OTHER OFFICERS

There are three other officers under the Lord Chancellor as Speaker of the House of Lords.

(1) *The Clerk of the Parliament:* His duties are similar to those of the clerk of the House of Commons, namely, to keep the record of the proceedings and judgements of the House, of Lords in a journal.

(2) *The Gentleman Usher of the Black rod,* whose duties are analogous to those of the Sergeant at arms in the House of Commons. He does the policing of the House.

(3) *The Sergeant at arms* is the attendant on the Lord Chancellor.

PARAMOUNTCY AND THE CLAIM OF THE INDIAN STATES TO BE INDEPENDENT

The announcement by Travancore and Hyderabad to declare themselves Independent Sovereign States on 15th of August when India becomes a dominion and the inclination shown by other States to follow their example has created a new problem. The problem is a crucial one and requires to be seriously considered. There are two aspects to the question. Can the States declare themselves Independent? Should they declare themselves Independent?

To begin with the first. The basis of the claim made by the States for a right to declare themselves independent lies in the Statement of 12th May 1946 issued by the Cabinet Mission in which they say that the British Government could not and will not in any circumstances transfer paramountcy to an Indian Government which means that the rights of the States which follow from their relationship to the Crown will no longer exist and that all the rights surrendered by the States to the paramount power will return to the States. The Statement of the Cabinet Mission that the Crown could not transfer paramountcy is obviously not a statement of political policy. It is a statement of law. The question is, is this a correct statement of the law as it applies to the States?

There is nothing original in the proposition set out by the Cabinet Mission. It is a mere repetition of the view propounded by the Butler Committee appointed in 1929 to examine the relationship between the Crown and the Indian States. As students of the subject know the Princes in the stand they took before the Butler Committee contended for two propositions:

(i) That Paramountcy could not override the *terms* and conditions contained in the Treaties between the Princes and the States but was limited by them.

(ii) That the relations embodied in Paramountcy were of a personal nature between the Crown and the Princes and could not, therefore, be transferred by the Crown to an Indian Government without the consent of the Princes.

The Butler Committee repudiated the first of these two contentions. It put the matter in most ruthless language by declaring that Paramountcy was Paramount and was not limited by any terms contained in the Treaties. As regards the second contention, strangely enough, the Butler Committee upheld. Whether it was to appease the Princes who were annoyed with the Committee for turning down the Princes' contention regarding Paramountcy it is no use speculating. The fact, however, remains that it gave immense satisfaction to the

Political Department of the Government of India and to the Princes.

The doctrine that Paramountcy cannot be transferred to an Indian Government is a most mischievous doctrine and is based upon an utter misunderstanding of the issues involved. The doctrine is so unnatural that the late Prof. Holdsworth, author of the History of English Law, had to exercise a great deal of ingenuity in defending it in the pages of the Law Quarterly Review for October 1930. Unfortunately, no Indian student of Constitutional Law has ever bothered to controvert his views with the result that they have remained as the last and final word on the subject. No wonder the Cabinet Mission adopted them as valid and acted upon them in settling the issue of British India *vs.*

Indian States. It is a pity that the Congress Working Committee, which was negotiating with the Cabinet Mission for a settlement, did not challenge the proposition enunciated by the Mission in regard to Paramountcy. But these circumstances cannot take away the right of Indians to examine the matter *de novo* and come to their own independent judgement and stand for it if they are convinced that their view is the right view, no matter what the Cabinet Mission has said.

The case against the position taken by the Cabinet Mission in regard to Paramountcy can be stated in the following propositions:

(1) Paramountcy merely is another name for what is called the prerogative of the Crown. It is true that Paramountcy as a prerogative of the Crown differs from the ordinary prerogative of the Crown in two respects—(a) The basis of the ordinary prerogative of the Crown lies in Common Law as distinguished from Statute Law while the basis of the Prerogative arising from Paramountcy lies in treaties supplemented by *usage,* (b) the Common Law prerogative of the Crown extends to all the subjects of the Crown resident in the

King's dominions and over aliens temporarily resident therein while Paramountcy as a prerogative extends only over the Indian States. Paramountcy is no doubt a distinct part of the prerogative of the Crown. Nonetheless, the fact remains that Paramountcy is a prerogative of the Crown.

(2) Being the prerogative of the King, the exercise of Paramountcy is subject to that part of the Municipal Law which is called the law of the Constitution

(3) According to the principle of the Constitutional Law, while the prerogative vests in the King, the King has no discretion in the exercise of his prerogative but can exercise it only in accordance with the advice given to him by his Ministers. The King cannot exercise it independently of the advice of his Ministers.

The last proposition enunciated above requires further elaboration. For, it may be asked on the advice of which Ministry is the Crown to act. The answer is on the advice of the Ministry of the Dominion concerned. Before the Statute of Westminster the British Empire constituted one single Dominion. Consequently, in the matter of the exercise of its prerogative rights, the Crown acted on the advice of the British Cabinet.

After the passing of the Statute of Westminster which carved out Canada, Australia, South Africa and Ireland as separate Dominions, the Crown, in the exercise of its prerogative rights acts on the advice of the Cabinet of the Dominion concerned. It is bound to do so. It cannot do otherwise. It follows that when India becomes a Dominion, the Crown will be bound to act in the exercise of its prerogative rights, *i.e.*, Paramountcy on the advice of the Indian Cabinet.

The protagonists of the theory, that Paramountcy cannot be transferred to the Government of India, rely on the omission from the Government of India Act 1935 of the provisions of section 39 of the Government of India Act of 1933 (they were reproduced in section 33 of the Government of India Acts,

1915—19) according to which the civil and military Government of India (as distinguished from the civil and military Government of British India) is vested in the Governor General in Council and argue that the omission is evidence in support of the conclusion that Paramountcy could not be transferred to an Indian Government. To say the least the argument is purile.

The Existence or nonexistence of such a provision in the Government of India Act is quite beside the point and proves nothing. The nonexistence of the clause does not prove that India can under no circumstances claim the right to advice the Crown in regard to the exercise of Paramountcy. Its existence in the Government of India Act does not mean that such a power was vested in it during 1833 to 1935 when it formed part of the Act for, that very clause contained the proviso whereby the Governor-General in Council was required to pay due obedience to all such orders as may be issued from the Secretary of State which means, even during 1833 to 1935, the ultimate authority to advice the Crown in the matter of the exercise of the prerogative was the Secretary of State for India in British India.

The different methods of disposing of Paramountcy adopted in the various Acts passed by Parliament relating to the governance of India between the 1833 to 1935 do not and cannot in any way affect the claim of the Indian people to advise the Crown in the exercise of Paramountcy. Under the Constitutional Law of the Empire only when a country has become a dominion, that it can claim the right to advise the Crown and the fact that before it became a dominion the Crown was differently advised is no bar to its claim. In the 1935 Act, India was not a country with responsible Government. But even if it was, India could not have claimed to advise the Crown in regard to the exercise of its prerogative rights regarding Indian States.

This is because the Constitutional Law of the British Empire makes difference between responsible Government and Dominion Status. In responsible Government, the right of the

Cabinet to advise the Crown and the obligation of the Crown to accept it is confined to cases of the exercise of the prerogative arising out of the internal affairs of the country. As to external affairs the British Cabinet retained the right to advise the Crown. But in the case of a Dominion, the Crown is bound to accept the advise of the Ministry with regard to all cases of the exercise of the prerogative whether it relates to internal affairs or external affairs.

That is why a dominion can make a treaty with a foreign country without the intervention of the British Cabinet. The fact that the Government of India was not permitted to advise the Crown in the exercise of its rights of Paramountcy does not mean that there is any inherent Constitutional incapacity which disentitles her from claiming the right to advise. The moment India gets the Status of a Dominion it automatically acquires the capacity to advise the Crown on Paramountcy. What has been stated above is no more than a summary of the Constitutional Law of the British Empire and the process of its evolution showing how a part of the Empire which acquires the Status of a Dominion becomes vested with the exclusive right to advise the Crown in the exercise of its prerogative. Why should this right be denied to India when she becomes a Dominion it is difficult to understand. On parity of reasoning, India should get the right to advise the Crown in the exercise of its prerogative as did Canada, Australia, South Africa and Ireland.

That Prof. Holdsworth came to a different conclusion is due not to any difference in the fundamental propositions of Constitutional Law stated above. Indeed he accepts them in toto. The reason why he came to a different conclusion is because he posed quite a different question for argument. The question posed by Prof. Holdsworth was whether the Crown could cede or transfer Paramountcy to an Indian Government. This is not the real issue. The real issue is whether the Indian Dominion can claim the advise to the Crown in the exercise of Paramountcy. In other words, we are not concerned with the question whether Paramountcy could be transferred. The issue with which we are concerned is how Paramountcy can be exercised. I am sure that if Prof. Holdsworth had realised what the real issue was, he could not have come to a different conclusion.

So far I have dealt with one part of the Cabinet Mission's statement where they say that the Crown could not transfer Paramountcy to an Indian Government. There remains for consideration the other parts of their statement in which they say that the Crown will not transfer Paramountcy to an Indian Government. According to the Cabinet Mission, Paramountcy will lapse. This is a most astounding statement and runs contrary to another well-established principle of the Constitutional Law.

According to this principle, the King cannot surrender or abandon his prerogative rights. If the Crown cannot transfer Paramountcy the Crown cannot also abandon it. The validity of this principle was admitted by the Privy Council in The Queen *vs.* Eduljee Byramjee decided in 1840 and reported in 5 Moore's P.C. p. 276 wherein they said (p. 294) that the Crown could not even by charter part with its prerogative. It is, therefore, obvious that the statement made by the Cabinet Mission that the Crown will not exercise Paramountcy is contrary to the Constitutional Law by which the Empire is governed. The Crown must continue to exercise Paramountcy.

It is of course true that the Crown can surrender its prerogative if permitted to do so by express statutory authority. The question is whether it would be legal and proper for the British Parliament to make a Law permitting the abandoning of Paramountcy. It would be open, I am sure, for Indians to argue that such a step by the British Parliament would neither be proper nor legal. It would not be legal for the simple reason that after India becomes Dominion, the Statute abrogating Paramountcy can be passed by the Dominion Parliament of India and the British Parliament would have no jurisdiction in this matter at all. Again a Statute passed by the Parliament of the Great Britain abrogating Paramountcy would be improper.

The reason is obvious. The army is the ultimate sanction for Paramountcy. This army has been the Indian Army for which British India has paid all along. Without the powerful army maintained by British India which was placed at the disposal of the Crown through his agent the Viceroy and Governor-General of India, the Crown would never have been able to build up and conserve the powers of Paramountcy.

These powers are of the nature of a Trust held by the Crown for the benefit of the people of India and it would be a gross breach of trust on the part of the British Parliament to pass a statute destroying this trust. Paramountcy is an advantage which is secured to it by treaty with the Princes. Independent India can, therefore, make valid claim for the inheritance of Paramountcy.

A question may be asked: What happens when India become Independent. The Crown disappears and the question of advising the Crown does not remain. Can Independent India claim to inherit the prerogative rights of the Crown? The answer is yes. She can. Independent India will be a succession State. For an answer to this question one must look to the provisions of International Law relating to succession among States. Oppenheim admits that a succeeding State can inherit certain rights of the preceding State. From Hall's International Law, it would appear that among other things, property and advantages secured to it by treaty can be inherited by a succession State. India as a succession State she can inherit certain rights. On this point the following extracts from Hall's International Law are relevant:

"And as the old State continues its life uninterruptedly, it possesses everything belonging to it as a person, which it has not expressly lost; so that property and advantages secured to it by treaty, which are enjoyed by it as a personal whole, or by its subjects in virtue of their being members of that whole, continue to belong to it. On the other hand, rights possessed in respect of the lost territory, including rights under treaties relating to cessions of territory and

demarcations of boundary, obligations contracted with reference to it alone, and property which is within it, and has, therefore, a local character, or which, though not within it, belongs to state institutions localised there, transfer themselves to the new state person."

The conclusion is that the Indian States will continue to be in the same position when India becomes Independent as they are now. They will be sovereign States to the extent they are, but they cannot be independent States so long as they remain under the suzerainty, as they must be, either of the Crown, if India remains a Dominion and under the suzerainty of the succession State, if India becomes independent. While the suzerainty remains they can never be independent.

The States may declare themselves independent. But they must realise that while the suzerainty lasts and it must continue even when India becomes independent, India will not recognise their independence nor can a foreign State accord them the status of an independent State. The only way by which, the Indian States can be free themselves from Paramountcy would be to bring about a merger of sovereignty and suzerainty. That can happen only when the I States join the Indian Union as constituent units thereof. The States' spokesmen ought to know this. But as they seem to have forgotten it is necessary to remind them of what happened at the R T C. In the beginning, the States were not prepared to join the Federation.

They agreed to join the Federation when they came to know that the Butler Committee had laid down the doctrine that Paramountcy was Paramount. This change of attitude was due to the realisation that to the extent the powers comprised in Paramountcy were handed over to the Federation to that extent Paramountcy would vanish. In fact, as most of us know, the Princes did raise the question to the then Secretary of State and asked him that the scope of Paramountcy should be limited to, by excluding the subjects included in List No. 1. The then Secretary of State had no answer to give and silenced the Princes by frowning upon them. Apart from the attitude of the then Secretary of State, the point remains that the Princes had seen the point that the dissolution of Paramountcy lay in joining the Federation. That point remains as valid now as it was then.

It would be wise on the part of the Indian States to follow that line and not to pursue the mirage of independence. The people of India should, therefore, repudiate the proposition enunciated by the Cabinet Mission that Paramountcy will lapse. They should insist that Paramountcy cannot lapse and that they are the heirs to that Paramountcy and will continue to exercise it, *vis-a-vis* such Indian States as do not join the Union even after the British have left. The States, on the other hand, should realise that their existence as Sovereign Indian States will not be worth 5 years purchase. It is in the interest of the Princes that they should join the Union and become Constitutional monarchs. Any Dewan who advises his Prince not to join the Union is really acting as the enemy of the Prince.

The joining of the Federation will no doubt involve the introduction of responsible Government but it has this advantage, *viz.*, that the Union will guarantee to the Princes the rights relating to dynastic succession which is the most that a Prince can expect. To be independent and to hope to get recognition and protection from the UNO is to live in one's own paradise. It is doubtful if the UNO will give recognition to Indian States ignoring the claim by India of suzerainty over them. But even if that happens, the UNO will never grant any assistance to an Indian State from external aggression or internal commotion without insisting that the State should first introduce responsible Government within its area. All these things are writ large on the wall. He who runs may read it. Those who refuse to read it will no doubt share the fate which befalls all those who are blinded by their self-interest

THE POWERS AND PRIVILEGES OF THE LORDS AND THE COMMONS

Both Houses of Parliament enjoy certain privileges in their collective capacity as constituent parts of Parliament and which are necessary for the support of their authority and for the proper exercise of their functions. Besides the privileges enjoyed collectively as members of the two Houses of Parliament, there are other privileges enjoyed by members in their individual capacity and which are intended to protect their person and secure their independence and dignity.

PRIVILEGES OF PARLIAMENT

Privileges of the House of Commons: The right to exclude strangers and to debate within closed doors is one of the privileges claimed by the House of Commons. The origin of this privilege lies in the existence of two different circumstances. One circumstance related to the seating arrangements for members in the House of Commons, which was so defective that strangers and members of Parliament were often mixed together. The result was that the strangers were often counted along with the members in divisions. To prevent this, the House claimed the right to exclude strangers. The second circumstance related to the system of espionage practised by the King over members of the House of Commons. In those days, as reporting of the speeches by the members in the House had not become systematic the King was anxious to know who were his friends and who were his enemies, employed spies, whose duty it was to report to the King the speeches made by members on the floor of the House. This was followed by intimidation of the members by the King or by other acts of displeasure, which had the effect of curtailing the independence of the members. And the only way by which the House could protect itself against the system of espionage practised by the King was to claim the right to exclude strangers.

Under this privilege it did not follow that strangers could not enter the House and listen to the debates. As a matter of fact, they did enter and listen to the debates. The effect of the privilege was that if a member took notice of their presence, the Speaker was obliged to order them to withdraw. This worked inconveniently because the objection of one member to the presence of strangers was enough to compel the Speaker to order them to withdraw. In 1875, therefore, the rule was altered by are solution of the House, which prescribed that if any member took notice of the presence of the strangers or to use technical language rose to address the Speaker "Sir, I spy strangers", the Speaker shall forthwith put the question that strangers be ordered to withdraw without permitting debate or amendment and take the sense of the House and act accordingly. This resolution while retaining the privilege of excluding strangers, makes its exercise subject to the wishes of the majority of the House, and not to the caprice of an individual member. The rule, however, gives the Speaker the power to order the withdrawal of strangers at any time on his own initiative and without a motion from any member of the House.

The House of Commons claims the privilege of secrecy of debates and have the right to prohibit the publication of their debates and their proceedings. In 1771, an incident occurred which put the privilege beyond debate. A certain printer who resided in the city of London printed the debates of the Commons without their permit. The Commons, having taken offence at this breach of their privilege, sent a messenger under the authority of the Speaker to arrest the printer. The printer in his turn handed over the messenger of the House of Commons to the custody of a constable for assaulting him in his own house. In the criminal proceedings that took place, the Mayor and the two aldermen of the city of London who constituted the bench held that the warrant of arrest issued by the House of Commons was not operative within the city on account of its charter and committed the messenger of the Commons though they left him out on bail.

The Commons sent for the Mayor and the aldermen who constituted the bench and their clerk who recorded the recognisance of the messenger in his book. They erased from the book the entry relating to the messenger's recognisance by tearing the page and committed the Mayor and the aldermen to the Tower of London for challenging the authority of the Warrant. Since then no one has ventured to offend against the privilege of the Commons relating to the secrecy of debates. The reports of the debates which one sees today are made on sufferance and published on sufferance, and they could be prohibited any time by the order of the House in that behalf. This was done on some occasions during the last war when many subjects were discussed on the floor of the House in secrecy without any reports being published of the debates.

Another privilege which the House of Commons claims is the right to provide for the proper Constitution of the House. Under this privilege, falls the consideration of three distinct questions.

Filling of Vacancies: While the holding of a general election for the summoning of a new Parliament is a Prerogative of the King, the filling up of vacancies during the continuance of a Parliament is a privilege of the House of Commons. Consequently, when a vacancy occurs, the writ for the return of a member to supply the vacancy is issued on a warrant by the Speaker in pursuance of an order by the House and not in pursuance of an order from the King. If Parliament is not sitting when the vacancy occurs, the Speaker is authorised to issue the writ subject to certain conditions.

The second question that falls within this privilege is the determination of disputed elections. This question formed for a long time a bone of contention between the King on the one hand and the Commons on the other. Each party claimed the right for itself to the exclusion of the other. Originally the writ issued to a constituency for an election was returned to Parliament, thereby recognizing the right of the Commons to fill a vacancy in that particular constituency.

Since the reign of Henry IV, it was returned to Chancery, thereby recognizing the right of the King to fill the vacancy. The matter thus alternated till 1604 when the Commons insisted that the right was theirs and a quarrel arose between them and

James 1. In that year, the King James I issued a proclamation directing that no bankrupt or out-law be elected to Parliament.

The County of Bucks elected one Mr. Goodwin. He was an outlaw and the King declared his election void and issued another writ. And Mr. Fortesque was returned. The Commons on their own motion resolved that notwithstanding the avoidance of his election by the King, Mr. Goodwin was duly elected a member of the House. The King on the other hand claimed the right to determine the issue. At a conference held between the King, the Lords and the Commons, the Lords advised the King to accept defeat and recognise the right of the Commons. The trial of disputed elections by the House became a source of trouble to the House and anxiety to the candidates because all such trials became matters of party politics and in 1868 the House was pleased by law to leave the adjudication of disputed elections to the Court of Law.

The third right which falls within the purview of this privilege is the right of the House to expel a member who has behaved in a manner which would render him unfit to sit in the House. Expulsion is not a disqualification and the member expelled may be again elected. It must be borne in mind that the right to be elected does not carry with it the right to sit. To be elected is a favour derived from the electors. To be allowed to sit is a favour within the competence of the House and cases have occurred in which persons have been duly elected to the House of Commons but who have not been able to take their seats in the House. The case of Wilkes is an illustration in point. Wilkes was elected four times in succession by the County of Middlesex and on all the four times, he was refused by the House a seat.

The next important privilege claimed by the House of Commons is the right to exclusive cognisance of matters arising within the House. Under this privilege, the House has the exclusive right to regulate its internal proceedings and concerns and the mode and manner of carrying on its business and that no Court could take cognisance of that, which passes within its walls. The nature and extent of this privilege are well-illustrated by the case of *Bradlaugh* vs. *Gosset.* The facts of this case are simple. On the 3rd of May 1880, Mr. Bradlaugh, who was elected a member from Northampton claimed to make the affirmation instead of the oath as he was an atheist. A Committee of the House of Commons reported that affirmation was confined to proceedings in a Court of Law and that the members of Parliament could not resort to it. Oath was the only thing that was open to them.

After this report, Mr. Bradlaugh came to the Speaker's table to take the oath. The house, however, objected on the ground that it would not be binding upon his conscience, and that it would be a mere formality. Another Committee was appointed to report whether Mr. Bradlaugh should be permitted to take the Oath. The Committee reported that he should not be permitted to take the oath but recommended that he should be allowed to affirm subject to its legality being tested in a Court of Law. In accordance with this, a motion was made to allow Mr. Bradlaugh to affirm to which an amendment was made disallowing him either to affirm or to take oath. Bradlaugh, however, insisted upon his right to take the oath, but the Speaker asked him to withdraw. He refused and the sergeant was asked to remove Mr. Bradlaugh. A scuffle ensued between Mr. Cosset, the sergeant and Mr. Bradlaugh in which Mr. Bradlaugh was very badly injured. A standing order was passed allowing affirmation.

Mr. Bradlaugh affirmed but the Court declared that affirmation was not permissible to a member of Parliament. His seat was thereafter vacated. Re-elected again in 1881, the same scene was repeated. Whenever he came to the table to take the oath, the House resolved that he be not allowed to do so. On one occasion by the direction of the Speaker, Mr. Bradlaugh was conducted by Sergeant Gosset beyond the precise of the House and subsequently expelled. Bradlaugh brought an action against Gosset in the Queen's bench division for an injunction to restrain Gosset from using force to prevent his taking the oath.. The House made the usual order for the defence of the sergeant. The Queen's bench division refused relief to Mr. Bradlaugh on the ground that the order under which Gosset acted related to the procedure of the House and that the Court had no power to interfere in such a matter. The House of Commons claims the privilege to protect its dignity and authority. It would be in vain to attempt any enumeration of the acts which might be construed by the House as an insult or an affront to its dignity. But certain principles may be laid down:

(1) Disobedience of any of the orders or rules which regulate the proceedings of the House is a breach of the privilege. Publication of debates contrary to the resolution of the House, wilful misrepresentation of the debates, publication of evidence taken before a select Committee until it has been reported to the House are examples of the breach of this rule.

(2) Disobedience to particular orders. Resolutions are agreed to at the beginning of each session which declare that the House will proceed with the utmost severity against persons who tamper with witnesses in respect of evidence to be given to the House or to any Committee thereof, who endeavour to deter or hinder persons from appearing or giving evidence and who give false evidence before the House on any Committee thereof, would be guilty of breach of privilege by reason of disobedience to particular orders.

(3) Indignities offered to the character or proceedings of Parliament or upon the honour of the House by libellous reflections would be a breach of the privilege. It is not to be supposed that only members of the public can be held guilty for a breach of privilege under this rule. Even members of Parliament could be made punishable if they commit the breach of this rule. In 1819, Mr. Hobhouse, who was an M. P., denounced the resistance offered by the House of Parliamentary Reforms, in a

pamphlet which he published anonymously. After his having acknowledged himself as the author of the pamphlet, the House held him guilty of the breach of privilege. In 1838, another instance occurred when Mr. Ocomed an M.P. at a public meeting laid a charge of foul perjury against members of the House in the discharge of their judicial duties in election committees.

(4) Interference with the members of the House in the discharge of their duties as members of the House.

It is an infringement of the privilege of the House to assault, insult or menace any member of the House in his coming or going from the House or on account of his behaviour in Parliament or to endeavour to compel members by force to declare themselves in favour of or against any proposition then pending or expected to be before the House or bribing members of parliament to vote in a particular manner.

PRIVILEGES OF INDIVIDUAL MEMBERS

(1) *Freedom from Arrest:* This privilege guarantees freedom from arrest for members during the continuance of the session and 40 days before the commencement and after its conclusion. Originally this privilege was not only enjoyed by members but also extended to their servants and their estates. It is now restricted to members only and that too to their persons.

(2) *Freedom of Speech:* The statute of William and Mary S2 C2 enacts that members shall enjoy complete freedom of speech in Parliamentary debates and proceedings and that nothing said by them shall be questioned or impeached in any Court or place out of Parliament.

METHODS OF PUNISHING BREACHES OF PRIVILEGE

There are five different ways in which the House can punish persons who are guilty of a breach of privilege. Incases of breach of privilege which are not grave, the House may release a person arrested for breach of privilege on mere admonition if he is prepared to tender apology. Or secondly, may release him on a reprimand. In cases of a grave character, the House can commit him to prison or inflict a fine or expel him. It is obvious that the last form of punishment namely, expulsion, can apply only to members of parliament who are guilty of a breach of privilege.

PRIVILEGES OF THE HOUSE OF LORDS

The privileges of the House of Lords are more or less the same as those of the Commons. It is, therefore, unnecessary to discuss them separately in detail. There is only one point of difference between the privileges of the Lords and the Commons which need to be mentioned and which relates to the source of their privileges. The privileges of the Commons are a gift from the King. They have to be claimed by the Speaker in the name of the Commons in the beginning of every newly elected Parliament. The privileges of the Lords belong to them in their own right. They are not derived from the King.

OFFICERS OF THE HOUSE

The House of Lords and the House of Commons possess certain Officers for the general conduct of their business and for the enforcement of their privileges. For the sake of clarity it might be desirable to discuss the status and the functions of the Officers of the two Houses separately.

THE HOUSE OF COMMONS

The Speaker: The Speaker is now elected by the House of Commons at its first meeting after the general election and continues to hold the place till the lifetime of the Parliament unless removed from Office by a resolution. Originally the King claimed and exercised a virtual right of selection. In 1679, there arose a conflict between the Charles II and the newly elected House of Commons on the right to choose the Speaker. The Commons chose Sir Edward Sey Mour and the King declined to accept him. The King suggested his own nominee to the Commons and the Commons in their turn refused to have him.

Eventually a compromise was arrived at, and another person who was an independent choice of the Commons was adopted by them as their Speaker. To him the King raised no objection. From this time onward, the right of the Commons to chose their own Speaker was not contested by the Crown.

THE FUNCTIONS OF THE SPEAKER

The Speaker of the House of Commons functions in three distinct capacities. As the Spokesman and representative of the House he performs the following duties.

(1) He demands its privileges and communicates its resolutions of thanks, ensures admonitions and reprimands.

(2) He issues warrants of commitments whenever a person is punished for breach of privilege. He issues warrants for attendance at the bar for being rebuked or sentenced by the House or for any other purpose as provided for in the order of the House.

(3) He issues writs for filling up vacancies—The Parliament Act of 1911 has imposed upon the Speaker a new function which did not belong to him before. Under the Act, he the functions as a judicial officer and in that capacity he has to certify whether any particular bill is a money bill or not.

The Speaker is also the Chairman of the House whenever the House meets to carry on its business. In his capacity as a Chairman he is required:

(1) To maintain order in debates.

(2) To decide questions upon points of order.

(3) To put the question under discussion to the House.

(4) To declare the determination of the House on the question.

OFFICERS UNDER THE SPEAKER

There are two Officers under the Speaker of the House of Commons. One is called the clerk of the House of Commons and the other is called the Sergeant at arms. The duty of the clerk of the Commons is to maintain a record of the proceedings of the House. He maintains what is called the journal of the House of Commons in which are noted all matters brought before the House and discusses by it in their order from day-to-day.

The Sergeant at arms is a sort of a Police Officer whose duty is to enforce the orders of the House and the Speaker in relation to internal order and to breach of privilege.

THE HOUSE OF LORDS

The Speaker: The Speaker of the House of Lords is not an elected person and the House of Lords has no right to elect its own Speaker. The Speaker of the House of Lords is by prescription the Lord Chancellor or the Lord Keeper of the Great Seal, who can act as Speaker in the absence of the Lord Chancellor. In their absence the place is taken by any one of the Deputy-Speakers of whom there are always several appointed by the King's Commission and if they should all be absent, the Lords elect a Speaker for the time being.

The Speaker of the House of Lords need not necessarily be a Peer, and that office may be discharged by a commoner and has been so discharged when a commoner happened to be the Lord Keeper of the Great Seal or when the Great Seal was in commission. It is singular that the President of this deliberative body is not necessarily a member of it, and the Woolsack on which the Speaker sits is treated as being outside the limits of the House of Lords, so as to permit the office being discharged by a person who is not a member of the House.

THE DUTIES OF THE SPEAKER IN THE LORDS

The position of the Speaker of the House of Lords is totally different from the position of the Speaker of the House of Commons. There is nothing common between them as far as their authority and function is concerned except that both are

Chairmen of a deliberative assembly. But so far as their function and authority is concerned, their position is fundamentally different. This is clear from standing order No. 20 which defines the duties of the Lord Chancellor as a Speaker of the House of Lords. The standing order says: "The Lord Chancellor when he speaks to the House is always to speak uncovered and is not to adjourn the House or to do anything else as mouth of the House, without the consent of the Lords first had, except the ordinary thing about bills which are of course wherein the Lords may likewise overrule, as for preferring one bill before another and such like, and in case of difference among the Lords, it is to be put to the question, and if the Lord Chancellor speak to anything particularly, he is to go to his own place as a Peer" and be it noted that the place of the Lord Chancellor if he is a Peer is to the left of the Chamber.

It is clear from the standing order how limited is the authority of the Speaker in the Lords.

(1) In the enforcement of rules for maintaining order the Speaker of the House of Lords has no more authority than any other Peer.

(2) He cannot decide points of order as is done by the Speaker of the House of Commons. If he is a Peer he may address the House on any point of order raised. But the decision on it is the decision of the Majority of the House.

(3) Owing to the limited authority of the Speaker in the Lords in directing the proceedings of the House, the right of a Peer to address the House depends not upon him as it does in the House of Commons but depends solely upon the will of the House. When two Peers rise at the same time, unless one immediately gives way to the other, the House calls upon one of them to speak and if each is supported by a party, there is no alternative but division. The issue is not decided by the Speaker, as is done in the House of Commons.

The result of his imperfect powers is that a Peer who is disorderly is called to order by another Peer perhaps of an opposite party and that an irregular argument is liable to ensue in which case, each last Speaker imputes disorder to his predecessor and recrimination takes the place of an orderly debate with the Lord Chancellor sitting but powerless to intervene, as his power is limited to the putting of questions and carrying on other formal business.

These are lectures on the English Constitution which I delivered to the students of the Government Law College, Bombay, in 1934-35. In publishing these lectures I have not forgotten how presumptuous it may be deemed for an Indian to attempt to expound the principles of the English Constitution. Sir Austen Chamberlain in the course of his cross-examination of a certain Indian witness who appeared before the Joint Committee on Indian Constitutional Reform observed: I listen to the witness with great respect when he talks of Indian conditions, but when he expounds the British Constitution he must permit me to remain of my own opinion (Minutes of Evidence, Vol. IIc, Q. 9812). There is undoubtedly a great deal of truth in this remark and it should make every Indian who wishes to write on the English Constitution pause.

An Indian, however, who wishes to enter into the field may well take courage from the fact that much of the English Constitution have been expounded by foreigners who have not only been heard with respect by Englishmen but whose writings have compelled a change of opinion. Be that as it may the remark made by Sir Austen Chamberlain need not come in my way. I am not expounding anything of my own. I am not expounding it to Englishmen. I am merely trying to make Dicey's English Constitution easier for Indian students to follow and to understand. From the standpoint of Indian students Dicey's treatise suffers from two defects.

It presupposes a knowledge of certain parts of the English Constitution. For instance it presupposes a knowledge of what is Parliament, how it is constituted and how it functions. This presupposition, howsoever justifiable it may be in the case of English students, would be without warrant in the case of Indian students who are called upon to take up the study of Dicey for the first time. Without a complete knowledge of this part of the English Constitution Indian student feels completely bewildered and fails to grasp the full import of such fundamental principles as supremacy of the rule of law or the role of conventions in the working of the Constitution. In order that the Indian student may follow in an intelligent way the exposition of Dicey regarding the operation of these principles the teacher is forced at every turn to present to the student the framework of the English Constitution which finds no place in Dicey's treatise.

Secondly, the English Constitution has grown enormously both as regards rules of law and also as regards conventions since the last edition of Dicey's English Constitution was published. The result of this growth has been felt in two different ways. It has rendered some of the illustrations given by Dicey quite inappropriate. Secondly, it has altered the character of the English Constitution especially the relations of the Crown and the British Parliament to the Dominions to such an extent that an Indian student who depends upon Dicey alone will not be up-to-date but will be missing a great deal that is vital in it. Except for additions of matter and changes of form there is nothing new in these lectures. They constitute a revision of Dicey's treatise on the English Constitution with a view to remove its defects and to adapt it to the needs of Indian students.

6

GANDHISM : THE DOOM OF THE UNTOUCHABLES

INTRODCUTION

What is Gandhism? What does it stand for? What are its teachings about economic problem? What are its teachings about social problem? At the outset it is necessary to state that some Gandhists have conjured up a conception of Gandhism which is purely imaginary. According to this conception Gandhism means return to the village and making the village self-sufficient. It makes Gandhism a mere matter of regionalism. Gandhism, I am sure, is neither so simple nor so innocent as regionalism is. Gandhism has a much bigger content than regionalism. Regionalism is a small insignificant part of it. It has a social philosophy and it has an economic philosophy. To omit to take into account the economic and social philosophy of Gandhism is to present deliberately a false picture of Gandhism.

The first and foremost requisite is to present a true picture of Gandhism. To start with Mr. Gandhi's teachings on social problem. Mr. Gandhi's views on the caste system—which constitutes the main, social problem in India—were fully elaborated by him in 1921-22 in a Gujarathi Journal called Navajivan. The article is written in Gujarathi. I give below an English translation of his views as near as possible in his own words. Says Mr. Gandhi:

1. I believe that if Hindu Society has been able to stand it is because it is founded on the caste system.
2. The seeds of Swaraj are to be found in the caste system. Different castes are like different sections of military division. Each division is working for the good of the whole.
3. A community which can create the caste system must be said to possess unique power of organisation.
4. Caste has a ready made means for spreading primary education. Every caste can take the responsibility for the education of the children of the Caste. Caste has a political basis. It can work as an electorate for a representative body. Caste can perform judicial functions by electing persons to act as judges to decide disputes among members of the same caste. With castes it is easy to raise a defence force by requiring each caste to raise a brigade.
5. I believe that interdining or intermarriage are not necessary for promoting national unity. That dining together creates friendship is contrary to experience. If this was true there would have been no war in Europe... Taking food is as dirty an act as answering the call of nature. The only difference is that after answering call of nature we get peace while after eating food we get discomfort. Just as we perform the act of answering the call of nature in seclusion so also the act of taking food must also be done in seclusion.
6. In India children of brothers do not intermarry. Do they cease to love because they do not intermarry? Among the Vaishnavas many women are so orthodox that they will not eat with the members of the family nor will they drink water from a common water pot. Have they no love? The Caste system cannot be said to be bad because it does not allow inter-dining or intermarriage between different Castes."

7. Caste is another name for control. Caste puts a limit on enjoyment. Caste does not allow a person to transgress caste limits in pursuit of his enjoyment. That is the meaning of such caste restrictions as interdining and intermarriage.
8. To destroy caste system and adopt Western European social system means that Hindus must give up the principle of hereditary occupation which is the soul of the caste system. Hereditary principle is an eternal principle. To change it is to create disorder. I have no use for a Brahmin if I cannot call him a Brahmin for my life. It will be a chaos if every day a Brahmin is to be changed into a Sudra and a Sudra is to be changed into a Brahmin.
9. The caste system is & natural order of society. In India it has been given a religious coating. Other countries not having understood the utility of the Caste System it existed only in a loose condition and consequently those countries have not derived from Caste system the same degree of advantage which India has derived.

These being my views I am opposed to all those who are out to destroy the Caste System."

In 1922, Mr. Gandhi was a defender of the caste system. Pursuing the inquiry, one comes across a somewhat critical view of the caste system by Mr. Gandhi in the year 1925. This is what Mr. Gandhi said on 3rd February 1925:

"I gave support to caste because it stands for restraint. But at present caste does not mean restraint, it means limitations. Restraint is glorious and helps to achieve freedom. But limitation is like chain. It binds. There is nothing commendable in castes as they exist today. They are contrary to the tenets of the shastras. The number of castes is infinite and there is a bar against intermarriage. This is not & condition of elevation. It is a state of fall."

In reply to the question: What is the way out Mr. Gandhi said:

"The best remedy is that small castes should fuse themselves into one big caste. There should be four such big castes so that we may reproduce the old system of four varnas."

In short, in 1925 Mr. Gandhi became an upholder of the Varna system.

The old Varna system prevalent in ancient India had society divided into four orders: (1) Brahmins, whose occupation was learning; (2) Kshatriyas whose occupation was warfare, (3) Vaishyas, whose occupation was trade and (4) Sudras, whose occupation was service of the other classes. Is Mr. Gandhi's Varna System the same as this old Varna system of the orthodox Hindus? Mr. Gandhi explained his Varna system in the following terms:

1. I believe that the divisions into Varna is based on birth.
2. There is nothing in the Varna system which stands in the way of the Sudra acquiring learning or studying military art of offence or defence. Contra it is open to a Kshatriya to serve. The Varna system is no bar to him.

   What the Vavna system enjoins is that a Sudra will not make learning a way of earning a living. Nor will a Kshatriya adopt service as a way of earning a living. [Similarly a Brahmin may learn the art of war or trade.. But he must not make them a way of earning his living. Contra a Vaishya may acquire learning or may cultivate the art of war. But he must not make them a way of earning his living.
3. The varna system is connected with the way of earning a living. There is no harm if a person belonging to one varna acquires the knowledge or science and art specialised in by persons belonging to other varnas. But as far as the way of earning his living is concerned he must follow the occupation of the varna to which he belongs which means he must follow the hereditary profession of his forefathers.

4. The object of the varna system is to prevent competition and class struggle and class war. I believe in the varna system because it fixes the duties and occupations of persons,
5. Varna means the determination of a man's occupation before he is born.
6. In the Varna system no man has any liberty to choose his occupation. His occupation is determined for him by heredity.

Turning to the field of economic life, Mr. Gandhi stands for two ideals:

One of these is the opposition to machinery. As early as 1921 Mr. Gandhi gave vent to his dislike for machinery. Writing in the Young India of 19th January 1921, Mr. Gandhi said:

> *"Do I want to put back the hand of the clock of progress? Do I want to replace the mills by hand-spinning and hand-weaving? Do I want to replace the railway by the country-cart? Do I want to destroy machinery altogether? These questions have been asked by some journalists and public men. My answer is: I would not weep over the disappearance of machinery or consider it a calamity."*

Hitherto when Indians have been talking about the reconstruction of Indian social and economic life they have been talking in terms of individualism versus collectivism, capitalism versus socialism, conservatism versus radicalism and so on. But quite recently a new 'ism' has come on the Indian horizon. It is called Gandhism. It is true that very recently Mr. Gandhi had denied that there is such a thing as Gandhism. This denial is nothing more than the usual modesty which Mr. Gandhi wears so well. It does not disprove the existence of Gandhism. There have been quite a number of books with the title of Gandhism without any protest from Mr. Gandhi. It has already caught the imagination of some people both inside and outside India. Some have so much faith in it that they do not hesitate to offer it as an alternative to Marxism.

The followers of Gandhism who may happen to read what is said in the foregoing pages may well ask; Mr. Gandhi may not have done what the Untouchables expected him to do; but does not Gandhism offer any hope to the Untouchables? The followers of Gandhism may accuse me of remembering only the short, slow, intermittent steps taken by Mr. Gandhi for the sake of the Untouchables and of forgetting the potential length of the principles enunciated by him. I am prepared to admit that it does sometimes happen that a person, who enunciates a long principle takes only a short step and that he may be forgiven for the short step in the hope that some day the principle will by its native dynamics force a long step covering all who were once left out. Gandhism is in itself a very interesting subject for study.

But to deal with Gandhism after having dealt with Mr. Gandhi is bound to he a tedious task and therefore my first reaction was to leave out the consideration of Gandhism and. Untouchables. At the same time, I could hardly remain indifferent to the facts that the effect of my omission to consider the subject might be very unfortunate.

For Gandhists, notwithstanding my exposure of Mr. Gandhi, might take advantage of it and continue to preach that if Mr. Gandhi has failed to solve the problem of the Untouchables still the Untouchables will find their salvation in Gandhism. It is because I wish to leave no room for such propaganda that I have overcome my original disinclination and engage upon discussion of Gandhism.

His opposition to machinery is well evidenced by his idolisation of charkha (the spinning wheel) and by insistence upon hand-spinning and hand-weaving. This opposition to machinery and his love for charkha is not a matter of accident. It is a matter of philosophy. This philosophy Mr. Gandhi took special occasion to propound in his presidential address at the Kathiawad Political Conference held on 8th January 1925. This is what Mr. Gandhi said:

"Nations are tired of the worship of lifeless machines multiplied ad infinitum. We are destroying the matchless living machines viz., our own bodies by leaving them to rust and trying to substitute lifeless machinery for them. It is a law of God that the body must be fully worked and utilised. We dare not ignore it. The spinning wheel is the auspicious symbol of Sharir Yajna— body labour. He who eats his food without offering this sacrifice steals it. By giving up this sacrifice we became traitors to the country, and banged the door in the face of the Goddess of Fortune."

Anyone who has read Mr. Gandhi's booklet on Hind Swaraj (Indian Home Rule) will know that Mr. Gandhi is against modern civilisation. The book was first published in 1908. But there has been no change in his ideology. Writing in 1921 Mr. Gandhi said:

"The booklet is a severe condemnation of 'modern civilisation.' It was written in 1908. My conviction is deeper today than ever. I feel that, if India would discard 'Modern civilisation' she can only gain by doing so."

In Mr. Gandhi's view: "Western civilisation is the creation of satan."

The second ideal of Mr. Gandhi is the elimination of class-war and even class struggle in the relationship between employers and employees and between landlords and tenants. Mr. Gandhi's views on the relationship between employers and employees were set forth by him in an article on the subject which appeared in the Navajivan of the 8th June 1921 from which the following is an extract:

Two paths are open before India, either to introduce the Western principle of 'Might is right' or to uphold the Eastern principle that truth alone conquers, that truth knows no mishap, that the strong and the weak have alike a right to secure justice. The choice is to begin with the labouring class. Should the labourers obtain an increment in their wages by violence? Even if that be possible, they cannot resort to anything like violence, howsoever legitimate may be their claims. To use violence for securing rights may seem an easy path, but it proves to be thorny in the long run. Those who live by sword die also by sword. The swimmer often dies by drowning. Look at Europe. No one seems to be happy there, for not one is contented. The labourer does not trust the capitalist and the capitalist has no faith in the labourer. Both have a sort of vigour and strength but even the bulls have it. They fight to the very bitter end. All motion is not progress. We have got no reason to believe, that the people of Europe are progressing. Their possession of wealth does not argue the possession of any moral or spiritual qualities.

What shall we do then? The labourers in Bombay made a fine stand. I was not in a position to know all the facts. But this much I could see that they could fight in a better way. The millowner may be wholly in the wrong. In the struggle between capital and labour, it may be generally said that more often than not the capitalists are in the wrong box. But when labour comes fully to realise its strength, I know it can become more tyrannical than capital. The millowners will have to work on the terms dictated by labour, if the latter could command intelligence of the former. It is clear, however, that labour will never attain to that intelligence. If it does; labour will cease to be labour and become itself the master. The capitalists do not fight on the strength of money alone. They do possess intelligence and tact.

The question before us is this: When the labourers, remaining what they are, develop a certain consciousness, what should be their course?' It would be suicidal 'if the labourers rely upon their numbers or brute-force, *i.e.*, violence. By so doing, they will do harm to industries in the country. If, on the other hand, they take their stand on pure justice and suffer in their person to secure It, not only will they always succeed but they will reform their masters, develop industries and both master and men will be as members of one and the same family.

Referring to the same theme on another occasion Mr. Gandhi said: "Nor was it otherwise before. Indians history is not one of strained relations between capital and labour."

Particularly noteworthy are the views of Mr. Gandhi on strike as a weapon, in the hand of the workers to improve their economic condition. Mr. Gandhi says: "Speaking, therefore, as one having handled large successful strikes, I repeat the following maxims, already stated in these pages, for the guidance of all strike leaders:

(1) There should be no strike without a real grievance.

(2) There should be no strike, if the persons concerned are not able to support themselves out of their own savings or by engaging in some temporary occupation, such as carding, spinning and weaving. Strikers should never depend upon public subscriptions or other charity.

(3) Strikers must fix an unalterable minimum demand, and declare it before embarking upon their strike.

"A strike may fail in spite of a just grievance and the ability of strikers to hold out indefinitely, if there are workers to replace them. A wise man, therefore, will not strike for increase of wages or other comforts, if he feels that he can be easily replaced. But a philanthropic or patriotic man will strike in spite of supply being greater than the demand, when he feels for and wishes to associate himself with his neighbour's distress. Needless to say, there is no room in a civil strike of the nature described by me for violence in the shape of intimidation, incendiarism or otherwise...Judged by the tests suggested by me, it is 'clear that friends of the strikers could never have advised them to apply for or receive Congress or any other public funds for their support. The value of the strikers' sympathy was diminished to the extent, that they received or accepted financial aid. The merit of a sympathetic strike lies in the inconvenience and the loss suffered by the sympathisers."

Mr. Gandhi's view on the relationship between landlords and tenants were expounded by him in the Young India of 18th

May 1921 in the form of instructions to the tenants of U.P. who had risen against their landlords. Mr. Gandhi said:

"Whilst the U. P. Government is crossing the bounds of propriety, and intimidating people, there is little doubt that the Kisans too are not making wise use of their newly found power. In several Zamindaries, they are said to have overstepped the mark, taken the law into their own hands and to have become impatient of anybody who would not do as they wish. They are abusing social boycott and are turning it into an instrument of violence. They are reported to have Stopped the supply of water, barber and other paid services to their Zamindars in some instances and even suspended payment of the rent due to them. The Kisan movement has received an impetus from Noncooperation but it is anterior to and independent of it. Whilst we will not hesitate to advise the Kisans when the moment comes, to suspend payment of taxes to Government, it is not contemplated that at any stage of Noncooperation we would seek to deprive the Zamindars of their rent. The Kisan movement must be confined to the improvement of status of the Kisans and the betterment of the-relations between the Zamindars and them. The Kisans must be advised scrupulously to abide by the terms of their agreement with the Zamindars, whether such is written or inferred from custom. Where a custom or even a written contract is bad, they may not try to uproot it by violence or without previous reference to the Zamindars. In every case there should be a friendly discussion with the Zamindars and an attempt made to arrive at a settlement."

Mr. Gandhi does not wish to hurt the propertied class. He is even opposed to a campaign against them. He has no passion for economic equality. Referring to the propertied class Mr. Gandhi said quite recently that he does not wish to destroy the hen that lays the golden egg. His solution for the economic conflict between the owners and workers, between the rich and the poor, between landlords and tenants and between the employers and the employees is very simple. The owners need not deprive themselves of their property. All that they need do is to declare themselves Trustees for the poor. Of course the Trust is to be a voluntary one carrying only a spiritual obligation.

Is there anything new in the Gandhian analysis of economic ills? Are the economics of Gandhism sound? What hope does Gandhism hold out to the common man, to the down-and out? Does it promise him a better life, a life of joy, and culture, a life of freedom, not merely freedom from want but freedom to rise, to grow to the full stature which his capacities can reach?

There is nothing new in the Gandhian analysis of economic ills in so far as it attributes them to machinery and the civilisation that is built upon it. The arguments that machinery and modern civilisation help to concentrate management and control into relatively few hands, and with the aid of banking and credit facilitate the transfer into still fewer hands of all materials and factories and mills in which millions are bled white in order to support huge industries thousands of miles away from their cottages, or that machinery and modern civilisation cause deaths, maimings and cripplings far in, excess of the corresponding injuries by war, and are responsible for disease and physical deterioration caused directly and indirectly by the development of large cities with their smoke, dirt, noise, foul air, lack of sunshine and outdoor life, slums, prostitution and unnatural living which they bring about, are all old and worn out arguments. There is nothing new in them. Gandhism is merely repeating the views of Rousseau, Ruskin, Tolstoy and their school.

The ideas which go to make up Gandhism are just primitive. It is a return to nature, to animal life. The only merit is their simplicity. As there is always a large corps of simple people who are attracted by them, such simple ideas do not die, and there is always some simpleton to preach them. There is, however, no doubt that the practical instincts of men—which seldom go wrong—have found them unfruitful and which society in search of progress has thought It best to reject.

The economics of Gandhism are hopelessly fallacious. The fact that machinery and modern civilisation have produced many evils may be admitted. But these evils are no argument against them. For the evils are not due to machinery and modern civilisation. They are due to wrong social organisation which has made private property and pursuit of personal gain matters of absolute sanctity. If machinery and civilisation have not benefited everybody the remedy is not to condemn machinery and civilisation but to alter the organisation of society so that the benefits will not be usurped by the few but will accrue to all.

In Gandhism the common man has no hope. It treats man as an animal and no more. It is true that man shares the constitution and functions of animals, nutritive, reproductive, etc. But these are not distinctively human functions. The distinctively human function is reason, the purpose of which is to enable man to observe, meditate, cogitate, study and discover the beauties of the Universe and enrich his life and control the animal elements in his life. Man thus occupies the highest place in the scheme of animate existence. If this is true what is the conclusion that follows? The conclusion that follows is that while the ultimate goal of a brute's life is reached once his physical appetites are satisfied, the ultimate goal of man's existence is not reached unless and until he has fully cultivated his mind. In short, what divides the brute from man is culture. Culture is not possible for the brute, but it is essential for man. That being so, the aim of human society must be to enable every person to lead a life of culture which means the cultivation of the mind as distinguished from the satisfaction of mere physical wants. How can this happen?

Both for society and as well as for the individual there is always a gulf between merely living and living worthily. In order that one may live worthily One must first live. The time and energy spent upon mere life, upon gaining of subsistence detracts from that available for activities, of a distinctively human nature and which go to make up a life of culture. How then can a life of culture be made possible? It is not possible unless there is sufficient leisure. For it is only when there is leisure that a person is free to devote himself to a life of culture.

The problem of all problems which human society has to face is how to provide leisure to every individual. What does leisure mean? Leisure means the lessening of the toil and, effort necessary for satisfying the physical wants of life. How can leisure be made possible? Leisure is quite impossible unless some means are found whereby the toil required for producing goods necessary to satisfy human needs is lessened. What can lessen such toil? Only when machine takes the place of man. There is no other means of producing leisure. Machinery and modern civilisation are thus indispensable for emancipating man from leading the life of a brute, and for providing him with leisure and making a life of culture possible. The man who condemns machinery and modern civilisation simple does not understand their purpose and the ultimate aim which human society must strive to achieve.

Gandhism may be well suited to a society which does not accept democracy as its ideal. A society which does not believe in democracy may be indifferent to machinery and the civilisation based upon it. But a democratic society cannot. The former may well content itself with life of leisure and culture for the few and a life of toil and drudgery for the many. But a democratic society must assure a life of leisure and culture to each one of its citizens. If the above analysis is correct then the slogan of a democratic society must be machinery, and more machinery, civilisation and more civilisation. Under Gandhism the common man must keep on toiling ceaselessly for a pittance and remain a brute. In short, Gandhism with its call of back to nature, means back to nakedness, back to squalor, back to poverty and back to ignorance for the vast mass of the people.

The division of life into separate functions and of society into separate classes may not be altogether obliterated. Inspite of many social and economic changes, in spite of the abolition of legal serfdom, legal slavery and the spread of the notion of democracy, with the extension of science, of general education through books, newspapers, travel and general intercourse in, schools and factories there remains and perhaps will remain enough cleavage in society into a learned and an ignorant class, a leisure and a labouring class.

But Gandhism is not satisfied with only notional class distinctions. Gandhism insists upon class structure. It regards the class structure of society and also the income structure as sacrosanct with the consequent distinctions of rich and poor, high and low owners and workers as permanent parts of social organisation. From the point of view of social consequences nothing can be more pernicious. Psychologically, class structure sets in motion influences which are harmful to both the classes. There is no common plane on which the privileged and the subject classes can meet. There is no endosmosis, no give and take of life's hopes and experiences.

The social and moral evils of this separation to the subject class are of course real and obvious. It educates them into slaves and creates all the psychological complex which follows from a slave mentality. But those affecting the privileged class, though less material and less perceptible, are equally real. The isolation and exclusiveness following upon the class structure creates in the privileged classes the anti-social spirit of a gang. It feels it has interests ' of its own ' which it makes its prevailing purpose to protect against everybody even against the interests of the State. It makes their culture sterile, their art showy „ their wealth luminous and their manners fastidious. Practically speaking in a class structure there is, on the one hand, tyranny, vanity, pride, arrogance, greed, selfishness and on the other, insecurity, poverty, degradation, loss of liberty, self-reliance, independence, dignity and self-respect. Democratic society cannot be indifferent to such consequences. But Gandhism does not mind these consequences in the least.

It is not enough to say that Gandhism is not satisfied with mere class distinctions. It is not enough to say that Gandhism believes in a class structure. Gandhism stands for more than that. A class structure which is a faded, jejune, effete thing a mere sentimentality, a mere skeleton is not what Gandhism wants. It wants class structure to function as a living faith. In this there is nothing to be surprised at. For class structure in Gandhism is not a mere accident. It is its official doctrine.

The idea of trusteeship which Gandhism proposes as a panacea by which the moneyed classes will hold their properties in trust for the poor is the most ridiculous part of it. All that one can say about it is that if anybody else had propounded it the author would have been laughed at as a silly fool who had not known the hard realities of life and was deceiving the servile classes by telling them that a little dose of moral rearmament to the propertied classes—those who by their insatiable cupidity and indomitable arrogance have made and will always make this world a vale of tears for the toiling millions—will recondition them to such an extent that they will be able to withstand the temptation to misuse the tremendous powers which the class structure gives them over servile classes.

The social ideal of Gandhism is either caste or varna. Though it may be difficult to say which, there can be no doubt that the social ideal of Gandhism is not democracy. For whether one takes for comparison caste or varna both are fundamentally opposed to democracy. It would have been something if the defence of caste system which. Gandhism offers was strong and honest. But his defence of the caste system is the most insensible piece of rhetoric one can think of. Examine Mr. Gandhi's arguments in support of caste and it will be found that everyone of them is specious if not puerile. To run through the arguments summarised earlier in this Chapter.

The first three arguments call for pity. That the Hindu Society has been able to stand while others have died out or disappeared is hardly a matter for congratulation. If it has survived it is not because of caste but because the foreigner who conquered the Hindus did not find it necessary to kill them wholesale. There is no honour in mere survival. What matters is the plane of survival. One can survive by unconditional surrender. One can survive by beating a cowardly retreat and one can survive by fighting. On what plane have the Hindus survived?

If they can be said to have survived after fighting and beating their enemies the virtue ascribed to the caste system by Mr. Gandhi could be admitted. The history of the Hindus has been one of surrender—abject surrender. It is true others have surrendered to their invaders. But in their case surrender is followed by a revolt against the foreign ruler. The Hindus have not only never withstood the onslaught of the foreign invader, they have never even shown the capacity to organise a rebellion to throw off the foreign yoke. On the other hand the Hindus have tried tc make slavery comfortable. On this one may well argue the contrary namely that this helpless condition of the Hindus is due entirely to the caste system.

Argument in para 4 is plausible. But it cannot be said that caste is the only machinery for discharging such functions as the spread of primary education or the judicial settlement of disputes. Caste is probably the worst instrument for the discharge of such functions. It can be easily influenced and easily corrupted. Such functions have been discharged in other countries much better than they have been in India although they have had no caste system. As to using the caste as basis for raising military units the idea is simply fantastic. Under the occupational theory underlying the caste system this is unthinkable. Mr. Gandhi knows that not a single caste in his own Province of Gujarat has ever raised a military unit. It did not do it in the present World War. But it did not do so even in the last World War, when Mr. Gandhi toured through Gujarat as a Recruiting Agent of British Imperialism. In fact under the caste system a general mobilisation of the people for defence is impossible since mobilisation requires a general liquidation of the occupational theory underlying the caste system.

Arguments contained in paras 6 and 6 are as stupid as they are revolting. The argument in para 5 is hardly a good argument. It is quite true the family is an ideal unit in which every member is charged with love and affection for another member although there is no intermarriage among members of a family. It may even be conceded that in a Vaishnava family members of the family do not interdine and yet they are full of love and affection for one another. What does all this prove? It does not prove that interdining and intermarrying are not necessary for establishing fraternity. What it proves is that where there are other means of maintaining fraternity —such as consciousness of family tie—interdining and intermarriage are not necessary. But it cannot be denied that where—as in the caste system—no binding force exists intermarriage and interdining are absolutely essential. There is no analogy between family and caste, Inter-caste dinner and inter-caste marriage are necessary because there are no other means of binding the different castes together while in the case of a family there exists other forces to bind them together. Those who have insisted upon the ban against interdining and inter-marriage have treated it as a question of relative values.

They have never elevated it to the level of a question of absolute value. Mr. Gandhi is the first one to do it. Inter-dining is bad and-even if it was capable of producing good it-should not be resorted to and why? Because eating is a filthy act, as filthy as answering the call of nature! The caste system has been defended by others. But this is the first time I have seen such an extraordinary if not a shocking argument used to support it. Even the orthodox may say, "Save us from Mr. Gandhi," It shows what a deep-dyed Hindu Mr. Gandhi is. He has outdone the most orthodox of orthodox Hindus. It is not enough to say that it is an argument of a cave man. It is really an argument of a mad man.

The argument in favour of the caste system outlined in para 7 is not worth much in terms of building up moral strength. The caste system no doubt prohibits a man from satisfying his lust for a woman who is not of his caste. The caste system no doubt prohibits a man from satisfying his craving for food cooked in the house of a man who is not of his caste. If morality consists of observing restraints without regard to the sense or sensibility of restraints then the caste system, may be admitted to be a moral system. But Mr. Gandhi does not see that these easy restraints are more than balanced by vast liberties permitted by Hinduism. For Hinduism places no restraint upon a man marrying hundred women and keeping hundred prostitutes within the ambit of his caste. Nor does it stop him from indulging in his appetite with his castemen to any degree.

The argument in para 8 begs the whole question. The hereditary system may be good or may not be good. It may be agreeable to some. It may be disagreeable to others. Why elevate it into an official doctrine? Why make it compulsory? In Europe it is not an official doctrine and it is not compulsory. It is left to the choice of an individual most of whom do follow the profession of their ancestors and some don't. Who can say that compulsory system has worked better than the voluntary system? If a comparison of the economic condition of the people in India and the people of Europe is any guide there would be very few rationally-minded people who would be found to support the caste system on this ground. As to the difficulty in changing nomenclature to keep pace with frequent changes in occupation it is only artificial, it arises out of the supposed necessity of having labels for designating persons following a particular profession.

The class labels are quite unnecessary and could well be abolished altogether without causing difficulty. Besides what happens today in India? Men's callings and their class labels are not hi accord. A Brahmin sells shoes. Nobody is disturbed because he is not called a Chamar. A Chamar becomes an officer of the State. Nobody is disturbed because he is not called a Brahmin. The whole argument is based on a misunderstanding. What matters to society is not the label by which the individual's class is known but the service he offers.

The last argument set out in para 9 is one of the most astounding arguments I have heard in favour of the caste system. It is historically false. No one who knows anything about the Manusmriti can say that the caste system is a natural system. What does Manusmriti show? It shows that the caste system is a legal system maintained at the point of a bayonet. If it has survived it is due to (1) prevention of the masses from the possession of arms; (S) denying to the masses the right to education and (3) depriving the masses of the right to property. The caste system far from natural is really an imposition by the ruling classes upon the servile classes.

That Mr. Gandhi changed over from the caste system to the varna system does not make the slightest difference to the charge that Gandhism is opposed to democracy. In the first place, the idea of varna is the parent of the idea of caste. If the idea of caste is a pernicious idea it is entirely because of the viciousness of the ides of varna.

Both are evil ideas and it matters very little whether one believes in varna or in caste. The idea of varna was most mercilessly attacked by the Buddhists who did not believe in it. Orthodox or the Sanatan Vedic Hindus had no rational defence to offer. All that they could say was that it was founded on the authority of the Vedas and that as the Vedas were infallible so was the varna system.

This argument was not enough to save the varna system against the rationalism of the Buddhists. If the idea of the varna survived it was because of the Bhagavad Gita, which gave a philosophical foundation to the varna system by arguing that the varna was based on the innate qualities of man. The Bhagavad Gita made use of the Sankhya philosophy to bolster and buttress the varna idea which would have otherwise petered away by making sense of a thing that is absolute nonsense. Bhagavad Gita had done enough mischief by giving a fresh lease of life to the varna system by basing it upon a new and plausible foundation, namely that of innate qualities.

The varna system of the Bhagavad Gita has at least two merits. It does not say that it is based on birth. Indeed it makes a special point that each man's varna is fixed according to his innate qualities. It does not say that the occupation of the son shall be that of the father. It says that the profession of a person shall be according to his innate qualities, the profession of the father according to the father's innate quality and that of the son according to the son's innate qualities. But Mr. Gandhi has given a new interpretation of the varna system. He has changed it out of recognition. Under the old orthodox interpretation caste connoted hereditary occupation but varna did not. Mr. Gandhi by his own whim has given a new connotation to the varna. With Mr. Gandhi varna is determined by birth and the profession of a varna is determined by the principle of heredity so that varna is merely another name for caste. That Mr. Gandhi changed from caste to varna does not indicate the growth of any new revolutionary ideology. The genius of Mr. Gandhi is elvish, always and throughout. He has all the precocity of an elf with no little of its outward guise. Like an elf he can never grow up and grow out of the caste ideology.

Mr. Gandhi sometimes speaks on social and economic subjects as though he was a blushing Red. Those who will study Gandhism will not be deceived by the occasional aberrations of Mr. Gandhi in favour of democracy and against capitalism. For Gandhism is in no sense a revolutionary creed. It is conservatism in excises. So far as India is concerned, it is a reactionary creed blazoning on its banner the call of Return to Antiquity. Gandhism aims at the resuscitation and reanimation of India's dread, dying past.

Gandhism is a paradox. It stands for freedom from foreign domination, which means the destruction of the existing political structure of the country. At the same time it seeks to maintain intact a social structure which permits the domination of one class by another on a hereditary basis which means a perpetual domination of one class by another. What is the explanation of this paradox? Is it a part of a strategy by Mr. Gandhi to win the wholehearted support of the Hindus, orthodox and unorthodox, to the campaign of Swaraj? If it is the latter, can Gandhism be regarded as honest and sincere? Be that as it may there are two features of Gandhism which are revealing but to which unfortunately no attention has so far been paid. Whether they will make Gandhism more acceptable than Marxism is another matter. But as they do help to distinguish Gandhism from Marxism, it may be well to refer to them.

The first special feature of Gandhism is that its philosophy helps those who have, to keep what they have and to prevent those who have not from getting what they have a right to get. No one who examines the Gandhian attitude to strikes, the Gandhian reverence for Caste and the Gandhian doctrine of Trusteeship by the rich for the benefit of the poor can deny that this is upshot of Gandhism. Whether this is the calculated result of a deliberate design or whether it is a matter of accident may be open to argument. But the fact remains that Gandhism is the philosophy of the well-so-do and the leisure class. The second special feature of Gandhism is to delude people into accepting their misfortunes by presenting them as best of good fortunes. One or two illustrations will suffice to bring out the truth of this statement.

Tbe Hindu sacred law penalized the Sudras (Hindus of the fourth class) from acquiring wealth. It is a law of enforced poverty unknown in any other part of the world. What does Gandhism do? It does not lift the ban. It blesses the Sudra for his moral courage to give up property! It is well worth quoting Mr. Gandhi's own words. Here they are:

"The Sudra who only serves (the higher caste) as a matter of religious duty, and who will never own any property, who indeed has not even the ambition to own anything, is deserving of thousand obeisance. The very Gods will shower down flowers on him.

Another illustration in support is the attitude of Gandhism towards the scavenger. The sacred law of the Hindus lays down that a scavenger's progeny shall live by scavenging. Under Hinduism scavenging was not a matter of choice, it was a matter of forced What does Gandhism do? It seeks to perpetuate this system by praising scavenging as the noblest service to society!! Let me quote Mr. Gandhi: As a President of a Conference of the Untouchables, Mr. Gandhi said:

> *"I do not want to attain Moksha. I do not want to be reborn. But if I have to be reborn, I should be born an untouchable, so that I may share their sorrows, sufferings and the affronts levelled at them, in order that I may endeavour to free myself and them from that miserable condition. I, therefore prayed that if I should be born again, I should do so not as a Brahmin, Kshatriya, Vaishya, or Sudra, but as an Atisudra."*

1 love scavenging. In my Ashram, an eighteen years old Brahmin lad is doing the scavenger's work in order to teach the Ashram scavenger cleanliness. The lad is no reformer. He was born and bred in orthodoxy. But he felt that his accomplishments were incomplete until he had become also a perfect sweeper, and that if he wanted the Ashram sweeper to do his work well, he must do it himself and set an example. "You should realise that you are cleaning Hindu Society."

Can there be a worse example of false propaganda than this attempt of Gandhism to perpetuate evils which have been deliberately imposed by one class over another? If Gandhism preached the rule of poverty for all and not merely for the Sudra the worst that could be said about it is that it is a mistaken idea. But why preach it as good for one class only?

Why appeal to the worst of human failings, namely, pride and vanity in order to make him voluntarily accept what on a rational basis he would resent as a cruel discrimination against him? What is the use of telling She scavenger that even a Brahmin is prepared to do scavenging when it is clear that according to Hindu Shastras and Hindu notions even if a Brahmin did scavenging he would never be subject to the disabilities of one who is a born scavenger? For in India a man is not a scavenger because of his work. He is a scavenger because of his birth irrespective of the question whether he does scavenging or not.

If Gandhism preached that scavenging is a noble profession with the object of inducing those who refuse to engage in it, one could understand it. But why appeal to the scavenger's pride and vanity in order to induce him and him only to keep on to scavenging by telling him that scavenging is a noble profession and that he need not be ashamed of it? To preach that poverty is good for the Sudra and for none else, to preach that scavenging is good for the Untouchables and for none else and to make them accept these onerous impositions as voluntary purposes of life, by appeal to their failings is an outrage and a cruel joke on the helpless classes which none but Mr. Gandhi can perpetuate with equanimity and impunity. In this connection one is reminded of the words of Voltaire who in repudiation of an 'ism' very much like Gandhism said: "Oh! mockery to say to people that the suffering of some brings joy to others and works good to the whole I What solace is it to a dying man to know that from his decaying body a thousand worms will come into life?"

Criticism apart) this is the technique of Gandhism, to make wrongs done appear to the very victim as though they were his privileges. If there is an 'ism' which has made full use of religion as an opium to lull the people into false beliefs and false security, it is Gandhism. Following Shakespeare one can well say: Plausibility I Ingenuity! Thy name is Gandhism.

Such is Gandhism. Having known what is Gandhism the answer to the question, 'Should Gandhism become the law of the land what would be the lot of the Untouchables under it,' cannot require much scratching of the brain. How would it compare with the lot of the lowest Hindu? Enough has been said to show what would be his lot should the Gandhian social order come into being. In so far as the lowest Hindu and the Untouchable belong to the same disinherited class, the Untouchable's lot cannot be better. If anything it might easily be worse. Because in India even the lowest man among the Caste Hindus—why even the aboriginal and Hill Tribe man—though educationally and economically not very much above the Untouchables is still superior to the Untouchables. It is not he regards himself as superior to the Untouchables. The Hindu society accepts his claim to superiority over the Untouchables. The Untouchable will therefore continue to suffer the worst fate as he does now namely, in prosperity he will be the last to be employed and in depression the first to be fired.

What does Gandhism do to relieve the Untouchables from this fate? Gandhism professes to abolish Untouchability. That is hailed as the greatest virtue of Gandhism. But what does this virtue amount to in actual life? To assess the value of this anti-Untouchability which is regarded as a very big element in Gandhism, it is necessary to understand fully the scope of Mr. Gandhi's programme for the removal of Untouchability. Does it mean anything more than that the Hindus will not mind touching the Untouchables? Does it mean the removal of the ban on the right of the Untouchables to education? It would be better to take the two questions separately.

To start with the first question, Mr. Gandhi does not say that a Hindu should not take a bath after touching the Untouchables. If Mr. Gandhi does not object to it as a purification of pollution then it is difficult to see how Untouchability can be said to vanish by touching the Untouchables. Untouchability centres round the idea of pollution by contact and purification by bath to remove the pollution. Does it mean social assimilation with the Hindus? Mr. Gandhi has most categorically stated that removal of Untouchability does not mean inter-dining or inter-marriage between the Hindus and the Untouchables. Mr. Gandhi's anti-Untouchability means that the Untouchables will be classed as Sudras instead of being classed as Ati-Sudras There is nothing more in it. Mr. Gandhi has not considered the question whether the old Sudras will accept the new Sudras into their fold. If they don't then the removal of Untouchability is a senseless proposition for it will still keep the Untouchables as a separate social category. Mr. Gandhi probably knows that the abolition of Untouchability will not bring about the assimilation of the Untouchables by the Sudras. That seems to be the reason why Mr. Gandhi himself has given a new and a different name to the Untouchables. The new name registers by anticipation what is likely to be the fact. By calling the Untouchables Harijans Mr. Gandhi has killed two birds with one stone. He has shown that assimilation of the Untouchables by the Sudras is not possible. He has also by his new name counteracted assimilation and made it impossible.

Regarding the second question, it is true that Gandhism is prepared to remove the old ban placed by the Hindu Shastras on the right of the Untouchables to education and permit them to acquire knowledge and learning. Under Gandhism the Untouchables may study law, they may study medicine, they may study engineering or anything else they may fancy. So far so good. But will the Untouchables be free to make use of their knowledge and learning? Will they have the right to choose their profession? Can they adopt the career of lawyer, doctor or engineer? To these questions the answer which Gandhism gives is an emphatic 'no.' The Untouchables must follow their hereditary professions.

That those occupations they are unclean is no answer; That before the occupation became hereditary it was the result of force and not volition does not matter...The argument of Gandhism is that what is once settled is settled for ever even if it was wrongly settled. Under Gandhism the Untouchables are to be eternal scavengers. There is no doubt that the Untouchables would much prefer the orthodox system of Untouchability. A compulsory state of ignorance imposed upon the Untouchables by the Hindu Shastras made scavenging bearable. But Gandhism which compels an educated Untouchable to do scavenging is nothing short of cruelty. The grace in Gandhism is a curse in its worst form. The virtue of the anti-Untouchability plank in Gandhism is quite illusory. There is no substance in it.

What else is there in Gandhism which the Untouchables can accept as opening a way for their ultimate salvation? Barring this illusory campaign against Untouchability Gandhism is simply another form of Sanatanism which is the ancient name for militant orthodox Hinduism. What is there in Gandhism which is not to be found in orthodox Hinduism? There is caste in Hinduism, there is caste in Gandhism. Hinduism believes in the law of hereditary profession, so does Gandhism. Hinduism enjoins cow-worship. So does Gandhism. Hinduism upholds the law of karma, predestination of man's condition in this world, so does Gandhism. Hinduism accepts the authority of the Shastras. So does Gandhism. Hinduism believes in avatar or incarnations of God. So does Gandhism. Hinduism believes in idols, so does Gandhism. All that Gandhism has done is to find a philosophic justification for Hinduism and' its dogmas. Hinduism is bald in the sense that it is just a set of rules which bear on their face the appearance of a crude and cruel system. Gandhism supplies the philosophy which smoothens its surface and gives it the appearance of decency and respectability and so alters it and embellishes it as to make it even attractive. What philosophy does Gandhism propound to cover the nudity of Hinduism? This philosophy can be put in a nutshell.

It is a philosophy which says that "All that is in Hinduism is well, all that is in Hinduism is necessary for public good." Those who are familiar with Voltaire's Candide will recognise that it is the philosophy of Master Pangiloss and recall the mockery Voltaire made of it. The Hindus are of course pleased with it. No doubt it suits them and accords with their interest. Prof. Radhakrishnan—whether out of genuine feeling or out of sycophancy we need not stop to inquire—has gone to the length of describing Mr. Gandhi as * God on earth.' What do the Untouchables understand this to mean? To them it means that: "This God by name Gandhi came to console an afflicted race: He saw India and changed it not saying all is well and will be, if the Hindus will only fulfil the law of caste. He told the afflicted race, 'I have come to fulfil the law of caste.' Not a title, not a jot shall I allow to abate from it."

What hope can Gandhism offer to the Untouchables? To the Untouchables Hinduism is a veritable chamber of horrors. The sanctity and infallibility of the Vedas, Smritis and Shastras, the from law of caste, the heartless law of karma and the senseless law of status by birth are to the Untouchables veritable instruments of torture which Hinduism has forged against the Untouchables. These very instruments which have mutilated, blasted and blighted the life of the Untouchables are to be found intact and untarnished in the bosom of Gandhism. How can the Untouchables say that Gandhism is a heaven and not a chamber of horrors as Hinduism has been? The only reaction and a very natural reaction of the Untouchables would be to run away from Gandhism.

Gandhists may say that what I have stated applies to the old type of Gandhism. There is a new Gandhism, Gandhism without caste. This has reference to the recent statement of Mr. Gandhi that caste is an anachronism. Reformers were naturally gladdened by this declaration of Mr. Gandhi. And who would not be glad to see that a man like Mr. Gandhi having such terrible influence over the Hindus, after having played the most mischievous part of a social reactionary, after having stood out as the protagonist of the caste system, after having beguiled and befooled the unthinking Hindus with arguments which made no distinction between what is fair and foul should have come out with this recantation? But is this really a matter for jubilation? Does it change the nature of Gandhism?

Does it make Gandhism a new and a better 'ism' than it was before. Those who are carried away by this recantation of Mr. Gandhi, forget two things. In the first place all that Mr. Gandhi has said is that caste is an anachronism. He does not say it is an evil. He does not say it is anathema. Mr. Gandhi may be taken to be not in favour of caste. But Mr. Gandhi does not say that he is against the Varna system. And what is Mr. Gandhi's varna system? It is simply a new name for the caste system and retains all the worst features of the caste system.

The declaration of Mr. Gandhi cannot be taken to mean any fundamental change in Gandhism. It cannot make Gandhism acceptable to the Untouchables. The Untouchables will still have ground to say:

"Good God I Is this man Gandhi our Saviour?"

MR. GANDHI AND THE EMANCIPATION OF THE UNTOUCHABLES

In response to the invitation of the Chairman of the Indian section of the Institute of Pacific Relations, I wrote in August last year a Paper on the Problem of the Untouchables of India for the Session of the Conference which was due to be held on December 1942 at Mont' Tramblant in Quebec in Canada. The Paper is printed in the proceedings of the Conference. Ever since it became known that I had written such a Paper, the leaders of the Untouchables and Americans interested in their problem have been pressing me to issue it separately in the form of a book and make it available to the general public. It was not possible to refuse the demand. At the same time I could not without breach of etiquette publish the paper until the proceedings of the Conference were made public.

I am now told by the Secretary of the Pacific Relations Conference that the proceedings have been made public and there can be no objection to the publication of my Paper if I desired it. This will explain why the Paper is published nearly 10 months after it was written.

Except for a few verbal alterations the Paper is printed as it was presented to the Conference. The Paper will speak for itself. There is only one thing I would like to add. It is generally agreed among the thoughtful part of humanity that there are three problems which the Peace Conference is expected to tackle. They are (1) Imperialism, (2) Racialism, (3) Anti-semitism and (4) Free Traffic in that merchandise of death popularly called munitions. There is no doubt these are the plague glands in which nation's cruelty to nation and man's inhumanity to man have their origin.

There is no doubt that these problems must be tackled if a new and a better world is to emerge from the ashes of this terrible and devastating war. What my fear is that the problem of the Untouchables may be forgotten as it has been so far, That would indeed be a calamity. For the ills which the Untouchables are suffering if they are not as much advertised as those of the Jews, are not less real. Nor are the means and the methods of suppression used by the Hindus against the Untouchables less effective because they are less bloody than the ways which the Nazis have adopted against the Jews. The Anti-semitism of the Nazis against the Jews is in no way different in ideology and in effect from the Sanatanism of the Hindus against the Untouchables.

The world owes a duty to the Untouchables as it does to all suppressed people to break their shackles and to set them free. I accepted the invitation to write this Paper because I felt that it was the best opportunity to draw the attention of the world to this problem in comparison to which the problem of the Slaves, the Negroes and the Jews is nothing. I hope the publication of this Paper will serve as a notice to the Peace Conference that this problem will be on the Board of Causes which it will have to bear and decide and also to the Hindus that they will have to answer for it before the bar of the world.

22, Prithviraj Road,

New Delhi.

B.R. Ambedkar

1st September 1943.

JOINT V/S SEPARATE ELECTORATES

The Hindus have after a long struggle accepted the view that a purely territorial constituency will not do in a country like India. In the previous discussion regarding the controversy between territorial constituency and communal constituency as two rival methods of bringing about a truly representative legislature was unnecessary. But I stated the case for and against because I felt that the foreigners who are not aware of Indian Political conditions ought to know the basic conceptions underlying that controversy. Unfortunately, however, the fact is that although the Hindus have accepted the basic argument in favour of communal scheme of representation they have not accepted all what the Untouchables are demanding.

The Untouchables demand that their representation shall be by separate electorates. A separate electorate means an electorate composed exclusively of Untouchable voters who are to elect an Untouchable as their representative to the legislature. The Hindus agree that certain number of seats are to be reserved for Untouchables to be filled only by Untouchables. But they insist that the Untouchables who is to be the representative of the Untouchables in the Legislature should be elected by a mixed electorate consisting both of the Hindus as well as of the Untouchables and not by an electorate exclusively of the Untouchables. In other words there is still a controversy over the question of joint versus separate electorates. Here again I want to set out the pros and cons of this controversy. The objection to separate electorate raised by the Hindus is that separate electorate means the fragmentation of the nation. The reply is obvious. First of all, there is no nation of Indians in the real sense of the word.

The nation does not exist, it is to be created, and I think it will be admitted that the suppression of a distinct and a separate community is not the method of creating a nation. Secondly, it is conceded-as the Hindus have done-that Untouchables should be represented in that Legislature by Untouchable then it cannot be denied that the Untouchable must be a true representative of the Untouchable voters. If this is a correct position then separate electorate is the only mechanism by which real representation can be guaranteed to the Untouchables. The Hindu argument against separate electorate is insubstantial and unsupportable. The premises on which the political demands of the Untouchables are based are admitted by the Hindus. Separate electorate is only a consequence which logically follows from those premises.

How can you admit the premise and deny the conclusion? Special electorates are devised as a means of protecting the minorities. Why not permit a minority like the Untouchables to determine what kind of electorate is necessary for its protection? If the Untouchables decide to have separate electorates why should their choice not prevail? These are questions to which the Hindus can give no answer. The reason is that the real objection to separate electorates by the Hindus is different from this ostensible objection raised in the name of a nation. The real objection is that separate electorate does not permit the Hindus to capture the seats reserved for the Untouchables. On the Other hand the joint electorate does. Let me illustrate the point by a few examples of how joint and separate electorate would work in the constituency. Take the following constituencies from the Madras Presidency.

The figures of the voting strength given in the above table for the seven constituencies taken at random in the Madras Presidency are illuminating. A scrutiny of the above figures is sufficient to show any disinterested person that if there is a separate electorate for the Untouchables in these seven constituencies they would be in a position to elect a man in whom they had complete confidence and who would be independent to fight the battle of the Untouchables on the floor of the Legislature against the representatives of the Hindus. If, on the other hand, there is a joint electorate in these constituencies the representative of the Untouchables would be only a nominal representative and not a real representative, for no Untouchable who did not AGree to be a nominee of the Hindus and a tool in their hands could be elected in a joint electorate in which the Untouchable voter was out numbered in ratio of 1 to 24 or in some cases 1 to 49. The joint electorate is from the point of the Hindus to use a familiar phrase a "rotten borough" in which the Hindus get the right to nominate an Untouchable to set nominally as a representative of the Untouchables but really as a tool of the Hindus. It will be noticed that the Hindu in opposing the so-called communal Scheme of the Untouchables with his so-called National Scheme is not fighting for a principle nor is be fighting for the nation. He is simply fighting for his own interests. He is fighting to have in his hands the undivided control over political power. His first line of defence is *not* to allow any shares to be drawn up so that like the Manager of the Hindu joint family he can use the whole for his benefit. That is why he fought for purely territorial constituencies. Failing that he takes his second line of defence. He wants that if he is made to concede power he must not lose control over it. This is secured by joint electorates and frustrated by separate electorates. That is why the Hindu objects to separate electorates *and* insists on joint electorates.

The end of the so-called National Scheme may not be communal but the result undoubtedly is.

THE EXECUTIVE

The second political demand of the Untouchables is that they must not only be represented to the Legislature but they must also be represented in the executive. This demand is also opposed by the Hindus. The argument of the Hindus takes two forms. One is that the executive must represent the majority of the Legislature and secondly the men in the Executive must be competent to hold places in the executive. I propose to deal with the second argument first. It is an argument which is fundamentally sound. But it is equally necessary to realise that in a representative Government this argument cannot be carried too far. For as Professor Dicey has argued, "It has never been a primary object of constitutional arrangement to get together the best possible parliament in intellectual capacity. Indeed, it would be inconsistent with the idea of representative Government to attempt to form a parliament far superior in intelligence to the mass of the nation."

The stress upon competency is needless. Nobody has said that ignorant people should be made Ministers simply because they are Untouchables. Given the right to representation in the cabinet the Untouchables, there is no doubt, will elect the most competent people amongst them-there are a number of than in every province-to fill those places. Again why apply this limiting condition to the Untouchables only? Like the Untouchables the Muslims are also claiming the right to be represented in the cabinet. Why have the Hindus not insisted upon such a limiting condition against the Muslims' claim? This shows that the objection of the Hindus is not based on reason. It is an excuse.

Coming to the second argument the Hindus are simply misusing the words majority and minority. They seem to forget that majority and minority are political categories. As political categories there is no fixed majority or a fixed minority. Political majorities and political minorities are fluid bodies and what is a majority today may become a minority tomorrow, and what is a minority today may become a majority tomorrow. The difference between the Hindus and the Untouchables cannot be said to be a difference of this sort. There is no endosmosis between the Untouchables and Hindus as there is between the Majority and Minority.

There is another characteristic of a majority and minority relationship, which would make them inapplicable to the relationship which subsists between the Hindus and the Untouchables. The majority and minority are divided by a difference only-difference in the point of views. They are not separated by a fundamental and deadly antagonism as the Hindus are from the Untouchables. There is a third characteristic of Majority and Minority relationship which is not to be found in the relationship that subsists between the Hindus and the Untouchables.

A minority grows into a minority and a majority in becoming a majority absorbs so much of the sentiment of the minority that the minority is satisfied with the result and does not feel the urge of fighting out the issue with the majority. Now all these considerations are quite foreign to the relationship between the Hindu Majority and the Untouchable minority. They are fixed as permanent communities. They are not merely different but they are antagonistic. To speak of them as majority and minority would be as true and as useful as would be to speak of the Germans being a majority and the French being a minority.

PUBLIC SERVICES

The Untouchables demand that a certain proportion of posts in the public services of the country shall be reserved for them, subject to the rule of minimum qualification. The Hindus object to this demand as they do to the other demands of the Untouchables. The stand they take is that the interests of the State require that capacity, efficiency and character should be the only consideration and that caste and creed should have no place in making appointment to public offices. There is no dispute regarding character as a necessary qualification. Nor is there any dispute regarding capacity and efficiency.

The only point of dispute, and it is a very important point, is whether caste and creed should form a consideration which must be taken into account in the recruitment for public services. Relying upon the educational qualification as the only test of efficiency, the Hindus insist that public offices should be filled on the basis of competitive examination open to persons of all Castes and Creeds. They argue that such a system serves both purposes. It serves the purpose of efficiency. Secondly it does not prohibit the entry of the Untouchables in the Public Services of the country.

The Hindus seek to give to their opposition to the demand of the Untouchable an appearance of fairness by relying upon efficiency and competitive examination. Here again the argument is quite beside the point. The question is not whether the competitive system of Examination is or is not the proper method of getting efficient persons in public services. The question is whether the competitive system simply because it is open to all castes and creeds will enable the Untouchables to get a footing in the Public Service. That depends upon the educational system of the State.

Is it sufficiently democratic? Are the facilities for education sufficiently widespread and sufficiently used to permit persons from all classes to come forth to compete? Otherwise, even with the system of open competition large classes are sure to be left out in the cold. This basic condition is conspicuous by its absence in India. Higher education in India is the monopoly of Hindus and particularly of high Caste Hindus. By reason of Untouchability the Untouchables are denied the opportunity for Education. By reason of their poverty higher education necessary for higher posts in the public service-and higher posts in the public service are the only things that matter because they have a strategic value-is not within their reach.

The State will not take the financial responsibility of giving them higher education-they are demanding it by their resolution and the Hindus will not extend the benefit of their charities to the Untouchables-Hindu Charity being shamefully communal-so that to ask the Untouchables to rely upon the results of competitive examination for entry into the public services is to practise a fraud upon than. The position taken up by the Untouchables is in no sense unreasonable. They admit the necessity for maintaining efficiency. That is why in their resolution they themselves say that their demand shall be subject to the rule of minimum qualification. In other words what the Untouchables demand is that a minimum qualification should be prescribed for every post in the public service and if two persons apply for such a post and the Untouchables has the minimum qualification he should be preferred to a Hindu even though the Hindu may have a qualification higher than the minimum qualification. It, of course, does mean that the basis for appointment should be minimum qualification and not the higher qualification. This may sound queer to those who do not mind if their test of efficiency gives certain communities a monopoly of public service. But did not Campbell-Bannerman say that self-government was better than good government? What else are the Untouchables demanding? They are prepared to recognise the need of having an efficient Government.

That is why they are ready to accept the requirement of minimum qualifications for entry in the public services of the country. What the untouchables are not prepared to do is to forego self-government for good government Good Government based on highest qualification will be a communal government, for the Hindus alone can claim qualifications higher than minimum qualifications. This is what they do not want. What they say is that minimum qualifications are enough for efficient government and since it makes self-government possible, minimum qualification should be the rule for entry in Public Service. It ensures self-government as well as efficient government.

SEPARATE SETTLEMENTS

Resolution No. IV referred to in the foregoing part of this paper is to my mind quite self-explanatory and not much detailed comment is necessary to explain its purport. Nor is it possible in the compass of this short paper to deal with it in more than general terms. The demand for separate settlements is the result of what might be called "The New Life Movement" among the Untouchables. The object of the movement is to free the Untouchables from the thralldom of the Hindus. So long as the present arrangement continues it is impossible for the Untouchables either to free themselves from the yoke of the Hindus or to get rid of their Untouchability.

It is the close-knit association of the Untouchables with the Hindus living in the same villages which marks them out as Untouchables and which enables the Hindus to identify them as being Untouchables. India is admittedly a land of villages and so long as the village system provides an easy method of marking out and identifying the Untouchable, the Untouchable has no escape from Untouchability. It is the village system which perpetuates untouchability and the Untouchables therefore demand that it should be broken and the Untouchables who are as a matter of fact socially separate should be made separate geographically and territorially also, and be grouped into separate villages exclusively of Untouchables in which the distinction of the high and the low and of Touchable and Untouchable will find no place.

The second reason for demanding separate settlements arises out of the economic position of the Untouchables in the village. That their condition is most pitiable no one will deny. They are a body of landless labourers who are entirely dependent upon such employment as the Hindus may choose to give them and on such wages as the Hindus may find it profitable to pay. In the villages in which they live they cannot engage in any trade or occupation, for owing to untouchability no Hindu will deal with them. It is therefore obvious that there is no way of earning a living which is open to the Untouchables so long as they live as a dependent part of the Hindu village. This economic dependence has also other consequences besides the condition of poverty and degradation which proceeds from it.

The Hindu has a code of life, which is part of his religion. This code of life gives him many privileges and heaps upon the Untouchable many indignities which are incompatible with the sanctity of human life. By the New Life Movement which has taken hold of the Untouchables, the Untouchables all over India are fighting against the indignities and injustices which the Hindus in the name of their religion have heaped upon them. A perpetual war is going on every day in every village between the Hindus and the Untouchables. It does not see the light of the day. The Hindu Press is not prepared to advertise it lest it should injure the cause of their freedom in the eyes of the world. The silent struggle is however a fact. Under the village system the Untouchable has found himself greatly handicapped in his struggle for free and honourable life. It is a contest between the economically and socially strong Hindus and an economically poor and socially small group of Untouchables.

That the Hindus most often succeed in pulling down Untouchables is largely due to many causes. The Hindu has the Police and the Magistracy on his side. In a quarrel between the Untouchables and the Hindus the Untouchables will never get protection from the Police or justice from the Magistrate. The Police and the Magistracy are Hindus, and they love their class more than their duty. But the chief weapon in the armoury of the Hindus is economic power which they possess Over the poor Untouchables living in the village. The economic processes by which the Hindus can hold down the Untouchables in their struggle for equality are well described in the Report made by a Committee appointed by the Government of Bombay in 1928 to investigate into the grievances of the Depressed Classes and from which the following extracts are made. It illuminates the situation in a manner so simple that even foreigners who do not know the mysteries of the Hindu social system may understand what tyranny the Hindus can practise upon the Untouchables. The committee said:

"Although we have recommended various remedies to secure to the Depressed Classes their rights to all public utilities we fear that there will be difficulties in the way of their exercising them for a long time to come. The first difficulty is the fear of open violence against them by the orthodox classes, It must be noted that the Depressed Classes form a small minority in every village, opposed to which is a great majority of the orthodox who are bent on protecting their interests and dignity from any supposed invasion by the Depressed Classes at any cost. The danger of prosecution by the Police has put a limitation upon the use of violence by the orthodox classes and consequently such cases axe rare.

"The second difficulty arises from the economic position in which the Depressed Classes are found today. The Depressed Classes have no economic independence in most parts of the Presidency. Some cultivate the lands of the orthodox classes as their tenants at will Others live on their earnings as farm labourers employed by the orthodox classes and the rest subsist on the food or grain given to them by the orthodox classes in lieu of service rendered to them as village servants. We have heard of numerous instance where the orthodox classes have used their economic power as a weapon against those Depressed Classes in their villages, when the latter have dared to exercise their rights, and have evicted them from their land, and stopped their employment and discontinued their remuneration as village servants. This boycott is often planned on such an extensive scale as to include the prevention of the Depressed Classes from using the commonly used paths and the stoppage of sale of the necessaries of life by the village Bania. According to the evidence, sometimes small causes suffice for the proclamation of a social boycott against the Depressed Classes. Frequently it follows on the exercise by the Depressed Classes of their right to the use of the common well, but cases have been by no means rare where a stringent boycott has been proclaimed simply because a Depressed Class man has put on the sacred thread, has bought a piece of land, has put on good clothes or ornaments, or has carried a marriage procession with the bridegroom on the horse through the public street."

This demand for separate settlements is a new demand which has been put forth by the Untouchables for the first time. It is not possible to say as yet as to what attitude the Hindus will take to this demand. But there is no doubt that this is the most vital demand made by the Untouchables, and I am sure that whatever may happen with regard to the other demands they are not likely to yield on this. The Hindus are prone to think that they and the Untouchables are joined together by the will of God as the Bible says the husband is joined to his wife and they will say in the language of the Bible that those whom God is pleased to join let no man put asunder. The Untouchables are determined to repudiate any such view of their relations with the Hindus. They want the link to be broken and a complete divorce from the Hindus effected without delay.

The only questions that arise are those of the cost it will involve in and time it will take. As to cost, the Untouchables say it should be financed by Government It will no doubt fall for the most part on the Hindus. But there is no reason why the Hindus should not bear the same. The Hindus own everything. They own the land in this country. They control trade, and they also own the State. Every source of revenue and profit is controlled by them. Other communities and particularly the Untouchables are just hewers of wood and drawers of water. The social system helps the Hindus to have a monopoly of everything. There is no reason why they should not be asked to pay the cost of this scheme when they practically own the country.As to time, it matters very little even if the transplantation of the Untouchables to new settlements takes 20 years. Those who have been the bounded slaves of the Hindus for a thousand years may well be happy with the prospect of getting their freedom by the end of 20 years.

TOTAL POPULATION OF THE UNTOUCHABLES

The Decennial Census in India was at one time a very simple and innocent operation which interested only the Malthusians. None else took interest in it. Today the Census is a matter of a first rate concern to everybody. Not only the professional politician but the general public in India regards it as a matter of very grave concern. This is so because politics in India has become a matter of numbers. It is numbers which give political advantage, to one community over another which does not happen anywhere else in the world. The result is that the Census in India is deliberately cooked for securing political advantages which numbers give.

In this cooking of the Census the Hindus, the Muslims and the Sikhs have played their part as the chief chefs of the kitchen. The Untouchables and the Christians, who are also interested in their numbers, have no hand in the cooking of the Census, for the simple reason that they have no place in the administrative services of the country which deal with the operations of the Census.

On the other hand the Untouchables are the people who are quartered, cooked and served by the Hindus, Muslims and the Sikhs at every Decennial Census. This has happened particularly in the last Census of 1940. The Untouchables of certain parts of the Punjab were subjected to systematic tyranny and oppression by the Sikhs. The object was to compel them to declare in the Census returns that they are Sikhs even though they are not. This reduced the number of the Untouchables and swelled the number of the Sikhs.

The Hindus on their part carried on a campaign that nobody should declare his or her caste in the Census return. A particular appeal was made to the Untouchables. It was suggested to them that it is the name of the Caste that proclaims to the world that they are Untouchables and if they did not declare their caste name but merely said that they were Hindus, they would be treated just like other Hindus and nobody would know that they were really Untouchables. The Untouchables fell a victim to this stratagem and decided not to declare themselves as Untouchables in the Census return but to call themselves merely as Hindus.

The result was obvious. It reduced the number of Untouchables and swelled the ranks of the Hindus. To what extent the cooking of the Census has taken place it is difficult to say. But there can be no doubt that the degree to which cooking was resorted to was considerable. The Census has been cooked all over. But it is the Untouchables who have suffered most from the cooking of the Census. That being so, the Census figure regarding the total population of the Untouchables in British India cannot be accepted as giving a correct total. But one cannot be far wrong if it was said that the present number of the Untouchables to British India is round about 60 million people.

THE IMPORTANCE OF THE UNTOUCHABLES

Most parts of the world have had their type of what Ward calls the lowly. The Romans had their slaves, the Spartans their helots, the British their villeins, the Americans their Negroes and the Germans their Jews. So the Hindus have their Untouchables. But none of these can be said to have been called upon to face a fate which is worse than the fate which pursues the Untouchables. Slavery, serfdom, villeinage have all vanished. But Untouchability still exists and bids fair to last as long as Hinduism will last. The Untouchable is worse off than a Jew. The sufferings of the Jew are of his own creation. Not so are the sufferings of the Untouchables. They are the result of a cold calculating Hinduism which is not less sure in its effect in producing misery than brute force is. The Jew is despised but is not denied opportunities to grow. The Untouchable is not merely despised but is denied all opportunities to rise. Yet nobody seems to take any notice of the Untouchables-some 60 millions of souls-much less espouse their cause.

If there is any cause of freedom in this Indian turmoil for independence it is the cause of the Untouchables. The cause of the Hindus and the cause of the Musalmans is not the cause of freedom. Theirs is a struggle for power as distinguished from freedom. Consequently it has always been a matter of surprise to me that no party and no organisation devoted to the cause of freedom has so far interested itself in the Untouchables. There is the American Weekly called "The Nation". There is the British Weekly called "Statesman". Both are powerful. Both are friends of India's freedom. I would mention the American Labour and British Labour among organised bodies among the supporters of India's freedom.

So far as I know none of these have ever championed the cause of the Untouchables. Indeed what they have done is what no lover of freedom would do. They have just identified themselves with the Hindu body calling itself the Indian National Congress. Now everybody in India, outside the Hindus, knows that whatever may be its title it is beyond question that the Congress is a body of middle class Hindus supplied by the Hindu Capitalists whose object is not to make Indians free but to be independent of British control and to occupy places of power now occupied by the British.

If the kind of Freedom which the Congress wants was achieved there is no doubt that the Hindus would do to the Untouchables exactly what they have been doing in the past In the light of this apathy the Indian branch of the Institute of International Affairs may well be congratulated for having invited a paper for submission to the Institute of Pacific Relations, discussing the position of the Untouchables in India in the New Constitution. I must confess that this invitation for a statement on the position of the Untouchables under the new constitution came to me as an agreeable surprise and a great relief and it is because of this, that notwithstanding the many things with which lam preoccupied, I agreed to find time to prepare this paper.

THE POLITICAL DEMANDS OF THE UNTOUCHABLES

The problem of the Untouchables is an enormous problem. As a matter of fact I have been for sometime engaged on a work dealing with this problem which will run into several hundred pages. All that I can do within the limits of this paper is to set out in a brief compass what the nature of the problem is and the solution which the Untouchables have themselves propounded. It seems to me that I cannot do better than begin by drawing attention to the following Resolutions which were passed at the All-India Scheduled Castes Conference held in the city of Nagpur on the 18th and 19th July 1942:

CONSENT ESSENTIAL TO CONSTITUTION

"This Conference declares that no constitution will be acceptable to the Scheduled Castes unless:

(i) it has the consent of the Scheduled Castes,

(ii) it recognises the fact that the Scheduled Castes are distinct and separate from the Hindus and constitute an important element in the national life of India, and

(iii) contains within itself provisions which will give to the Scheduled Castes a real sense of security under the new constitution and which are set out in the following resolutions."

ESSENTIAL PROVISIONS IN THE NEW CONSTITUTION

"For creating this sense of security in the Scheduled Castes: this Conference demands that the following provisions shall be made in the new Constitution:

(1) That in the budget of every provincial Government an annual sum as may be determined upon by agreement be set apart for promoting the primary education among

the children of the Scheduled Castes and another annual sum for promoting advanced education among them, and such sums shall be declared to be the first charge on the revenues of the Province.

(2) That provision shall be made by law for securing representation to the Scheduled Castes in all Executive Governments-Central and Provincial-the proportion of which shall be determined in accordance with their number, their needs and their importance.

(3) That provision shall be made by law for securing representation to the Scheduled Castes in the Public Services the proportion of which shall be fixed in accordance with their number, their needs and their importance. This Conference further insists that in the case of security services such as Judiciary, Police and Revenue, provision shall be made that the proportion fixed for the Scheduled Castes shall, subject to the rule of minimum qualification, be realised within a period of ten years.

(4) That provision shall be made by law for guaranteeing to the Scheduled Castes representation in all Legislatures and Local bodies in accordance with their number, needs and importance.

(5) That provision shall be made by law whereby the representation of the Scheduled Castes in all Legislatures and Local Bodies shall be by the method of Separate Electorates.

(6) That provision shall be made by law for the representation of the Scheduled Castes on all Public Service Commissions, Central and Provincial."

SEPARATE SETTLEMENTS

"It is the considered opinion of this conference,

(a) That so long as the Scheduled Castes continue to live on the outskirts of the Hindu village, with no source of livelihood and in small number as compared to

Hindus, they will continue to remain Untouchables and subject to the tyranny and oppression of the Hindus and will not be able to enjoy free and full life.

(b) That for the better protection of the Scheduled Castes from the tyranny and oppression of the Caste Hindus, which may take a worse form under Swaraj which cannot but be a Hindu Raj, and

(c) To enable the Scheduled Castes to develop to their fullest manhood, to give them economical and social security as also to pave the way for the removal of untouchability.

This Conference has after long and mature deliberation come to the conclusion that a radical change must be made in the village system now prevalent in India and which is the parent of all the ills from which the Scheduled Castes are suffering for so many centuries at the hands of the Hindus. Realising the necessity of these changes this conference holds that along with the Constitutional changes in the system of Government there must be a change in the village system now prevalent, made along the following lines:

(1) The constitution should provide for the transfer of the Scheduled Castes from their present habitation and form separate Scheduled Caste villages away from and independent of Hindu village.

(2) For the settlement of the Scheduled Castes in new villages a provision shall be made by the constitution for the establishment of a Settlement Commission.

(3) All Government land which is cultivable and which is not occupied shall be handed over to the Commission to be held in trust for the purpose of making new settlements of the Scheduled Castes.

(4) The Commission shall be empowered to purchase new land under the Land Acquisition Act from private owners to complete the scheme of settlement of Scheduled Castes,

(5) The constitution shall provide that the Central Government shall grant to the settlement commission

a minimum sum of Rupees five crores per annum to enable the Commission to carry out their duty to this behalf.

CASTE AND CONSTITUTION

It might well be asked why should such questions as are raised by these demands of the Untouchables find a place in the Constitution? Nowhere in the world have the makers of constitution been compelled to deal with such matters. This is an important question and I admit that an answer is required on the part of those who raise such questions and insist that they are of constitutional importance. The answer to this question is to my mind quite obvious. It is the character of the Indian Society which invests this question with constitutional importance. It is the Caste system and the Religious system of the Hindus which is solely responsible for this. This short statement may not suffice to give an adequate explanation to foreigners of the social and political repercussions of the Hindu Caste and Religious systems.

But it is equally true that in the brief compass of this paper it is impossible to deal exhaustively with the repercussion of the caste system on the constitution. I would refer for a full and complete exposition of the subject to my book on the Annihilation of Castes which I wrote some time ago. For I believe it will shed sufficient light on the social and economical ramification of the Caste and Religious system of the Hindus In this Paper I will content myself with making the following general observations. In framing a constitution the Social structure must always be kept in mind. The political structure must be related to the social structure. The operation of the social forces is not confined to the social field. They pervade the political field also. This is the view point of the Untouchables and I am sure this is incontrovertible.

The Hindus are quite conscious of this argument and also of its strength. But what they do is to deny that the structure of the Hindu Society is in any way different from the structure of European society. They attempt to meet the argument by saying that there is no difference between the Caste system of the Hindus and the Class system in Western Society. This is of course palpably false and discloses a gross ignorance both of the Caste system as well as of the Class system. The Caste system is a system which is infested with the spirit of isolation and in fact it makes isolation of one Caste from another a matter of virtue. There is isolation in the Class system but it does not make isolation a virtue nor does it prohibit social intercourse. The Class system it is true produces groups. But they are not akin to Caste groups.

The groups in the Class System are only non-social while the Castes in the Caste system are in their mutual relations definitely and positively anti-social. If this analysis is true then there can be no denying the fact that the social structure of Hindu Society is different and consequently its political structure must be different. What the Untouchables are asking, to put it in general terms, is a proper correlation of means to ends. End may be the same. But because the end is the same it does not follow that the means must also be the same. Indeed ends may remain the same and yet means must vary according to time and circumstances. Those who are true to their ends must admit this fact and must agree to adopt different means if they wish that the end they have in view is not stultified.

In this connection there is another thing which I would like to mention. As I have said, it is the Caste basis of Hindu society which requires that its political structure should be different and suited to its social structure. There are people who admit this but argue that caste can be abolished from Hindu society. I deny that.

Those who advocate such a view think that caste is an institution like a Club or a Municipality or a County Council. This is a gross error. Caste is Religion, and religion is anything but an institution. It may be institutionalised but it is not the same as the institution in which it is embedded. Religion is an influence or force suffused through the life of each individual moulding his character, determining his actions and reactions, his likes and dislikes.

These likes and dislikes, actions and reactions are not institutions which can be lopped off. They are forces and influences which can be dealt with by controlling them or counteracting them. If the social forces are to be prevented from contaminating politics and perverting it to the aggrandisement of the few and the degradation of the many then it follows that the political structure must be so framed that it will contain mechanisms which will bottle the prejudices and nullify the injustice which the social forces are likely to cause if they were let loose.

So far I have explained in a general way why the peculiar social structure of the Hindu Society calls for a peculiar political structure and why the marker of the Indian Constitution cannot escape problems which did not plague the makers of Constitution in other countries. Let me now take the specific question, namely why it is necessary that in the Indian Constitution the Communal Scheme must find its place and why in the Public Services for the Untouchables should be specified and should be assigned to them as their separate possession. The justification for these demands is easy and obvious. It arises from the undeniable fact that what divides the Untouchables from the Hindus is not mere matter of difference on nonessentials.

It is a case of fundamental antagonism and antipathy. No evidence of this antipathy and antagonism is necessary. The system of Untouchability is enough evidence of the inherent antagonism between the Hindus and the Untouchables. Given this antagonism it is simply impossible to ask the Untouchables to depend upon and trust the Hindus to do them justice when the Hindu get their freedom and independence from the British. Who can say that the Untouchable is not right in saying that he will not trust the Hindu? The Hindu is as alien to him as a European is and what is worse the European alien is neutral but the Hindu is most shamefully partial to his own class and antagonistic to the Untouchables.

There can be no doubt that the Hindus have all these ages despised, disregarded and disowned the Untouchables as belonging to a different and contemptible strata of Society if not to a different race. By their own code of conduct the Hindus behave as the most exclusive class steeped in their own prejudices and never sharing the aspirations of the Untouchables with whom they have nothing to do and whose interests are opposed to theirs.

Why should the Untouchables entrust their fate to such people? How could the Untouchables be legitimately asked to leave their interest into the hands of a people who as a matter of fact are opposed to them in their motives and interests, who do not sympathise with the living forces operating among the Untouchables, who are themselves not charged with their wants, carvings and desires, who are inimical to their aspirations, who in all certainty will deny justice to them and to discriminate against them and who by reason of the sanction of their religion have not been and will not be ashamed to practise against the Untouchables any kind of inhumanity. The only safety against such people is to have the political rights which the Untouchables claim as safeguards against the tyranny of the Hindu Majority defined in the Constitution. Are the Untouchables extravagant in demanding this safety?

SOME QUESTIONS TO THE HINDUS AND THEIR FRIENDS

In the midst of this political controversy one notices that the Hindus are behaving differently towards different communities. The Untouchables are not the only people in India who are demanding political safeguards. Like the Untouchables the Muslims and the Sikhs have also presented their political demands to the Hindus. Both the Musulmans and the Sikhs can in no sense be called helpless minorities. On the contrary they are the two most powerful communities in India. They are educationally quite advanced and economically well placed. By their social standing they are quite as high as the Hindus. Their organisation is a solid structure and no Hindu will dare to take any liberties with them much less cause any harm to them.

What are the political demands of the Muslims and the Sikhs? It is not possible to set them out here. But the general opinion is that they are very extravagant and the Hindus resent them very much. In contrast with this the condition and the demands of the Untouchables are just the opposite of the condition of the Muslims and the Sikhs. They are a weak, helpless and despised minority. They are at the mercy of all and there are not a few occasions when Hindus, Muslims and Sikhs combine to oppress them. Of all the Minorities they need the greatest protection and the strongest safeguards. Their demands are of the modest kind and there is nothing in them of that overinsurance which may be said to characterise the demands of the Muslims and the Sikhs.

What is the reaction of the Hindus to the demands of the Muslims, the Sikhs and the Untouchables? Notwithstanding the extravagance of their demands the Hindus are ever ready to conciliate the Musalmans and the Sikhs, particularly the former. They not only want to be correct in their relationship with the Musalmans, they are prepared to be considerate and even generous. Mr. Rajagopalachari's political exploits are too fresh to be forgotten.

Suddenly he enrolled himself as a soldier of the Muslim League and proclaimed a war on his own kin and former friends and for what? Not for their not failure to grant the reasonable demands of the Muslim but for their conceding the most extravagant one, namely Pakistan!! What is Mr. Rajagopalachari's response to the demands of the Untouchables? So far I am aware there is no response. He does not even seem to be áware that there are 60 million Untouchables in this country and that they too like the Muslims are demanding political safeguards. This attitude of studied silence and cold indifference of Mr. Rajagopalachari is typical of the whole body of Hindus. The Hindus have been opposing the political demands of the Untouchables with the tenacity of a bulldog and the perversity of a renegade. The Press is theirs and they make a systematic attempt to ignore the Untouchables.

When they fail to ignore them they buy their leaders; and where they find a leader not open to purchase they systematically abuse him, misrepresent him, blackmail him, and do everything possible that lies in their power to suppress him and silence him: Any such leader who is determined to fight for the cause of the Untouchables he and his followers are condemned as anti-National. So exasperated the Hindus become by the political demands of the Untouchables that they in their rage refuse to recognise how generous the Untouchables are in consenting to be ruled by a Hindu Majority in return for nothing more than a few political safeguards. The Hindus are not aware of what Carson said to Redmond when the two were negotiating for a United Ireland. The incident is worth recalling. Redmond said to Carson "Ask any safeguards you like for the Protestant Minority of Ulster, I am prepared to give them; but let us have a United Ireland under one constitution." Carson's reply was curt and brutal.

He said without asking for time to consider the offer "Damn your safeguards, I don't want to be ruled by you". The Hindus ought to be thankful that the Untouchables have not taken the attitude which Carson took. But far from being thankful they are angry because the Untouchables are daring to ask for political rights. In the opinion of the Hindus the Untouchables have no right to ask for any rights. What does this difference of attitude on the part of the Hindus to the political demands of the different communities indicate? It indicates three things: (1) They want to get all power to themselves, (2) They are not prepared to base their political institutions on the principle of justice, (3) Where they have to surrender power they will surrender it to the forces of truculence and the mailed first but never to the dictates of justice.

This attitude of the Hindus forms the tragic scene of Indian politics. Unfortunately this is not the only tragic scene with Indian Politics. There is another equally tragic in character. It concerns the friends of the Hindus in foreign countries, The

Hindus have created many friends for themselves all over the world by their clever propaganda, particularly in America, "the land of liberty". The tragedy is that these friends of the Hindus are supporting a side without examining whether it is the side which they in point of justice ought to support No American friends of the Hindus have, so far as I know, asked what do the Hindus stand for?

Are they fighting for freedom or are they fighting for power? If the Hindus are fighting for power, are the American friends justified in helping the Hindus? If the Hindus are engaged in a war for freedom, must they not be asked to declare their war aims? This is the least bit these American friends could do. Since the American friends have thought it fit to respond to the Hindu call for help it is necessary to tell these American friends of the Hindus what wrong they will be doing to the cause of freedom by their indiscriminate and blind support to the Hindu side. What I want to say follows the line of argument which the Hindus themselves have taken. Since the war started the Hindus, both inside and outside the Congress, demanded that the British should declare their war aims. Day in and day out the British were told, "If you want our help, tell us what you are fighting for?

If you are fighting for freedom, tell us if you will give us freedom in the name of which you are waging this war" There was a stage when the Hindus were prepared to be satisfied with a promise from the British that India will have the benefit of freedom for which the British are waging. They have gone a stage further. They are no longer content with a promise. Or to put it in the language of a Congressman, "They refuse to accept a postdated cheque on a crashing Bank". They wanted freedom to be given right now, before the Hindus would consent to give their voluntary support to the War effort. That is the significance of Mr. Gandhi's new slogan of "Quit India". Mr. Churchill on whom the responsibility of answering these questions fell replied, that his war aim was victory over the enemy. The Hindus were not satisfied.

They questioned him further "What are you going to do after you get that victory? What social order you propose to establish after the war?" There was a storm when Mr. Churchil replied that he hoped to restore traditional Britain. These were legitimate questions I agree. But do not the friends of Hindus think that if it is legitimate to ask the very same questions to Mr. Churchill it is also legitimate to ask the very same questions to Mr. Gandhi and the Hindus? The British had declared war against Hitler. Mr. Gandhi has declared war against the British. The British have an Empire. So have the Hindus. For is not Hinduism a form of I imperialism and are not the Untouchables a subject race, owing there allegiance and their servitude to their Hindu Master?

If Churchill must be asked to declare his war aims how could anybody avoid asking Mr. Gandhi and the Hindus to declare their war aims. Both say their war is a war for freedom. If that is so both have a duty to declare what their war aims are. What does Mr. Gandhi propose to do after he gets his victory over the British. Does he propose to use the freedom he hopes to get to make the Untouchables free or will he allow the freedom he gets to be used to endow the Hindus with more power than they now possess, to hold the Untouchables as their bondsmen? Will Mr. Gandhi arid Hindus establish a New Older or will they be content with rehabilitation of the traditional Hindu India, with its castes and its untouchability, with its denial of Liberty, Equality and Fraternity, should think that these questions should be asked by those American friends to Mr. Gandhi and the Hindus who are helping them in this so-called war for Freedom.

These questions are legitimate and pertinent. It is only answers to such questions which will enable these American friends to know whether Mr. Gandhi's war is a war for freedom or a war for power. These questions are not merely pertinent and legitimate, they are also necessary. The reason is obvious to those who know the Hindus. The Hindus have an innate and inveterate conservatism and they have a religion which is incompatible with liberty, equality and fraternity *i.e.* with democracy. Inequality, no doubt, exists everywhere in the world.

It is largely to conditions and circumstances. But it never has had the support of religion. With the Hindus it is different. There is not only inequality in Hindu Society but inequality is the official doctrine of the Hindu religion. The Hindu has no will to equality. His inclination and his attitude are opposed to the democratic doctrine of one man one value. Every Hindu is a social Tory and political Radical. Mr. Gandhi is no exception to this rule. He presents himself to the world as a liberal but his liberalism is only a very thin veneer which sits very lightly on him as dust does on one's boots. You scratch him and you will find that underneath his liberalism he is a blue blooded Tory. He stands for the cursed caste. He is a fanatic Hindu upholding the Hindu religion. See how the Hindus read the famous American Declaration of Independence of 1776. The Hindu is mad with joy when he reads the Declaration to say-

That whenever any Form of Government become destructive of these ends, it is the Right of the People to alter or to abolish it, and to institute new Government, laying its foundation on such principles and organising its powers in such form, as to them shall seem most likely to effect their Safety and Happiness.'

But he stops there. He never bothers about the earlier part of that Declaration which says:

> *"We hold these truths to be self-evident, that all* men *are created equal, that they are endowed by their Creator with certain unalienable Rights, that among these are Life, Liberty and the pursuit of Happiness. That to secure these rights. Governments are instituted among Men, deriving their just powers from the consent of the governed."*

The implementation of this Declaration has no doubt been a tragic episode in the history of the United States. There have been two views about this document Some hold that it is a great spiritual document. Others have held that it immoralises many untruths. In any case this charter of human Liberty was not applied to the Negroes. What is however important to note is the faith underlying the Declaration. There is no doubt about it and certainly no doubt about the faith of Jefferson, the author of this Declaration. He never forgot that while enunciating along principle, his country decided to take a short step. He wrote, "I am sorry for my countrymen." It may be no recompense to the Negroes.

But it is by no means small comfort to know that the conscience of the country is not altogether dead and the flame of righteous indignation may one day bust forth. The Negroes may laugh at this. But the fact is that even this much comfort the Untouchables cannot hope to have from the Hindus. People today are proud of the fact that the Hindus are a solid mass. But strange as it may appear, to the Untouchables of India, this is more a matter of dread than comfort-as the "Solid South" is to the Negroes in the United States. Where could anyone find in India among the Hindus any person with a sense of shame and a sense of remorse such as was felt by Jefferson? I should have thought the Hindus would be too ashamed of this stigma of Untouchability on them to appear before the world with a demand for their freedom. That they do clamour for freedom-the pity is that they get support-is evidence that their conscience is dead, that they feel no righteous indignation, and to them Untouchability is neither a moral sit) nor a civil wrong. It is just a sport as cricket or hockey is.

The friends of Mr. Gandhi will no doubt point to him and his work. But what has Mr. Gandhi done to reform Hindu Society that his work and life be cited by democrats as a witness of hope and assurance 7 His friends have been informed of the Harijan Sevak Sangh and they continue to ask, "Is not Mr. Gandhi working to uplift the Harijans?" Is he? What is the object of this Harijan Sevak Sangh? Is it to prepare the Untouchables to win their freedom from their Hindu masters, to make them their social and political equals? Mr. Gandhi had never had any such object before him and he never wants to do this, and I say that he cannot do this. This is the task of a democrat and a revolutionary. Mr. Gandhi is neither. He is a Tory by birth as well as by faith. The work of the Harijan Sevak Sangh is not to raise the Untouchables. His main object, as every self-respecting Untouchable knows, is to make India safe for Hindus and Hinduism. He is certainly not fighting the battle of the Untouchables.

On the contrary by distributing through the Harijan Sevak Sangh petty gifts to petty Untouchables he is buying, benumbing and drawing the laws of the opposition of the Untouchables which he knows is the only force which will disrupt the caste system and will establish real democracy in India. Mr. Gandhi wants Hinduism and the Hindu caste system to remain intact. Mr. Gandhi also wants the Untouchables to remain as Hindus. But as what 7 not as partners but as poor relations of the Hindus. Mr. Gandhi is kind to the Untouchables. But for what? Only because he wants to kill, by kindness, them and their movement for separation and independence from Hindus. The Harijan Sevak Sangh is one of the many techniques which has enabled Mr. Gandhi to be a successful humbug.

Turn to Pandit Jawaharlal Nehru. He draws his inspiration from the Jeffersonian Declaration; but has he ever expressed any shame or any remorse about the condition of the 60 millions of Untouchables? Has he anywhere referred to them in the torrent of literature which comes out from his pen? Go to the youth of India, if you want. The youths who fill the Universities and who follow the Pandit's lead are ever ready to fight the political battle of India against the British. But what do these children of the leisured class Hindus have done to redress the wrongs their forefathers have done to the Untouchables? You can get thousands of Hindu youths to join political propaganda but you cannot get one single youth to take up the cause of breaking the caste system or of removing Untouchability. Democracy and democratic life, justice and conscience which are sustained by a belief in democratic principle are foreign to the Hindu mind. To leave democracy and freedom in such Tory hands would be the greatest mistake democrats could commit

It is therefore very necessary for the American friends of the Hindus to ask Mr. Gandhi and the Hindus to declare their War aims, so that they may be sure that the fight of the Hindus against British is really and truly a fight for freedom. The Congress and the Hindus will no doubt refer their inquiring foreign friends to the Congress Resolutions regarding minority rights.

But I would like to warn the American friends of the Hindus not to be content with the "glittering generalities" contained in congress declaration of Minority Rights. To declare the rights of the minority is one thing and to have them implemented is another. And why should the friends of the Hindus if they are really friends of freedom, not insist on implementation straight away? Are not the Hindus saying that they would not be satisfied with mere declaration of freedom from the British? Are they not asking for immediate implementation? If they want the British to implement their War aims, why should the Hindus be not prepared to implement their war aims?

American friends of the Hindus, I am sure, will not be misled by the Hindu propaganda that this war of the Hindus against the British is a War for freedom. Before helping the Hindus they must get themselves satisfied that the Hindus who are urging that their war against the British is a war for freedom will not turn out to be the enemies of the freedom of millions of Indians like the Untouchables. That is the plea I am making on behalf of the 60 millions of the Untouchables of India. And above all let not the American friends think that checks and balances in a Constitution-the demand for checks and balances suited to Indian conditions-are not necessary because the struggle is carried on by a people and is carried on in the name of freedom. Friends of democracy and freedom cannot afford to forget the words of John Adams when he said-

"We may appeal to every page of history we have hitherto turned over, for proof irrefragable that the people when they have been unchecked, have been as unjust, tyrannical, brutal, barbarous, and cruel as any king or Senate possessed of uncontrollable power: the majority has eternally and without one exception usurped over the rights of the minority."

If all Majorities must be subjected to checks and balances how much more must it be so in the case of the Hindus?

In 1933, Mr. Gandhi took up two movements. First was the Temple-entry Movement. He took personal responsibility for seeing through these two measures. One was the opening of the Guruvayur temple. The other was the passing of the Temple-entry Bill sponsored by Mr. Ranga Iyer in the Central Legislature. Mr. Gandhi said that he would fast unto death if the trustee of the Guruvayur temple did not throw it open to the Untouchables by a certain date.

The Guruvayur temple still remains closed to the Untouchables but Mr. Gandhi has not fulfilled his vow of going on, fast. Surprising as it may be he has done nothing to get the temple declared open to the Untouchables although it is now thirteen years since he took the vow. Mr. Gandhi virtually coerced the Governor-General to give his sanction to the introduction of the Temple-entry Bill. The Congress party in the Central legislature which was pledged to carry through the Bill refused to support it when the stage of referring it to a Select Committee came on the ground that the Bill gave offence to the Hindus and in the election that was pending the Hindus would seek revenge on the Congress and defeat it at the poll if the Congress supported the Bill. To the great chagrin of Mr. Ranga Iyer, the Congress party let him down, by leaving the Bill to die. Mr. Gandhi did not mind this. He even went to the length of justifying the conduct of the Congress Party.

The other movement which Mr. Gandhi sponsored in 1933 was the establishment of the Harijan Sevak Sangh with a network of branches all over India. There were three motives which lay behind the organisation of the Sangh. First was to prove that Hindus had enough charitable spirit towards the Untouchables and that they would show it by their generous contributions towards their uplift. The second motive was to serve the Untouchables by helping them in the many difficulties with which they were faced in their daily life. The third motive was to create in the minds of the Untouchables a sense of confidence in the Hindus from whom they were estranged in matters political. None of the three objects has been realized.

In the first flush the Hindus contributed a total of about 8 lakhs of rupees for the Sangh which is of course nothing as compared to the crores they have contributed for general political purposes. After that they have gone dry. The Sangh is now depending for its finances either on Government grants or on the income derived from the sale of Mr. Gandhi's autographs or on the munificence of some wealthy merchant who makes a contribution, to the Sangh, not because he loves the Untouchables but because he thinks it profitable to please Mr. Gandhi. The branches of the Sangh are being closed every year. The Sangh is contracting and contracting so rapidly that very soon it will have only a centre and no circumference. That the Hindus have lost interest in the Sangh is not the only regrettable aspect of this activity of Mr. Gandhi.

The Sangh has not been able to secure the good will and the cooperation of the Untouchables for whose benefit it is supposed to have been, started. This is due to various reasons. The work of the Sangh is of the most inconsequential kind. It does not catch anyone's imagination. It neglects most urgent purposes for which the Untouchables need help and assistance. The Sangh rigorously excludes the Untouchables from its management. The Untouchables are no more than beggars mere recipients of charity. The result is that the Untouchables feel no concern for the Sangh. They look upon it as a foreign body set up by the Hindus with some ulterior motive. Here was an opportunity for Mr. Gandhi to make the Sangh a real bridge between the Hindus and the Untouchables. He could make it a virile institution by improving its programme of work and by allowing the Untouchables to participate in its working Mr. Gandhi has done nothing of the kind. He has allowed the Sangh to languish. It is dying peacefully and may perish even during the lifetime of Mr. Gandhi.

There need be no surprise if this survey of Mr. Gandhi's anti Untouchability campaign, of his sayings and his doings baffles and puzzles the reader. There need be no wonder if the reader were to pause and ask a few questions on the lines set out below to clear his own mind:

(1) In 1921, Mr. Gandhi collected 1 crore and 35 lakhs of rupees for the Tilak Swaraj Fund. Mr. Gandhi insisted that there was no possibility of winning Swaraj unless Untouchability was removed. Why did he not protest when only a paltry sum of Rs. 43,000 was given to the cause of the Untouchables?

(2) In 1922 there was drawn up the Bardoli Programme of constructive work. Uplift of the Untouchables was an, important item in, it. A Committee was appointed to work out the details. The Committee never functioned a lid was dissolved and the uplift of the Untouchables as an item in the constructive programme was dropped. Only Rs. 800 were allotted to the Committee for working expenses. Why did Mr. Gandhi not protest against this niggardly and step-motherly treatment of the Committee by the Congress Working Committee? Why did not Mr. Gandhi support Swami Shradhanand who was fighting with the Congress Working Committee for large funds being assigned to the Committee? Why did not Mr. Gandhi protest against the dissolution of the Committee? Why did not Mr. Gandhi appoint another Committee? Why did he allow the work for the Untouchables to drop out as though it was of no importance?

(3) Mr. Gandhi had at the very outset of his campaign for Swaraj insisted that there were five conditions precedent for winning Swaraj: (i) Hindu-Moslem Unity; (ii) Removal of Untouchability; (iii) Universal adoption of hand-spun and hand-woven khadi; (iv) absolute non-

violence and (v) complete noncooperation. Mr. Gandhi had not only laid down these conditions but had told Indians that without the fulfilment of these conditions there could be no Swaraj. In 1922, he fasted for the sake of Hindu-Moslem unity. In 1924, he made production of hand-spun yarn the basis of franchise for Congress membership. Why did he not make nonobservance of Untouchability the basis of Congress franchise in 1924 or at any time subsequent thereto?

(4) Mr. Gandhi has gone on fast many a time to achieve a variety of objects which are dear to him. Why has Mr. Gandhi nut fasted even once for the sake of the Untouchables?

(5) Mr. Gandhi has devised satyagraha as a weapon to redress wrongs and to win freedom and has practised it against the British Government. Why has not Mr. Gandhi started satyagraha even once against the Hindus on behalf of the Untouchables for securing admission to wells, temples and other public places to which access is denied by the Hindus?

(6) Following Mr. Gandhi's lead the Untouchables started satyagraha from 1929 onwards against the Hindus for admission to wells and temples. Why did Mr. Gandhi condemn their satyagraha?

(7) Mr. Gandhi declared that he would fast if the Guruvayur temple was not thrown open to the Untouchables by the Zamorin. The temple has not been thrown open. Why did not Mr. Gandhi go on fast?

(8) Mr. Gandhi in 1982 threatened the British Government with dire consequences if the Governor-General did not give permission to Mr. Ranga Iyer to introduce his Temple-entry Bill on behalf of the Congress Party in the Central Legislature. As fresh elections to the Central Legislature were announced the Congress Party withdrew its support to the Bill and Mr. Ranga lyer had to drop it. If Mr. Gandhi was earnest and sincere about

Temple-entry, why did Mr. Gandhi support the action of the Congress Party? What was more important—Temple-entry for the Untouchables or Electoral victory to the Congress?

(9) Mr. Gandhi knows that the difficulty of the Untouchables does not lie in their not having civic rights. Their difficulty lies in the conspiracy of the Hindus who threaten them with dire consequences if the Untouchables dare to exercise them. The real way of helping the Untouchables is to have some organisation for the protection of civic rights which will undertake the duty of prosecuting Hindus who assault the Untouchables or proclaim social and economic boycott against them and thereby prevent them from exercising their civic rights. Why did not Mr. Gandhi include this as one of the objects of the Harijan Sevak Sangh?

(10) Before Mr. Gandhi came on the scene the Depressed Classes Mission Society was formed by the caste Hindus for the uplift of the Untouchables. The moneys were subscribed by the Hindus. Yet the Society's affairs were conducted by Joint Boards consisting of Hindus and Untouchables. Why has Mr. Gandhi excluded the Untouchables from the management of the Harijan Sevak Sangh?

(11) If Mr. Gandhi is the real friend of the Untouchables, why did he not leave it to the Untouchables to decide whether political safeguards were the best means for their protection? Why did he go to the length of making a pact with the Muslims in order to isolate and defeat the Untouchables? Why did Mr. Gandhi declare a fast unto death the object of which was to deprive the Untouchables of the benefit of the Communal Award by this extreme form of coercion?

(12) After having accepted the Poona Pact, why did not Mr. Gandhi keep faith with the Untouchables by telling the Congress not to despoil the politics of the Untouchables

by contesting the seats reserved for the Untouchables by getting such Untouchables elected as were prepared to become the tools of the Hindus?

(13) After having accepted the Poona Pact why did not Mr. Gandhi keep up the gentleman's agreement and instruct the Congress High Command to include representatives of the Untouchables in, the Congress Cabinets?

(14) Why did Mr. Gandhi disapprove of the appointment by Dr. Khare of Mr. Agnibhoj—a member of the Scheduled Castes—as a minister in the Congress Cabinet in the C. P. when Mr. Agnibhoj was in every way qualified to be a Minister? Did Mr. Gandhi say that he was opposed to the creation of such high ambitions among persons belonging to the Scheduled Castes?

What is the explanation that Mr. Gandhi has to offer? What is the explanation that Mr. Gandhi's friends have to offer? Mr. Gandhi's anti-untouchability campaign is marked by so many twists and turns, inconsistencies and contradictions, attacks and surrenders, advances and retreats that the whole campaign has become a matter of mystery. Few have a belief in its efficacy and quite a large number hold that there is not enough earnestness and sincerity behind it. Some explanation is therefore necessary.

It is more for the sake of Mr. Gandhi's reputation for earnestness and sincerity that for the sake of giving a clear understanding of Mr. Gandhi's aims and methods to the reader that one would like Mr. Gandhi and his friends to explain the points raised in the foregoing questions.

It would no doubt be interesting to know what Mr. Gandhi and his friends may have to say in reply to these questions. Everybody interested in this question will naturally be looking forward to it. It will not however do for anyone else to anticipate the reply and then dead with it. They 'must be left to frame it in their own way and select their own time to do so. In the meantime one may well ask what the Untouchable have to say about Mr. Gandhi and his anti-untouchability campaign. It us not difficult to state what view the Untouchables take of Mr. Gandhi's anti-untouchability campaign.

Do the Untouchable regard Mr. Gandhi as being in earnest? The answer is in the negative. They do not regard Mr. Gandhi as being in earnest. How can they? How can they look upon, a man being in earnest who when in 1921 the whole country was aroused to put the Bardoli programme in action remained completely indifferent to the anti-untouchability part of it? How could they look upon a man as being in earnest who, when out of 1 crore and 25 lakhs of Swaraj Fund, found that only 43 thousands rupees were allotted to the cause of the Untouchables did not raise any protest at this niggardly treatment of a long neglected cause?

How can they regard a man as being in earnest who when, in 1924 he got an opportunity to impose upon the Hindus the obligation to remove Untouchability did not do so even though he had the power and the occasion to enforce it? Such a step would have served three purposes. It would have put the nationalism of Congressmen to test. It would have helped to remove Untouchability, and it would have proved that Mr. Gandhi was sincere in his talks about the evil of Untouchability and its being a sin and a stigma on Hinduism. Why did not Mr. Gandhi do it? Does this not show that Mr. Gandhi was more interested in the spread of spinning than in the removal of Untouchability? Does this not show that removal of Untouchability was the least part of Mr. Gandhi's programme and that it was not even last?

Does it not show that the statements by Mr. Gandhi that Untouchability is a blot on Hinduism and that there will be no Swaraj without the removal of Untouchability were just empty phrases with no earnestness behind them? How could they believe in the earnestness of a person who takes a vow to fast if the Guruvayar temple is not opened to the Untouchables but will not go on fast even when the temple remains closed? How could they accept a man to be in earnest when he sponsors a Bill for securing Temple-entry and subsequently becomes a party to dropping it.? How could they accept the earnestness of a man who contents himself with saying the he will not go into a temple if it is not open to the Untouchables when what is required of him is to adopt every means to get the temples thrown open to the Untouchables? How could they believe in the earnestness of a man who is ready to fast for everything but will not fast for the Untouchables? How can they believe in the earnestness of a man who is prepared to practise dstyagraha for everything and against everybody but who will not practise it against the Hindus for the sake of the Untouchables? How can they believe in the earnestness of a man who does nothing more than indulge in giving sermons, on the evils of Untouchability?

Do they regard Mr. Gandhi as honest and sincere? The answer is that they do not regard Mr. Gandhi as honest and sincere. At the outset of his campaign for Swaraj Mr. Gandhi told the Untouchables not to side with the British. He told them not to embrace Christianity or any other religion. He told them that they could find salvation in Hinduism. He told Hindus that they must remove Untouchability as a condition precedent to Swaraj. Yet in 1921 when only a paltry sum out of the Tilak Swaraj Fund was allotted to the Untouchables, when the Committee to plan the uplift of the Untouchables was unceremoniously wound up Mr. Gandhi did not raise a word of protest.

Mr. Gandhi had under his command a sum of Rs. 1 crore and 25 lakhs belonging to the Tilak Swaraj Fund. Why did Mr. Gandhi not insist upon a substantial portion of this amount being earmarked for the uplift of the Untouchables? That Mr. Gandhi showed almost complete indifference to the cause of the Untouchables is beyond dispute. What is surprising is the explanation which Mr. Gandhi offered for his indifference. He said that he was busy in planning a campaign to win Swaraj and that he had no time to spare for the cause of the Untouchables. He not only did not blush at his explanation but he offered a moral justification for his indifference to the cause of the Untouchables. He took the stand that there was nothing wrong in his devoting himself entirely to the political cause of India to the exclusion of the cause of the Untouchables for in his opinion the good of the whole includes the good of the part and that as the Hindus are slaves of the British, slaves cannot emancipate slaves. Phrases such as 'slaves of slaves' and 'greater includes the less' may be admirable dialectics, though they cannot have more truth than the saying that because the country's wealth has increased, therefore everybody's wealth has increased. But we are not considering Mr. Gandhi's ability as a dialectician. We are testing his sincerity. Can we accept a man's sincerity who evades his responsibility and contents himself with an excuse? Can the Untouchables believe that Mr. Gandhi is the champion of their cause?

How can they regard Mr. Gandhi as honest and sincere if they consider Mr. Gandhi's conduct towards them and towards the Muslims and Sikhs in the matter of constitutional safeguards?

Mr. Gandhi used to justify his discrimination between the Scheduled Castes and other Minorities in the matter of constitutional safeguards by another plea. The plea was that there were historical reasons, which compel him to recognise the Muslims and the Sikhs. He has never explained what those reasons are. They cannot be other than those, which hold the Muslims and the Sikhs as the fragments of old ruling communities. One does not mind Mr. Gandhi having succumbed to such puerile and undemocratic arguments, though he could have insisted that he would treat all minorities on equal basis and would not give any weight to such illogical and irrelevant considerations.

The question is: How could the admission of such a plea have prevented Mr. Gandhi from opposing the demand of the Scheduled Castes? Why did Mr. Gandhi regard himself as bound by no other reasons except the historical reasons? Why did not Mr. Gandhi think that if historical reasons were decisive in the case of Muslims and Sikhs, moral reasons were decisive in the case of the Untouchables? The fact is that the plea of historical reasons is a hollow plea. It was not a plea at all. It was an excuse for not conceding the demand of the Untouchables.

Mr. Gandhi is never so much disgusted as he is when he is confronted with the question of Majority versus Minority. He would like to forget it and ignore it. But circumstances will not let him do either and he is often forced to deal with the issue. The last time he dealt with it was on the 21st October 1989 in the form of an Editorial in the Harijan under the heading "The Fiction of Majority." The article is full of venom and Mr. Gandhi has not hesitated to pour all the ridicule he could on those who were constantly raising the question. In the article he vehemently denied that the Muslims are a Minority. He denied that the Sikhs are a Minority and denied that the Indian Christians are a Minority. His contention was that they were not minorities in the technical sense of Oppressed Communities they were minorities they were to in the numerical sense only, which meant that they were no minorities at all. What did Mr. Gandhi have to say about the Scheduled Castes? Could he deny their contention that they are a Minority? Let me quote Mr. Gandhi's own words. Mr. Gandhi said:— "I have endeavoured to show that there is no such things as real minorities in India whose rights can be endangered by India becoming independent. With the exception of the Depressed Classes there is no minority which is not able to Take care of itself."

Here is an, admission, on, the part of Mr.Gandhi that the Scheduled Castes are a minority in, the real sense of the word and that they are the only minority in India who will not be able to take care of themselves in, a free India governed by a Hindu Communal Majority. Notwithstanding this inner conviction Mr. Gandhi maintained in a most vehement manner that he would not concede any political safeguards to the Untouchables. How can the Untouchables accept such a man as sincere and honest?

Mr. Gandhi opposed the demands of the Untouchables for political safeguards at the Round Table Conference. He did everything to defeat the object of the Untouchables. To weaken, the force behind their demand and isolate them he tried to buy over the Muslims by offering to concede the whole of their fourteen demands. Mr. Gandhi at the meeting of the Minorities Sub-Committee had said: "Who am I to oppose the demand of the Untouchables if the Committee gave it its approval."

It was wrong for Mr. Gandhi to have tried to defeat the verdict of the Committee by offering to give the Muslims their full demand formulated in. Mr. Jinnah's fourteen points in return for their agreeing to oppose the demands of the Scheduled Castes!! His was a most subtle piece of strategy. He offered the Musalmans a most difficult choice between having their 14 points and withdrawing their support to the demand of the Untouchables or siding with the Untouchables and losing their 14 points. In the end Mr. Gandhi's strategy failed and neither did the Musalmans lose their 14 points nor did the Untouchables lose their case. But the episode remains as a witness to Mr. Gandhi's perfidy. What else can be the appropriate description of the conduct of a man who offers criminal inducement to another for getting him to break his promise, who calls a person his friend and then contrives to stab him in the back? How can such a man be regarded by the Untouchables as honest and sincere?

Mr. Gandhi left the decision of the communal question to the arbitration of the British Prime Minister. Notwithstanding Mr. Gandhi's efforts to defeat the Untouchables His Majesty's Government conceded them their political demands. As a party to the arbitration Mr. Gandhi was bound to abide by the decision. But Mr. Gandhi decided to defy it and he did it by going on a fast unto death. Mr. Gandhi shook India and the world outside by his Fast unto Death. The object of the Fast was to compel the British Government to withdraw the Constitutional Safeguards which the British Prime Minister had proposed in his Award for the protection of the Untouchables under the new Constitution. One of Mr. Gandhi's disciples has described the fast as an Epic Fast. Why it should be described as an Epic Fast it is not easy to follow. There was nothing heroic about it. It was the opposite of heroic. It was an adventure. It was launched by Mr. Gandhi because he believed that both the Untouchables and the British Government would quake before his threat of fast unto death, and surrender to his demand.

Both were prepared to call off his bluff and as a matter of fact did call it off. All his heroism vanished the moment Mr. Gandhi found that he had overdone the trick. The man who started by saying that he would fast unto death unless the safeguards to the Untouchables were completely withdrawn and the Untouchables reduced to the condition of utter helplessness without rights and without recognition was plaintively pleading "My life is in your hands, will you save me?" Mr. Gandhi's over impatience to sign the Poona Pact—though it did not cancel the Prime Minister's Award as he had demanded but only substituted another and a different system of constituent safeguards—is the strongest evidence that the hero had lost his courage and was anxious to save his face and anyhow save his life.

There was nothing noble in the fast. It was a foul and filthy act. The Fast was not for the benefit of the Untouchables. It was against them and was the worst form of coercion against a helpless people to give up the constitutional safeguards of which they had become possessed under the Prime Minister's Award and agree to live on the mercy of the Hindus. It was a vile and wicked act. How can the Untouchables regard such a man as honest and sincere?

After having gone on a fast unto death, he signed the Poona Pact. People say that Mr. Gandhi sincerely believed that political safeguards were harmful to the Untouchables. But how could a honest and sincere man who opposed the political demands of the Untouchables who was prepared to use the Muslims to defeat them, who went on a Fast unto Death, in the end accept the very same demands—for there is no difference between the Poona Pact and the Communal Award—when he found that there was no use opposing, as opposition would not succeed? How can an honest and sincere man accept as harmless the demands of the Untouchables which once he regarded as harmful?

Do the Untouchables regard Mr. Gandhi as their friend and ally? The answer is in the negative. They do not regard him as their friend. How can they? It may be that Mr. Gandhi honestly believes that the problem of the Untouchables is a social problem. But how can they believe him to be their friend when he wishes to retain caste and abolish Untouchability it being quite clear that Untouchability is only an extended form of caste and that therefore without abolition of caste there is no hope of abolition of Untouchability? It may be that Mr. Gandhi honestly believes that the problem of Untouchables can be solved by social processes.

But how can the Untouchables regard a man as their friend who develops a fanatic and frantic opposition to political processes being employed when everyone was agreed that the use of political processes cannot mar the effect of social process and may be depended upon to help and accelerate the solution of the problem. How could a man be regarded as the friend of the Untouchables when he does not believe the Untouchables reaching to places of power and authority in the State. In this controversy over political safeguards Mr. Gandhi could have pursued any of the following courses. He could have been the champion of the Untouchables. As such, he should not only have welcomed their demand for safeguards but he should have proposed them himself without waiting for the Untouchables to do so. Not only should he have proposed them himself but he should have fought for them.

For, what could give greater happiness to a genuine champion of the Untouchables than to see that provision was made to enable them to become members of the Legislature, Ministers of Executive, and occupants of high offices in the

State? Surely, if Mr. Gandhi is a champion of the Untouchables these are the very provisions he should have fought for. Secondly, if he did not wish to be the champion of the Untouchables, he could have been their ally. He could have helped them by giving them his moral and material support. Thirdly, if Mr. Gandhi did not like to play the part of a champion and was averse to be even an ally of the Untouchables, the next thing he could have done consistent with his proclaimed and much advertised sympathies for the Untouchables, was to be their friend. Again as a friend he could have taken up the attitude of benevolent neutrality—declining to fight but ready to render all help for getting the demand for safeguards accepted. Failing benevolent neutrality he could have taken the attitude of strict neutrality and could have told the Untouchables to get the safeguards if the Round Table Conference was prepared to give them and that he would neither help nor hinder. Abandoning all these sober considerations Mr. Gandhi came out as an, open enemy of the Untouchables. How can the Untouchables regard such a man as their friend and ally?

That Mr. Gandhi's anti-untouchability campaign has failed is beyond cavil. Even the Congress papers admit it. I give below a few quotations from some of them:

On 17th August 1939 Mr. B. K. Gaikwad, a member of the Scheduled Castes in the Bombay Legislative Assembly, asked a question as to how many temples in the Bombay Presidency were thrown open to the Untouchables since 1932 when. Mr. Gandhi started, his Temple-entry movement. According to the figures given by the Congress Minister the total number of temples thrown open was 142. Of these 121 were ownerless temples standing on the wayside. Which were under the care of nobody in particular and which nobody used as places of worship. Another fact revealed was that not a single temple was thrown open to the Untouchables in Gujarat, the district which is the home of Mr. Gandhi.

Writing on 10th March 1940 the Harijan Bandu, Mr. Gandh's Gujarathi paper, said; "The Untouchability of the 'Harijans" in the matter of entry into schools persists nowhere so much still as in Gujarat."

The Bombay Chronicle in its issue of 27th August 1940 reproduced an extract from a monthly letter of the Harijan Sevak Sangh. It "States that Harijans of Godhavi in Ahmedabad District were so persecuted by caste Hindus for sending their children to Local Board School that ultimately 42 Harijan families left that place...and went to the Taluka town of Sanand."

On 27th August 1948, Mr. M. M. Nandgaonkar, a leader of the Untouchables residing in Thana in the Bombay Presidency and ex-Vice President of Thana Municipality was refused tea in a Hindu hotel. The Bombay Chronicle commenting upon this incident in its issue dated 28th August 1948 said:

> *"When Gandhiji fasted in 1932, some feverish attempts were made to have some temples and hotels opened to Harijans, Now the actual position is nearly what it used to be before with regard to temple entry and access to, hotels. The cleanest Harijan is not admitted to temples and hotels. Yet many anti-Untouchability workers take a complacent view of these disabilities and patronisingly talk of 'uplift first' for Harijans, saying that when Harijans learn to be clean, their civic disabilities will fall off automatically. This is rank nonsense."*

Writing on the proceedings of the All-India Scheduled Castes Federation held in Cawnpore in January 1944 the Bombay Chronicle in its issue of 4th February 1944 said:

> *"But such is the passivity of Hindu society that both caste and Untouchability still thrive. Nay, several Hindu leaders... misguided by the interested propaganda by certain Britishers, still plead that there is some mysterious virtue in caste because Hindu culture has remained today. Else, they argue, caste would not have survived the shocks of centuries... It is most tragic to find that, in spite of all that Gandhiji and other reformers have done, Untouchability still persists to no small extent. It is most rampant in villages. Even in a city like Bombay, a person known to be*

a sweeper, let alone a scavenger, however clean dressed he may be, is not allowed to enter a caste Hindu restaurant, nay, even an Iran's restaurant for tea."

The Untouchables have always said that Mr. Gandhi's anti-Untouchability campaign has failed. After 25 years of labour, hotels have remained closed, wells have remained closed, temples have remained closed and in very many parts of India—particularly in Gujarat—even schools have remained closed. The extracts produced from the papers form therefore a very welcome testimony especially because the papers are Congress papers. As they fully corroborate what the Untouchables have been saying on the point, nothing further need be said on the subject except to ask one question.

Why has Mr. Gandhi failed? According to me, there are three reasons which has brought about this failure. The first reason is the Hindus to whom he makes his appeal for the removal of Untouchability do not respond. Why is this so? It is a common experience that the words a man uses and the effect they produce are not always commensurate. What he says has its momentum indefinitely multiplied, or reduced to nullity, by the impression that the hearer for good reason or bad happens to have formed of the spirit of the speaker. This gives a clue to know why Mr. Gandhi's sermons on Untouchability have completely failed to move the Hindus, why people hear his after-prayer sermons for few minutes and then go to the comic opera and why there is nothing more to it. The fault is not entirely of the Hindu public.

The fault is of Mr. Gandhi himself. Mr. Gandhi has built up his reputation of being a Mahatma on his being an harbinger of political freedom and not on his being a spiritual teacher. Whatever may be his intentions, Mr. Gandhi is looked upon as an apostle of Swaraj. His anti-Untouchability campaign is looked upon as a fad if not a sideshow. That is why the Hindus respond to his political biddings but never to his social or religious preaching. The momentum of his anti-Untouchability campaign must therefore remain a nullity. Mr. Gandhi is a political shoemaker. He must stick to his political last. He thought he could take up the task of solving the social question. That was a mistake. A politician is not the man for it. That is why the hope held out to the Untouchables that Mr. Gandhi's sermons will do the trick has failed.

The second reason is that Mr. Gandhi does not wish to antagonise the Hindus even if such antagonism was necessary to carry out his anti-Untouchability programme. A few instances will illustrate Mr. Gandhi's mentality.

Most of Mr. Gandhi's friends give credit to Mr. Gandhi for sincerity and earnestness for the cause of the Untouchables and expect the Untouchables to believe in it on the mere ground that Mr. Gandhi is the one man who keeps on constantly preaching to the Hindus the necessity of removing Untouchability. They have lost sight of the old proverb that an ounce of practice is worth a ton of preaching and have never cared to ask Mr. Gandhi to explain why does he not cease to preach to the Hindus the necessity of removing Untouchability and launch a campaign of satyagraha or start a fast. If they would ask for such an explanation they would know why Mr. Gandhi merely contents himself with sermons on Untouchability.

The true reasons why Mr. Gandhi will not go beyond sermons were revealed to the Untouchables for the first time in, 1929 when the Untouchables in the Bombay Presidency opened a campaign of satyagraha against the Hindus for establishing their civic rights in the matter of temple-entry and taking water from public wells. They hoped to get the blessings of Mr. Gandhi in as much as satyagraha was Mr. Gandhi's own weapon to get wrongs redressed.. When appealed to for support, Mr. Gandhi surprised the Untouchables by issuing a statement condemning their campaign of satyagraha against the Hindus. The argument urged by Mr. Gandhi was very ingenious. He stated that Satyagrahs was to be used only against foreigners; i it must not be used against one's own kindred or countrymen and as the Hindus were the kindred and countrymen of the

Untouchables by rules of satyagraha the latter were debarred from using the weapon against the former!! What a fall from the sublime to the ridiculous! By this Mr. Gandhi made nonsense of satyagraha. Why did Mr. Gandhi do this? Only because he did not want to annoy and exasperate the Hindus.

As a second piece of evidence, I would refer to what is known as the Kavitha incident Kavitha is a village in the Ahmedabad District in Gujarat. In 1935, the Untouchables of the village demanded from the Hindus of the village that their children should be admitted in the common school of the village along with other Hindu children. The Hindus were enraged at this outrage and took their revenge by proclaiming a complete social boycott. The events connected with this boycott were reported by Mr. A. V. Thakkar, who went to Kavitha to intercede with the Hindus on behalf of the Untouchables. The story told by him runs as follows:

"The Associated Press announced on the 10th inst. that the Caste Hindus of Kavitha agreed to admit Harijan boys to the village school in Kavitha and that matters were amicably settled. This was contradicted on the 13th instant by the Secretary of the Ahmedabad Harijan Sevak Sangh, who said in his statement that the Harijans had undertaken (privately of course) not to send their children to the school. Such an undertaking was not given, voluntarily, but was extorted from them by the Caste Hindus, in this case the Garasias of the village; who had proclaimed a social boycott against poor Harijans-weavers, chamars and others, who number over 100 families. They were deprived of agricultural labour, their animals of grazing in the pasture land and their children of buttermilk. Not only this, but a Harijan leader was compelled to take an oath by Mahadev that he and others would not hereafter even make an effort to reinstate their children in the school. The so-called settlement was brought about in this way."

But even after the bogus settlement reported on the 10th and the complete surrender by poor Harijans, the boycott was not lifted up to the 19th and partly up to the 22nd from the weavers, it was lifted somewhat earlier from the head of the chamars, as Garasias themselves could not remove the caresses of their dead animals, and thus had to come to terms with the Chamars earlier. As if the enormities perpetrated so far were not enough, kerosine was poured into the Harijans' well, once on the 15th instant, and again on the 19th instant. One can imagine what terrorism was thus practised on poor Harijans because they had dared to send their children to sit alongside of the ' princely ' Garasia boys.

I met the leaders of the Garasias on the rooming of the 22nd. They said they could not tolerate the idea of boys of Dheds and Chamars sitting by the side of their own boys. I met also the District Magistrate of Ahmedabad on the 23rd with a view to finding out if he would do something to ease the situation, but without any result.

> *"Harijan boys are thus practically banned from the village school with nobody to help them. This has caused despondency among the Harijans to such an extent that they are thinking of migration in a body to some other village."*

This was a report made to Mr. Gandhi. What did Mr. Gandhi do? The followings is the advice Mr. Gandhi gave to the Untouchables of Kavitha:

> *"There is no help like self-help. God helps those who help themselves. If the Harijans concerned will carry out their reported resolve to wipe the dust of Kavitha off their feet, they will not only be happy themselves but they will pave the way for others who may be similarly treated. If people migrate in search of employment how much more should they do so in search of self-respect? I hope that well-wishers of Harijans will help these poor families to vacate inhospitable Kavitha." Mr. Gandhi advised the Untouchables of Kavitha to vacate. But why did he not advise Mr. Thakkar to prosecute the Hindus of Kavitha and help the Untouchables to vindicate their rights?" "Obviously, he would like to uplift the Untouchables If he can but not by offending*

the Hindus. What good can such a man do to promote the cause of the Untouchables? All this shows that Mr. Gandhi is most anxious to be good to the Hindus. That is why he opposes satyagraha against the Hindus. That is why he opposed the political demands of the Untouchables as he believed that they were aimed against them. He is anxious to be so good to the Hindus that he does not care if he is thereby becoming good for nothing for the Untouchables. That is why Mr. Gandhi's whole programme for the removal of Untouchability is just words, words and words and why there is no action behind it."

The third reason is that Mr. Gandhi does not want the Untouchables to organise and be strong. For he fears that they might thereby become independent of the Hindus and weaken the ranks of Hindus. This is best illustrated by the activities of the Harijan Sevak Sangh. The whole object of the Sangh is to create a slave mentality among the Untouchables towards their Hindu masters. Examine the Sangh from any angle one may like and the creation of slave mentality will appear to be its dominant purpose.

The work of the Sangh reminds one of the mythological demoness Putana described in the Bhagavad—a companion to the Mahabharata. Kamsa the king of Mathura, wanted to kill Krishna, as it was predicted that Kamsa will die at the hands of Krishna. Having come to know of the birth of Krishna, Kamsa asked Putana to undertake the mission to kill Krishna while he was yet a baby. Putana took the form of a beautiful woman and went to Yashoda, the foster mother of Krishna and having applied liquid poison to her breast pleaded to be employed as a wet nurse for suckling the baby Krishna and thus have the opportunity to kill it.

The rest of the story it is unnecessary to pursue. The point of the story is that the real purpose is not always the same as the ostensible purpose and a nurse can be a murdress. The Sangh is to the Untouchables what Putana was to Krishna. The Sangh under the pretence of service is out to kill the spirit of independence from among the Untouchables. The Untouchables, in the early stages of their agitation, had taken the support of some well-meaning Hindus and had followed their leadership. By the time of the Round Table Conference, the Untouchables had become completely self-reliant and independent. They were no longer satisfied with charity from the Hindus.

They demanded what they said was their right. There is no doubt that it is to kill this spirit of independence among the Untouchables that Mr. Gandhi started the Harijan Sevak Sangh. The Harijan Sevak Sangh by its petty services has collected a swarm of grateful Untouchables who are employed to preach that Mr. Gandhi and the Hindus are the saviours of the Untouchables. Daniel O'Connel the Irish leader once said that no man can be grateful at the cost of his honour, no woman can be grateful at the cost of her chastity and no country can be grateful at the cost of its liberty. The Untouchables are too simple-minded to know that the cost of the service which the Harijan Sevak Sangh offers to render is loss of independence. This is exactly what Mr. Gandhi wants.

The worst part of the activities of the Harijan Sevak Sangh is the help rendered to the Untouchable students kept in the hostels maintained by the Sangh. These Untouchable students remind me of Bhisma and Kocha, two prominent characters which figure in the Mahabharata. Bhisma proclaimed with great show that the Pandavas were right and the Kauravas wrong. Yet when it came to a war between the two he fought on the side of the Kauravas and against the Pandavas. When asked to justify his conduct he was not ashamed to say that he fought for the Kauravas because they fed him. Kocha belonged to the community of the Devas who were engaged in a war against the Rakshasas. The spiritual head of the Rakshasas knew a mantra (incantation) by which he could revive a dead Rakshasa.

The Devas were losing the battle since their head did not know the mantra and could not revive their dead. The Devas planned to send Kacha to the head of the Rakshasas with instructions somehow to learn the mantra and come back. Kacha in the beginning could not succeed. Ultimately he entered into an agreement with Devayani the daughter of the spiritual head of the Rakshasas that if she helped him to acquire the mantra he would be prepared to marry her. Devayani succeeded in fulfilling her part of the contract. But Kacha refused to perform his part alleging that the interests of his community were more important than his promise to her.

Bhisma and Kacha, in my opinion, are typical of the morally depraved characters who know no other purpose but to serve their own interests for the time being. The Untouchable students in the Harijan hostels are acting the part of both Bhisma and Kacha. During their stay in the hostels they play the part of Bhisma by singing the praises of Mr. Gandhi and the Congress. When they come out of the hostels they play the part of Kacha and denounce Mr. Gandhi and the Congress. I am extremely pained to see this. Nothing worse could happen to the youth of the Untouchables than this moral degeneration. But this is the greatest disservice which his Harijan Sevak Sangh has done to the Untouchables. It has destroyed their character. It has destroyed their independence. This is what Mr. Gandhi wants to happen.

Take a fourth illustration. The Sangh is run by the Caste Hindus. There are some Untouchables who have demanded that the institution should be handed over to the Untouchables and should be run by them. Others have demanded that the Untouchables should have representation on the governing Board. Mr. Gandhi has flatly refused to do either on two very ingenious grounds which no man with the greatest cunning could improve. Mr. Gandhi's first argument is that the Harijan Sevak Sangh it an act of penance on the part of the Hindus for the sin of observing Untouchability. It is they who must do the penance.

Therefore the Untouchable can have no place in running the Sangh. Secondly Mr. Gandhi says the money collected by him is given by the Hindus and not by the Untouchables and as the money is not of the Untouchables, the Untouchables have no right to be on the Governing Body. The refusal of Mr. Gandhi may be tolerated but his argument's are most insulting and a respectable Untouchable will be forgiven if he refuses to have anything to do with the Sangh. One should have thought that the Harijan Sevak Sangh was a Trust and the Untouchables its beneficiaries. Any trio in law would admit that the beneficiaries have every right to know the aims and objects of the Trust, its funds and whether the objects are properly carried out or not. The beneficiaries have even the right to have the Trustees removed for breach of trust. On that basis it would be impossible to deny the claim of the Untouchables for representation on the Managing Board. Evidently Mr. Gandhi does not wish to accept this position.

A self-respecting Untouchable who has no desire to cringe and who does not believe in staking the future of the "Untouchables on the philanthropy of strangers cannot have any quarrel with Mr. Gandhi, He is quite prepared to say that if meanness is a virtue then Mr. Gandhi's logic is superb and Mr. Gandhi is welcome to the benefit of it. Only he must not blame the Untouchables if they boycott the Sangh.

These however could not be the real reasons for not allowing the Untouchables to run the Sangh. The real reasons are different. In the first place, if the Sangh was handed over to the Untouchables Mr. Gandhi and the Congress will have no means of control over the Untouchable'?. The Untouchables will cease to be dependent on the Hindus. In the second place, the Untouchables having become independent will cease to be grateful to the Hindus. These consequences will be quite contrary to the aim find object, which have led Mr. Gandhi to found the Sangh, He wants to create among the Untouchables what is known among Indian Christians as the mission compound mentality. That is why Mr. Gandhi does not wish to hand over the Sangh to the control and management of the Untouchables. Is this consistent with a genuine desire for the emancipation of the Untouchables? Can Mr. Gandhi be called a liberator of the Untouchables? Does this not show that Mr. Gandhi is more anxious to tighten the tie which binds the Untouchables to the apron strings of the Hindus than to free them from the thralldom of the Hindus?

These are the reasons why Mr. Gandhi's anti-Untouchability campaign has failed.

To sum up, can it be said that Mr. Gandhi has recovered the title deeds to humanity which the Untouchables have lost? Obviously not. Those title deeds are still with the Hindus. He has done nothing to recover them. Nor has be helped the Untouchables to recover them. On the contrary, Mr. Gandhi has put every obstacle in their way. The Untouchables feel that their title deeds to humanity—"which means their emancipation from their thralldom of the Hindus can be secured by them by political power, and by nothing else. Mr. Gandhi, on the other hand, believes that his preaching and the charity and zeal of the Hindus are sufficient panacea for all the ills of the Untouchables. Can the Untouchables rely on a sustained flow of Hindu charity and Hindu zeal? Charity which has its fury is worth talking about.

Zeal which has its vengeance is worth building upon. But which friend of the Untouchables can ask them to depend upon the miserable measure 'of Hindu charity and the Hindu zeal? Untouchability has been in existence for the last two thousand years during which period the Hindus have day in and day out sucked the very blood of the Untouchables and have mutilated them and trodden upon them in every way.

During these two thousand years what amount of charity have the Hindus done to the Untouchables? Only 8 lakhs and that too when Mr. Gandhi personally went round the country with a begging bowl!!! Having put his programme to test, Mr. Gandhi might have shown, his willingness to concede the Untouchables' demand for political power as their only means of salvation. Indeed so obvious is the justice of this demand that a man with no more than common sense could have understood that executive power in the hands of the Untouchables could do more in a year than the whole order of preaching friars could be relied upon, to do in, a century.

But the very idea of political power to the Untouchables is hateful to Mr. Gandhi. Why should not the Untouchables say "'Beware of Mr. Gandhi' when they know that he would not allow the use of political processes for the emancipation of the Untouchables though Mr.Gandhi is fully alive to the fact that the social processes on which he laid so much store for helping them have completely failed.

In this connection one is reminded of the attitude of President Lincoln in the American Civil War towards the two questions of union and slavery. This attitude is well revealed by the correspondence that passed in 1862 between, Mr. Horace Greelcy and President Lincoln., In, a letter addressed to the President entitled "The Prayer of Twenty Millions," Mr. Greeley said:

> *"On the face of this wide earth, Mr. President, there is not one disinterested, determined, intelligent champion of the Union cause who does not feel that all attempts to put down the rebellion and at the same time uphold its inciting cause (namely slavery) are preposterous and futile."*

To this, President Lincoln's reply was: If there be those who would not save the Union unless they could at the same time save slavery, I do not agree with them.

If there be those who would not save the Union unless they could at the same time destroy slavery, I do not agree with them.

My paramount object is to save the Union, and not wither to save or to destroy slavery.

If I could save the Union without freeing any slave, I would do it. If I could save it by freeing all the slaves, I would do it and if I could do it by freeing some and leaving others alone, I would also do that.

These were the views of President Lincoln about Negro slavery and its relation to the question of Union. They certainly throw a very different light on one who is reputed to be the liberator of the Negroes. As a matter of fact he did not believe in the emancipation of the Negroes as a categorical imperative. Obviously the author of the famous Gettysberg oration about Government of the people, by the people and for the people would not have minded if his statement had taken the shape of government of the black people by the white people and for the white people provided there was union. Mr. Gandhi's attitude towards Swaraj and the Untouchables resembles very much the attitude of President Lincoln towards the two questions of the Negroes and the Union,. Mr. Gandhi wants Swaraj as did President Lincoln want Union. But he does not want Swaraj at the cost of disrupting the structure of Hinduism which is what political emancipation of the Untouchables means as President Lincoln did not want to free the slaves if it was not necessary to do so for the sake of the Union.

There is of course this difference between Mr. Gandhi and President Lincoln. President Lincoln was prepared to emancipate the Negro slaves if it was necessary to preserve the Union. Mr. Gandhi's attitude is in marked contrast. He is not prepared for the political emancipation, of the Untouchables even if it was essential for winning Swaraj. Mr. Gandhi's attitude is let Swaraj perish if the cost of it is the political freedom of the Untouchables.

Some Untouchables are probably under the impression that all this is a matter of the dead past and that Mr. Gandhi having accepted the Poona Pact cannot now oppose the political demands of the Untouchables for as a party to the Poona Pact Mr. Gandhi must be assumed to have conceded that the Untouchables are a separate element m the national life of India, This is a complete misunderstanding. For there are grounds to„ believe that the Poona Pact has made no difference m Mr. Gandhi's view and he still maintains the same attitude to the Untouchables' claim for political safeguards as he did at the Round Table (conference and before the Poona Pact. These grounds have their foundation in the fact that when His Majesty's Government declared in 1940 that the Untouchables are a separate clement in the National life of India and that their consent to the Constitution, is necessary Mr. Gandhi came out with "a protest.

When the Viceroy Lord Linlithgow referred to the Untouchables as a separate element and said that their consent to the Constitution was necessary, Mr. Gandhi said: "I felt that the putting up by the Viceroy, and then the Secretary of State of want of agreement by the Congress with the Princes, the Muslim League and even the Scheduled Classes as a barrier to the British recognition of India's right to freedom was more than unjust to the Congress and the people".

The introduction of the Scheduled Classes in the controversy has made the unreality of the case of the British Government doubly unreal. They know that these are the special care of the Congress, and that the Congress is infinitely more capable of guarding theirs interests than the British Government. Moreover, the Scheduled Classes are divided into as many castes as the Caste Hindu Society. No single Scheduled classes member could possibly and truthfully represent the innumerable castes.

The argument advanced by Mr. Gandhi is puerile. It may be pointed out that in the hurry he made in stating his opposition to the position assigned to the Scheduled Castes by the Viceroy, Mr. Gandhi forgot that if the Scheduled Castes are divided into many wastes and no single caste could represent them all, the case of the Muslims and the Indian Christians is in no way different. The Muslims are divided into three groups: (1) Sunnis; (2) Shias and (8) Momins each of which consists: of many castes who interdine but do not intermarry. Indian Christians are divided into (1) Catholics, and (2) Protestants. Catholics are again subdivided into (1) Caste Christians and (2) Non-caste Christians. Both Catholics and Protestants have castes which do not intermarry and caste Christians and Non-caste Christians do not even interline or go to the same church. This shows that Mr. Gandhi not withstanding his being a party to the Poona Pact is determined not to allow the Scheduled Castes being given the status of a separate element and that he is prepared to adopt any argument however desperate to justify his attitude of opposition.

In short Mr. Gandhi is still on the war path so far as the Untouchables are concerned. He may start the trouble over again. The time to trust him has not arrived. The Untouchables must still hold that the best way to safeguard themselves is to say 'Beware of Mr. Gandhi.'

HINDU OPPOSITION

The demands set forth in those resolutions fall into three categories (1) Political, (2) Educational and (3) Economic and Social.

Taking the political demands first it is obvious that they ask for three safeguards-

(1) That the Legislature shall not be merely representative of the people but it shall be representative separately of both categories Hindus as well as Untouchables.

(2) That the Executive shall not be merely responsible to the Legislature, which means to the Hindus, but shall also be responsible both to the Hindus as well *as* to the Untouchables.

(3) That the administration shall not be merely efficient but shall also be worthy of trust by all sections of the people and also of the Untouchables and shall contain sufficient number of representatives of the Untouchables holding key positions so that the Untouchables may have confidence in it.

These Political demands of the Untouchables have been the subject matter of great controversy between the Untouchables and the Hindus. Mr. Gandhi, the friend of the Untouchables, preferred to fast unto death rather than consent to them and although he yielded he is not reconciled to the justice underlying these demands. It will be well if I set out at this stage what the Hindu or the Congress Scheme of representative Government is. It is as follows:

(1) The Legislature to be elected by Constituencies which are to be purely territorial.

(2) The Executive to be drawn solely from the Majority party in the Legislature.

(3) The Administration to be run by a public service based entirely upon considerations of efficiency.

The Hindus of the Congress describe their own pet scheme as a National Scheme and call the scheme put forth by the Untouchables as the Communal Scheme. As I will show, there is no substance in this distinction. It is a case of damning what you do not like by the easy method of giving it a bad and a repelling name. Such tactics can't give strength to a case which is inherently weak. To expose its weakness let me examine the merits of the so called National Scheme. Before proceeding it might be desirable to note the points of agreement and the points of difference between the two. Both have the same object, inasmuch as both stand for a representative Legislature. The point of difference lies in the method of devising a scheme which will make the Legislature a truly representative Legislature. The so-called national, scheme insists upon the territorial constituency as being both proper and sufficient for producing a representative Legislature in India. What is called the Communal Scheme denies that a territorial constitution can produce a truly representative legislature in India in view of the peculiar social structure of the Indian Society as it exists today. The issue can a purely territorial constituency produce a really representative legislature in India. It is round this issue that the controversy has centred.

The so-called National Scheme of the Hindus generally appeals to the Westerner and he prefers it to the so-called Communal Scheme. This is largely because the Westerner knows and is accustomed only to the system of territorial constituency. But there can be no doubt that this so called National Scheme is on merits quite unsound and on motives worse than communal.

That it is unsound will be quite obvious to any One who will stop to examine the assumptions which are involved in the alleged efficacy and sufficiency of the territorial constituency. What are these assumptions? To mention only those which are most important,

(1) It assumes that the majority of voters in a constituency represents the will of the constituency as a whole.

(2) That it is enough to take stock of the general will of the constituency as expressed by the majority and that the will of any particular section however much it may be in conflict with the will of the majority may be ignored without remorse and without being guilty of any inequity.

(3) That the representative who is elected by the voters will represent the wishes and interests of the voters and that there is not the danger of the representative allowing the interest of his class to dominate and override the interests and wishes of the voter who elects him.

Every one of these assumptions is a false assumption unjustified by any theory and, unsupported by experience. The history of Parliamentary Government furnishes abundant proof in support of this assertion and even the history of England tells the same tale. It is wrong to suppose that the majority in all circumstances can be trusted to represent the will of all sections of people in the constituency. As a matter of fact it can never do so to any satisfactory degree. If at all, it can only give a very pale reflection of the general will and even that capacity for pale reflection must depend upon how numerous and varied are the interests which are consciously-shared by the different sections of the constituency and how full and free is the interplay between than.

It is obvious that where, as in India, there are no interest which are shared, where there is no full and free interplay and where there are no common cycles of participation for the different sections, one section large or small cannot represent the will of the other. The will of the majority is the will of the minority and nothing more, and no amount of logical ingenuity can alter the fact and to give effect to it is to allow full play to the tyranny of the Majority.

Again it is wrong to suppose that the representative elected to the Legislature will represent the wishes of the voters who elect him and forget or subordinate the interests of the class to which he belongs. The case of the representative is a case of divided loyalties. He is confronted with two-rather with three-conflicting duties: (1) a duty to himself, (2) a duty to the class to which he belongs, and (3) a duty to the voters who have elected him. Omitting (he first from our consideration it is common experience that the representative prefers the interests of his class to that of his voters. And why should any one expect him to act otherwise? It is in the nature of things that a man's self should be nearer to him than his constituency. There is a homely saying that man's skin sits closer to him than his shirt. To the members of the Legislature it is true more often than not that his class is his skin and the constituency is a shut which it is unnecessary to say is one degree removed than the skin.

The Hindu therefore in relying upon the territorial constituency is seeking-to base the political structure of India upon foundations which all political architects have declared to be unsound. The territorial constituency has long since been regarded even in European countries as a discredited piece of political mechanism. In great many European countries the representative system based on territorial constituency has been wound up and replaced by other systems of Government largely because the territorial system of representation produced neither good Government nor efficient Government In other countries where representative institutions have survived there is an acute discontent with the result produced by the system of territorial constituencies. The proposals for occupational and functional representation, the proposals for referendum and recall all furnish proof, if proof is really wanted, that there is a great body of enlightened and intelligent opinion which is definitely against the system of territorial constituency.

In these circumstances the question as to why the Hindu insists upon a political mechanism which is discredited everywhere excites a certain amount of curiosity. The reason he gives is that it is the only mechanism which is consistent with nationalism. I am not convinced that this is the real explanation. The real explanation to my mind is very different. The Hindu prefers the territorial constituency because he knows that it will enable him to collect and concentrate all political power in the hands of the Hindus, and who can deny that his calculation is incorrect? In a purely territorial constituency the contest, the Hindu knows, will be between a huge majority of Hindu voters and a small minority of Untouchable voters.

Given this fact the Hindu majority—if it is a purely territorial constituency-is bound to win in all constituencies. But the Hindus besides relying upon their majority can also rely upon other factors which cannot but work to strengthen that majority. Those factors have their origin in the peculiar nature of the Hindu Society. The Hindu Social system which places communities one above the other is a factor which is bound to have its effect on the result of voting. By the Hindu Social system the Communities are placed in an ascending scale of reverence and a descending scale of contempt. It needs no prophet to predict what effect these social attitudes will have cm voting. No Caste Hindu will cast a vote in favour of an Untouchable candidate, for to him he is too contemptible a person to go to the Legislature. On the other hand there will be found many voters among the Untouchables who would willingly cast their votes for a Hindu candidate in preference to an Untouchable candidate. That is because he is taught to revere the former more than himself or his Untouchable kinsmen. I am not mentioning the other means which are often resorted to for catching votes of the poor, illiterate, unconscious, unorganised body of voters which the Untouchables are.

A combination of all these circumstances is bound to work in the direction of augmenting the representation of the Hindus- Under a system of purely territorial constituencies it is quite certain the Hindus will have assured to them a majority. They can draw for their majority upon themselves as well as upon the Untouchables. It is equally certain that the Untouchables will lose all seats. They must; firstly because they are a minority, and secondly became the Hindus can successfully exploit the weaknesses of the Untouchables which makes them offer their votes to the Hindus as one offers burnt meat to his gods.

Understood in the light of these forces which are sure to make the territorial constituency, profitable to the Hindus by enabling them to loot the political power which the Untouchable would become possessed of if the Communal Scheme came into operation, there can be no doubt that the National Scheme is from the result side, if not from the motive side, worse than the Communal Scheme.

7

GAUTAMA BUDDHA AND DR. BHIMRAO AMBEDKAR

INTRODUCTION

Buddha was the first religious leader, who expounded peace and equality in the history of man. Five precepts (Panchsheeel) of Buddha's life are principles of building world peace the precepts Panchsheel based on Buddha's life would help to build world peace and harmony among the Nations. Our humanity is cultivated through our emotions. Each day we should look not only to be moved by others, But also to move them through kindness, patience and caring. Said Venerable Master Hsing Yun: It is my hope and prayer that we will always live a happy, joyful, peaceful life based on non-violence, truth, equality, love and compassion, this great message of Buddha is relevant today. The second great religion that originated in India is Buddhism. Ironically though Buddhism flourished overseas; in the land of its birth it was till recently nonexistent. It received a lease of life after independence, when Dr. B.R. Ambedkar decided to embrace Buddhism. A significant section of the scheduled castes followed Dr. Ambedkar and they today constitute an overwhelming portion of the adherents of Buddhism in India today. But they do not form part of the two traditional sects of Buddhism *viz.*, (Mahanayana and Hinayana) and are generally termed as Neo-Buddhists (Nava-Baudha). The history of Buddhism in India starts with that of its founder Gautama Buddha who lived in the 6th century BC.

Buddha was born in the Shakya clan that belonged to the warrior (Kshatriya) caste. His father was Shudhodana and his mother Maya. Before Buddha was born his mother had a dream in which a white elephant descended from heaven and entered her womb. Buddha was said to have been born in a grove named Lumbini near the ancient town of Kapilavastu. At birth the name given to him was Gautama, probably after the more ancient Vedic seer to whom some of the hymns in the Rig Veda are ascribed. Buddha was also known as Siddhartha which means 'he whose aim is accomplished'

The latter name seems to be a title given to him by his disciples although varying opinions are held on this issue. At his birth, a sage is said to have told King Shudhodana that Gautama would grow up to be a powerful king. But to become a king he should be kept away from the sorrows of life. And if perchance he happened to see any of the sorrows of life he would become an universal teacher. Keen as King Shudhodhana was to see Gautama to be a successful ruler, he built up special palace for Gautama from where he could set his eyes on none of the world's sufferings.

Even when the prince Gautama went out for stroll or ride, all unpleasant objects were removed so as to prevent Gautama's mind from being disturbed. But the prophesy of Gautama becoming an universal teacher was destined to be fulfilled. One day through some lapse, Gautama managed to slip out unnoticed from the palace. Riding through the streets of the city he saw for the first time in his life, a lame person, a sick person, a dead body and an ascetic.

These sights made a deep impact on his tender teenaged mind and he set thinking upon the cause of sufferings and sorrow. Consequently, Gautama began neglecting the affairs of the State which his father had assigned to him. Alarmed at his son's strange behaviour, King Shudhodana, to get his son off this brooding decided to marry him to a princess Yashodhara. Some times after marriage a son was born to them who was named Rahula.

But married life could not distract Gautama from his life's mission for long. When his patience was at the end of its tether, Gautama decided to forsake family life and one day he slipped out of his palace along with his servant Chandaka. After moving out of the city, Gautama cut off his hair removed his royal ornaments and jewels, his rich garments and sandals and gave them to Chandaka and bid him to return to the palace with the news of his (Gautama's) departure.

Gautama becomes the Buddha—the Enlightened One: Thus Gautama set out on his quest for the cause of sufferings (Klesha). He undertook severe austerities by fasting continuously. In this he was accompanied by five disciples. But his frail and pampered body could not stand up to this self-inflicted punishment and one day he fainted. Realizing that this was not the way to arrive at the truth, he gave up the austerities. Horrified at their Master's apostasy the five disciples left him. But undaunted, Gautama continued his quest for the cause of sufferings.

He seated himself under a fig tree (Mahabodhi tree) and decided not get up unless he found answers to his questions. His enlightenment is said to have come suddenly and was exceedingly simple—*viz.*, that all pain is caused—by desire, and therefore peace comes when one ceases to crave for anything. This thought was new at that age and it struck him with blinding force, and not only influenced his future life but left a lasting imprint on Buddhist philosophy. Freedom from all desires was said to release a person from the cycle of rebirth and lead to his salvation (Nirvana).

After this revelation Gautama started preaching to people and for this he travelled from place to place. He is said to have delivered his first sermon at a deer park (Isipatana) setting in motion, the wheel of law (Dharma-chakra or Dhammachakra in Pali).

As his teachings impressed people his following grew. Among his early converts were Sariputta, Mogallana and Ananda. He even received the patronage of rich traders like Anathapindika (*i.e.* feeder of poor) and powerful kings of the age like Ajatashatru of Magadh. After the revelation (Bodhi), Gautama came to be known as Buddha or Gautama Buddha. He was also known as Shakyamuni (Sage of the Shakyas). The tree under which he attained enlightenment is known as the Bodhi or Mahabodhi tree. But though he received an impressive following Buddha never claimed Divine status. Very few miracles are attributed to him.

"Miracles" by the Buddha: On one occasion a grieving lady carried her dead child to Buddha and asked him to revive it. This was a perfect setting for a miracle to be woven into religious folklore, but Buddhist records state that Buddha calmed the lady and told her that he would require three mustard seeds to revive her child. But the mustard seeds should be from a family where so far no one has ever died. To fulfil this seemingly simple request the lady went from house to house only to be told that sometime or the other, someone had died in every family. Gradually, the truth dawned upon the grieving lady and going to a cemetery, she laid down her child's body and taking its little hand in hers, she said "Beloved son, I thought that death has overtaken you alone, but no it overtakes all of us". She went back to Buddha and became his disciple.

The Buddhist Sangha and Morality: Buddhism is unique among religions in a fundamental sense. It does not advocate invocation of any God. Salvation can be attained by controlling one's desire; as desire is the cause of suffering.

The original Buddhism had neither God nor Devil. The emphasis was not on prayer but on controlling one's mind. In this sense it was more a worldly philosophy rather than a religion. But with the passage of time it acquired the nature of a religion complete with dogmas and rituals. Buddha's life-story is an eventful one. The most potent institution that Buddha established during his lifetime was the Sangha (monastic order) into which men were admitted irrespective of their caste. The members of the Sangha who were known as Bhikkus (beggars) had to lead a rigorous life devoid of all desires.

Their daily needs were limited to those necessary for physical survival. Their only possessions were a begging bowl, yellow coloured loin cloth, a walking stick if necessary and a pair of sandals for the more delicate. They were to sustain themselves by the alms they received but were forbidden from expressly begging for alms. Alms were to be accepted if given willingly and if not the Bhikkus were to move on to the next house. Thus came into being a clergy, but which unlike its Hindu counterpart was not based on caste and which was oriented towards missionary activities rather on the performance and upholding of rituals.

The break of Buddhism from other forms of worship that constituted Hinduism was almost complete in the lifetime of Buddha. This took the form of non-recognition of any personified Gods, spirits or the devil, and the near absence of rituals, repudiation of the caste system and the intense missionary activity of the monks which included rendering social service with the aim of alleviation of human suffering. Another significant aspect was that in the early stages all followers of Buddha were enrolled as members of the Sangha hence it was completely a missionary religion.

From its inception Buddhism received royal patronage. In the lifetime of Buddha Ajatashatru the king of north India's most powerful kingdom Magadh (in present-day Bihar) patronised Buddhism during Buddha's lifetime, and a few years after Buddha attained Nirvana (Salvation), the first religious council of the Buddhists was held at the town Rajagriha, which was the capital of Magadh from where Ajatashatru ruled. Councils such as this one were occasions for formulation and revision of the Buddhist religious code which was supposed to be adhered to by all followers. Thus it kept a check on the emergence of sub-sects- a tendency which is a hallmark of Hinduism.

The second such council was held at Vaishali also in Magadh, about a hundred years after the first council *i.e.* in the 5th century BC.

Relations Between Buddhism and Hinduism: Buddhism continued to grow steadily in the first few centuries after its birth. The reasons were its universal appeal, humane outlook, emphasis on missionary and social work and finally its peaceable methods that limited confrontation with the established local religions to a philosophical level.

Thus even kings who patronised Hinduism did not feel it necessary to make a distinction between Hinduism and Buddhism in policy matters. Buddhism normally returned the sympathy of the ruling power by giving it a moral legitimacy amongst the lay people. And although Brahmin orthodoxy did grudge the inroads made into itself by the new faith there hardly ever was there active confrontation between the two faiths.

On the contrary there was a exchange of beliefs and attitudes between Hinduism and Buddhism. The Hindu insistence of vegetarianism and non-violence (Ahimsa) are borrowed from Buddhism (and Jainism). Hinduism in turn tried to absorb Buddhism within itself by making Buddha one of the incarnations of Vishnu.

Major Royal Patrons—Samrat Ashoka, Maurya, Kanishka, Harsha Vardhana: The growth of Buddhism received a tremendous boost in the 3rd century BC. when Samrat Ashoka Maurya whose empire covered nearly the whole of India (including present-day Pakistan and Afghanistan) was converted to Buddhism.

Samrat Ashoka elevated Buddhism to the level of a state religion and sent missionaries not only to all parts of India but also to Sri Lanka, West Asia, Central Asia and China. In his days Buddhism is said to have spread in varying degrees up to Egypt and Southwestern Russia. Since the days of emperor Ashoka, Buddhist missionaries built majestic monasteries known as Viharas, Stupas and Chaityas.

The simple ascetic character of Buddhism had received its first dent under the pampering effect of royal patronage. The religion continued to grow nevertheless. During the reign of

Ashoka the third Religious Council was held at Pataliputra which was the capital of Ashoka's vast empire.

But that Ashoka was not inimical to Hinduism is evident from one of the titles that he took *viz.* Deva-naam-priya (Beloved of the Gods).

After the fall of the Maurya empire, Buddhism did not receive official patronage on a comparable scale for a long time. During the period after the Maurya empire, India was beset with invasions from the Indo-Greeks, Kushanas, Parthians, etc. But most of these invaders acculturized themselves in a few years after their coming and many of their kings embraced either Buddhism or Hinduism. Prominent among them were, Menander (Milinda) who was an Indo-Greek and to whom is ascribed the Buddhist treatise called Milinda-Panho (Questions of Menander) in which the king, posed certain questions to which answers were given by a Buddhist Sage called Nagasena.

The next major royal patron of Buddhism was Kushana who was a Mongol king who ruled north India, Pakistan and Afghanistan in the 1st century BC. In his reign) the fourth religious council was held at Jalandhara (Modern Jullundar in Indian Punjab). Now Buddhism had spread far and wide and had received royal patronage in varying degrees almost continuously from one king or another since Ashoka.

Split into Two Sects—Mahayana (Greater Vehicle) and Hinayana (Lesser Vehicle): By the time the fourth religious council was held, the religion had vertically split up into two schools. One school had elevated Buddha to the status of a God and introduced worship of the Buddha's image (idol), it also evolved elaborate rituals which were derived largely from Hinduism, and gave up the rigorous ascetic life in monasteries, discarded Pall and accepted Sanskrit as the literary medium.

These changes had far-reaching effects in narrowing the breach between Buddhism and Hinduism but at the cost of departing from the essence of the way of life that Buddha established. This school was called the Mahayana (Greater

Vehicle) school or the northern school of Buddhism. On the other hand the Hinayana (Lesser Vehicle) school stuck to the original character of Buddhism with its emphasis on rigorous and simple living although idol worship gradually made its way into Hinayana also. This school is also known as Theravada (from Staieryavada *i.e.* principle of stability) is mainly prevalent in Sri Lanka, Burma and Thailand.

Despite the split, Buddhism continued to grow steadily up to the reign of the Guptas.

Since the reign of the Gupta kings (3rd and 4th centuries C.E.) the growth of Buddhism came to a standstill and gradually the decline set in. The reasons for this decline could be many but the principal one was to be the absence of royal patronage since the Gupta period, although there was no persecution either.

The last known royal patron of Buddhism was Harsh Vardhana who ruled over a large part of northern India around the 7th century C.E. Harsha who was an ardent worshipper of the Hindu deity—Shiva, did not embrace Buddhism, but he extended many favours to the religion. During his reign the fifth religious council was held at Prayaga (Allahabad).

No significant event took place thereafter in the history of Buddhism. But it is certain that upto the beginning of the Gupta period the religion was on its ascendance and its following in India was significant. From the Gupta period Hinduism seems to have undergone a revival, partly under the patronage of the Gupta kings. Buddhism then onwards was definitely on the decline. The intellectual onslaught of Brahmanic philosophers like Adi Shankaracharya seems to have had its toll in emasculating what was once a cohesive and vibrant way of life. Whatever the reasons, it is certain that the following of Buddhism declined sharply during and after the Gupta period.

It survived nominally as an intellectual tradition kept alive by the select monks who controlled the monastic universities like the one at Nalanda. These universities were highly respected as seats of learning and attracted students from abroad. Fa Hien, Huien Tsiang and I-Tsing who came from China were said to have studied at Nalanda and other centres of Buddhist learning. But from the 5th century Onwards, Buddhism declined as the religion of the masses. Its following seems to have been absorbed into Hinduism, although this could have also been the result not of formal conversion but of a gradual relapse of the Buddhist laity into the parent religion. The portrayal of Buddha as an incarnation of the Hindu deity Vishnu, and the absorption of many Hindu attitudes by Mahayana Buddhism, along with the absence of royal patronage to Buddhism (and the extension of this patronage to Hinduism during Gupta times) must have contributed to this effect. Whatever Buddhists that remained constituted an elite who inhabited the Monasteries and rarely ventured out of them. Missionary activity was nearly absent.

Buddhism Resurrected in India in the 20th Century: In the mid 20th Century, Dr. B.R. Ambedkar, who was one of the architects of India's Constitution, gave Buddhism a fresh lease of life by embracing it a few years after India achieved independence. A significant number of members of those castes who were denied equal rights in the Hindu caste hierarchy also embraced Buddhism. Today an overwhelming proportion of Buddhists in India are these recent converts who term themselves as Nava-Baudha or Neo-Buddhists. A comparatively recent event of significance was the 6th religious council held at Rangoon in 1954 which came 1300 years after the 5th council held at, Prayaga in 643 C.E. in the reign of the last major pan-Indian emperor—Harsha Vardhana. The Rangoon council was also the first one to be held outside India.

Buddhism and Hinduism—Umbilical Marks: In the course of its eventful history Buddhism which began as a departure from the ritualism of the Hindu religion gradually adapted and absorbed many Hindu ideas and practices to the point that at times, the lines of distinction between the two religions (the parent and the offspring) were blurred. The objective of Nirvana towards which every Buddhist is supposed to strive is undoubtedly an adaptation of the Hindu concept of

Moksha. The difference is that for the attainment of Moksha righteous behaviour and the conformation of duties as assigned by the caste into which a person has been born is necessary, while for the attainment of Nirvana a person has to be free of all desires.

But the essence of both concepts is the release from the cycle of rebirth. The daily of life of the Buddhist Bhikkus (missionary ascetics) was evidently inspired by the concept and practice of Sanyasa which was the last phase of life a Hindu during which he was supposed to be free of all desires and to roam from place to place in search of spiritual enlightenment while spreading the gospel of rightousness among the people. The yellow coloured robes that the Buddhist Bhikkus donned were borrowed from the Saffron robes of the Hindu ascetic. Although as for the Buddhists the yellow colour was chosen to represent an autumn leaf which was once green but has inevitably turned yellow in conformation with the law that everything born has to decay and pass away.

Among the auxiliary Hindu practices which found their way into Buddhism, idol worship and the use of Sanskrit as the liturgical and scripfural language. The Buddhist conception of Buddha as a God and that in a later period after five thousand years when righteousness suffer an eclipse the Buddha will reappear on the earth. This Buddha who will be known as Maiterya will restore the rule of dhamma (law and religion). This idea implies belief in incarnations and re-incarnations on lines parallel to the Hindu concept of Kalki who, we are told, is to be the future incarnation of Lord Vishnu.

But all said and done though Buddhism precariously came close to Hinduism it maintained its distinct entity unlike the Jaina religion whose proximity to Hinduism nearly made it a part of Hinduism. In its appeal Buddhism was not, like its parent religion Hinduism, restricted to India and Indians but spread far and wide.

Thus in Buddhism, India gave birth to a major international religion, while the Hindus continued their way. Buddhism was the world's first missionary religion and won its triumphs through missionary activity. The ancient Buddhist monks who carried the Master's message of peace, love and universal brotherhood were pioneers in such a mission in Human history.

Buddhism is the only trans-national religion which has never preached malice against other faiths, nor have its followers ever indulged in a holy war against those of another faith. Buddhism has won its way by persuasion and never by the sword, nor has it ever used its position or power to compel conformity to its precepts.

And whatever its defects, it has unquestionably done much to benefit the human race by introducing and perpetuating a higher standard of conduct in life. One is inclined to bow before the Buddha, not in homage to a deity but in recognition to a superior craftsman in the art of living.

NAVAYANA BUDDHISM OF AMBEDKAR AND HIS FOLLOWERS

Ambedkar wrote The Buddha and His Dhamma with the intent of creating a single text for new Buddhists to read and follow. His introduction outlines four ways in which previous understandings of Buddhist doctrine are lacking: The Buddha could not have had his first great realization simply because he encountered an old man, a sick man, and a dying man. It is unreasonable and therefore false to assume that the Buddha did not have previous knowledge of something so common. The Four Noble truths "make the gospel of the Buddha a gospel of pessimism." If life is composed entirely of suffering then there is no incentive for change.

The doctrines of no-soul, karma, and rebirth are incongruous. It is illogical to believe that there can be karma and rebirth without a soul. The monk's purpose has not been presented clearly. Is he supposed to be a "perfect man" or a "social servant"? As these rather sweeping critiques of Buddhism suggest, Ambedkar was comfortable in the role of consciously restructuring his chosen religion to meet the needs of the Dalit community he spoke for. Several scholars have remarked upon and analysed this aspect of this article begins with an overview of Navayana Buddhism from two perspectives, that of Ambedkar himself, based on his "Buddhist gospel".

The Buddha and His Dhamma, and that of practioners in Maharashtra, based available academic scholarship. In the case of Ambedkar's understanding of Buddhism, I will focus mostly on the changes he made to more traditional presentations of Buddhism. In the case of Maharashtran practitioners, some broad conclusions can be drawn about their relationship to this relatively new religion. The centrality of the figure of Ambedkar in Navayana Buddhism, as well as Navayana Buddhist's lack of conformity with Ambedkar's understanding of Buddhist principles as articulated in The Buddha and His Dhamma, will guide me in my conclusions about the ways outside observers might want to move forward in the study of this relatively new religion.

Navayana Buddhism: For example, Adele Fiske and Christoph Emmrich undertook a detailed analysis of Ambedkar's use of the traditional Buddhists texts in Pali in writing *The Buddha and His Dhamma*. Fiske and Emmrich examined Ambedkar's references in the original version of *The Buddha and His Dhamma* and describe patterns of alteration from the presentation of Buddhism in the Pali canon that they characterize as omission, change in emphasis and changed meaning through interpolation or interpretation. Ambedkar made to traditional presentations of the Buddha's teachings and the way in which these changes might support Dalit activism. Ambedkar's first major reinterpretation involves the Buddha's reununciation of worldly life. Whereas traditional biographies of the Buddha emphasize the empathy the young prince felt when he first encountered human sufferring, Ambedkar highlights the strength of the Buddha's social conscience during a conflict over water rights.

According to Ambedkar, the Buddha advocated a rational and peaceful resolution of an inter-tribe water conflict but was unable to gain the necessary political leverage because he lacked majority vote. He then went into exile and became a renunciant because it was the only way to prevent his tribe from going to war with their neighbors. Ambedkar omits any mention of old age, sickness, and death (the forms of suffering the Buddha is usually understood to have encountered). In this way the Buddha's renunciation is motivated more by political exigencies rather than a desire to find the ultimate truth, and he becomes a figure not unlike a minority politician in contemporary India. The discussion of water rights was also a familiar topic after the Mahad Satyagraha. These changes, though unorthodox, create a character for the Buddha that might be easily understood by oppressed communities, specifically Dalits.

The Four Noble Truths: Ambedkar interprets the Four Noble truths similarly. "The centre of his Dhamma is man and the relation of man to man in his life on earth. This [the Buddha] said was his first postulate. His second postulate was that men are living in sorrow, in misery and poverty. The world is full of suffering and how to remove this suffering from the world is the only purpose of Dhamma. Nothing else is Dhamma. The recognition of the existence of suffering and to show the way to remove suffering is the foundation and basis of his Dhamma...A religion which fails to recognise this is no religion at all...The Buddha then told them that according to his Dhamma if every person followed (1) the Path of Purity; (2) the Path of Righteousness; and (3) the Path of virtue, it would bring about the end of all suffering." Ambedkar makes several obvious changes to early Buddhist doctrine. The first Noble Truth that life is suffering becomes the "second postulate," and the most important characteristic of Buddhism becomes its concern for human relationships. The second Noble Truth, that suffering arises from mental craving, is also described in social terms as "sorrow, misery and poverty." In turn he refers to the third Noble Truth regarding the cessation of suffering as the "removal of suffering." Christopher Queen's detailed analysis of Ambedkar's presentation of the Four Noble Truths reveals still more ways in which they have been altered to create a message of social activism. Queen notes that as the Buddha's teachings continue it becomes clear that the Path of Purity is the Five Precepts, the Path of Righteousness is the Eightfold Path, and the Path of Virture is the Ten Paramitas, or perfections.

Buddhism and the Caste System: These changes speak specifically to Dalits in a number of ways. First, there is a distinct element of anti-Brahmanism in Ambedkar's rendering of the Four Noble Truths. "Nothing else is *Dhamma,*" he states, and "a religion which fails to recognize this is no religion at all." Although Ambedkar does not criticize other religions in this section—as he does in other chapters of the book—this and other statements bear close resemblance to his earlier attack on Hinduism. Here, Ambedkar again legitimizes the use of Buddhism to oppose traditions that are unsatisfactory. Second, as Queen notes, Ambedkar seems to believe that the traditional presentation of suffering—which places the "blame" on the carvings of each individual—would alienate Buddhism from the socially and politically oppressed.

Thus suffering is described in transitory, but more graphic, terms as "sorrow", "misery", and "poverty." These largely social conditions are remedied quite differently from the traditional Buddhist understanding of suffering as an intricate network of mental carvings. This change also speaks of the fact that the traditional focus on craving might have lent itself to manipulation by people in power, who could advocate renunciation instead of response to the materially based claims of the dispossessed. Third, by placing the Four Noble Truths, the Eightfold Path, and the Ten Perfections in a social context he provides religious justification for peoples' social movements. Lastly, and perhaps most importantly, his definition of nirvana is not only easily understandable but also theoretically attainable within a single lifetime.

Concept of Rebirth and the Role of the Monk: Ambedkar's explanation of *karma* and rebirth further legitimizes both the source and the goal of social action. He defends the concept of rebirth but changes the concept of the soul. Each time a person is reborn his or her soul is divided and recombined with parts of many other peoples' souls. There is thus no single soul that is reborn over and over again. In this way Ambedkar establishes that there is no inheritance of traits from one lifetime to the next—a direct rebuttal to the widespread views of caste. This in turn negates the idea that current social injustices are a result of past misdeeds and assures Dalit converts that their new framework does not contain the possibility for religiously sanctioned hierarchy. He also explains that *karma* works only within one lifetime and cannot affect future lives.

A this-worldly emphasis on *karma* gives added significance to societal changes, as each life is now a unique and unrepeatable opportunity for change and growth. Whereas traditional conceptions of *karma* and rebirth render material changes insignificant on a cosmological scale, Ambedkar's reinterpretation implies that such changes actually have ultimate importance. In this way oppressed peoplés are vindicated in their sense of social outrage and are informed once again of the importance of political or social struggle. Ambedkar's reinterpretation of the role of the monk provides a final illustration that Buddhism takes a pro-active stance towards radical change. Monks should not be content merely to serve society—they are instead the active participants and creators of history.

He writes that the *bhikkhu*'s duties are to proselytize for Buddhism and serve the laity. The *bhikkhu* is commanded specifically to "fight to spread *Dhamma*." "We wage war, O disciples, therefore we are called warriors." Ambedkar's Buddha tells his disciples, "Where virtue is in danger do not avoid fighting, do not be mealy-mouthed." Monks are not hermetic ascetics who are focused on the attainment of otherworldly states. Rather they constitute the driving force behind a revolution in mind and body.

Ambedkar's Buddhism in Practice: The Buddhism one finds in daily life and practice can differ significantly from the principles described in The Buddha and his Dhamma. These differences vary according to location and socioeconomic situation and range from minute reinterpretations to fundamental contradictions. Polarizing concepts include karma, rebirth, dharma, meditation, spirituality, materialism, politics, individuality and social action. Varying social categories include the urban, rural, educated, uneducated, and in many cases, old and young. Thus, on the one hand forms of Navayana Buddhist practice can differ from each other quite significantly in terms of both form and content. This will be illustrated through a simple comparison between certain studies of rural Buddhists and members of the TBMSG. On the other hand, the figure of Ambedkar provides a clear and unifying link between different Buddhist practitioners.

Dalit Buddhist movement: Brahmans and traditional Hindu religiosity in writings such as *Annihilation of Caste*. It should therefore come as no surprise that some rural Buddhists have used their newfound self-confidence to engage in traditionally Hindu forms of worship, as many societal roles that are available for reclamation are also related to Hinduism in some way. The TBMSG is the Indian branch of the international Buddhist organization named the Friends of the Western Buddhist Order (FWBO), founded in London by Sangharakshita in 1967. The FWBO describes its purpose as "return[ing] to the basic principles of Buddhism and find[ing] ways of living them out in the context of the modern West." The FWBO became involved in the Indian Buddhist movement, particularly in Maharashtra, when several members of its order came to India to teach Buddhism in the late 1970's. The TBMSG now has twenty centres located throughout India and runs a network of social services organizations. Fitzgerald goes so far as to assert that Buddhists who are associated with the TBMSG represent the more "spiritual" side of Navayana Buddhism.

Their interpretation of Buddhism is compatible with Ambedkar's because it emphasizes rationality, moral action, and social reform. However, the TBMSG strives for total political nonpartisanship and many of its members view *nirvana* not in materialist terms but as a transcendent state of awareness. Johannes Beltz' study of the TBMSG in Maharashtra provides more information on the type of Buddhism that Fitzgerald seems to be describing. He interviewed several members of the TBMSG at a retreat centre outside Pune, many of who described a Buddhist message of increased spirituality. For example, one practitioner explained: "I was born Buddhist. But in reality, no one can be Buddhist without practising the *dhamma*. To be Buddhist from birth is not possible...I took refuge in the Buddha, the *dhamma*, and the *sangha*. I think that I am on the path of the Buddha. I want to become a *dhammamitra* (a lay leader in the TBMSG). A Buddhist is more than a physical man. He is spiritual...I would like to become 100% Buddhist."

Another told him: "I consider myself Buddhist because I believe not in God but in humanity. I practice Buddhism. I want to positively develop my personality and help others...Through meditation, we augment our state of consciousness to become better men." These statements embody the spirituality and humanism of Buddhism as envisioned by Sangharakshita, the founder of the FWBO. Meditation lies at the centre of individual practice, and only through knowing oneself does one enter a state where he or she truly begins to help others. In addition, these practitioners negate a materialistic understanding of the world. "A Buddhist is more than a physical man," one states, "He is spiritual." This explains why "no one can be Buddhist without practising the *dhamma*": meditation and action are two aspects of the same teaching, and to engage in one without the other is, according to the TBMSG, to ignore the meaning of Buddhism.

Several of the individuals Beltz interviewed also made a distinction between "Dalit Buddhists" who do not practice and "real Buddhists" who do. "The Dalit movement results in bad social conditions for untouchables," one *dhammachari* asserts, "It is for politics. The Dalit movement does not have a positive approach to Buddhism...My personal experience is different. I have developed my personality. I do not call myself Dalit. I consider myself Buddhist." An employee at the University of Pune went so far as to state, "The leaders of the Dalit movement are selfish and corrupt. They are demagogues and want to suppress other currents of Buddhist thought. They waste a lot of energy, time, and money...The TBMSG serenely runs the Buddhist movement and continues the work of Dr. Ambedkar with respect....There is no love between the activists."

Victory over Caste: The disparate practices of some Maharashtran Buddhists offer a cautionary statement for those who may be eager to equate Ambedkar's thinking about Buddhism directly with that of Dalit communities. Ambedkar, Ambedkar's Buddhism, and Buddhist communities are merely the loci for numerous personal and communal interactions that comprise the forms of Navayana Buddhism.

In theory, *The Buddha and His Dhamma* would serve as the philosophical, ideological, and religious template for Buddhists, and ones own experiences with Navayan. "*The Buddha* and His *Dhamma* is a true guide for all the Buddhists. It is the best basis for propagating the *Dhamma*, at least in India". There are plausible models that would explain how a narrative text such as *The Buddha and His Dhamma* could become the "just governance" for society that Ambedkar holds a good religion should be.

However, the above review suggests that *The Buddha and His Dhamma* does not occupy a central place in all Navayana Buddhists' lives. Given the differences in Navayana Buddhist practice, how are we to understand the religion as a whole? The element of Navayana Buddhism that seeks to separate itself from Hinduism provides one link between an uninformed adoption of Buddhism and an almost instantaneous increase in self-esteem and perception of selfworth. Even if converts do not remember each of Ambedkar's twenty-two vows, for example, they are bound to remember the central theme of rejection of Hinduism. Thus many Dalit Buddhists understand what Buddhism *is not* before they focus on what it *is*. The conversion experience can be powerful because the ideological victory over caste is expressed in concrete actions on the part of the convert. At the same time, however, the shift away from the Hindu caste system is highly nuanced. As Burra's study shows, the Mahar rejection of caste does not always entail rejection of Hinduism.

When the rural Buddhist studied align themselves with Buddhism they An Exemplary Prophet Lynch's interest lies in investigating why and how Ambedkar, a Mahar, was so fully accepted and integrated into Jatav culture. To this end, he provides several comparisons between Jatav myths of origin and a new "myth of origin" that was presented by Ambedkar. He views Ambedkar as a Weberian "exemplary prophet" who has now become the "chief hero" of the myth that he himself created. Lynch seems to imply that the entire "Neo-Buddhist myth" is encapsulated by Ambedkar's explanation of the origins of the caste system and the way in which Dalits ended up at its bottom. This would not hold true for other Buddhist communities such as the TBMSG, however. Alternatively, what if the figure of Ambedkar is the defining element of Navayana Buddhism? Even such differing communities as the rural Buddhists examined and the TBMSG share their veneration for him. A public debate between Gopal Guru, a Buddhist and professor at the University of Pune, and *Dhammacari* Lokamitra, a member of the TBMSG, supports this hypothesis. Though these men articulated very different opinions about the relative weight of the "spiritual" versus the "political" aspects of Buddhism, they both returned to Ambedkar for justification of their arguments. Lokamitra wrote, "I am afraid the project Gopal Guru is talking about is not that of Ambedkar but of those who have attempted to use Ambedkar's conversion to Buddhism to serve their own political ends".

Guru offered the following rejoinder: "Lokamitra and his TBMSG are free to sell their package of spiritual Buddhism and synthesise it with adopt a new social and psychological paradigm that can often be characterized foremost by the victory of equality over caste; only secondary is the victory of Buddhist practice over Hindu practice. As another possibility, Owen Lynch has applied an academic understanding of myth to the development of Navayana Buddhism. He uses it to explain the way that Ambedkar became a cultural hero and icon of Buddhism for the Jatavs in Agra, a group that has significant linguistic and cultural differences from the Mahars. He suggests that there is a "Neo-Buddhist" myth that provides motivation and strategy for the community it serves. Anything but not with Ambedkar's Buddhism. Because it does not allow such synthesis." Both judged the other's reasoning as flawed specifically on the grounds that it represents a misinterpretation of Ambedkar's message. As Guru acknowledged, he was bothered not so much by the TBMSG's false Buddhist doctrine as he is by the fact that it has been associated with Ambedkar. Ambedkar's figure fills in the gaps that are left by the explanations of origin and anti-Brahmanism. He is the inspiration, motivation, and justification for the Dalit Buddhist movement. His life illustrates the possibilities of the future, and since his death those possibilities have become the centre of much of contemporary Navayana Buddhism. Ambedkar is in this view both founder and standard-bearer of contemporary Navayana Buddhism.

Evaluation and Conclusions: In 1956 Dr. B.R. Ambedkar led over 50,000 Dalits in a mass conversion to Buddhism. This act was the first of many mass conversions of low cast Hindus to Buddhism. Today estimates range from between three million and ten million Buddhists in India, most of whom are Dalit. For years there was little scholarly material on Buddhism and the Ambedkarite movement, save a few examples such as the pioneering work of the American historian Eleanor Zelliot. Contrast this with a recent conference on Indic Religions in New Delhi held by the International Association of the History of Religions, where there were two entire panels composed of academics prepared to speak of their research on the subject "Dalits and Buddhism." "Navayana", "Dalit", or "Ambedkarite" Buddhism (depending on who is speaking) is also actively discussed by the worldwide "engaged Buddhist" community.

The intellectual discourse surrounding Ambedkar's understanding of Buddhism and those who follow in his foot steps has now grown to the point where it is able to have a fruitful dialogue even within itself. In turn, at this point it may be useful for outside observers of Navayana Buddhism to begin to consider not only *what* Navayana Buddhism is but also *how* and *why* we should examine it.

First, a discussion of Navayana Buddhist texts or canon must include all of Ambedkar's writing, not just *The Buddha and His Dhamma,* as a starting point. As the above examples highlight, Ambedkar's life is usually viewed as the embodiment, rather than the vehicle, of the Buddha's teachings. In theory, Ambedkar's significance leads to the logical conclusion that, just as most Buddhists' veneration of Ambedkar is not limited to the events surrounding his conversion, so too the texts which are understood as contributing to Navayana Buddhism should not be limited to *The Buddha and His Dhamma.* In practice, many Buddhists already impart religious significance to Ambedkar's other political and sociological works. This is readily apparent in D.C. Ahir's commentary on the Round Table Conference, for example, which views Ambedkar's comments as the embodiments of the principle of Right Speech. Clearly this inclusive approach may have its limits. Are we to view Ambedkar's doctoral dissertation at Columbia as religious texts? Likely not. Nor do anyone propose to delineate here between those texts that should be included in a Navayana Buddhist canon and those that should not. Rather this should be understood as an idea to generate discussion and a helpful approach to the study of Ambedkar's Navayana Buddhism as is conceived, that Buddhist practitioners will ultimately be the final arbiters in this matter. Second, where are the studies of urban, often professional, Navayana Buddhists and the corresponding surge in online Navayana Buddhist communities? In New Delhi, for example, one came to know several Buddhists whose meditation practice and highly informed understanding of Ambedkar and Buddhism bears little resemblance to the conversions described in some studies of rural Buddhists. There is a need for scholarship of these thriving Navayana Buddhist communities among those who do research in Marathi and Hindi.

Third, an attempt to describe Navayana Buddhism through appeal to the "essential" elements of Buddhism that may exist in early texts must be considered carefully. Surely there are continuities between traditional understandings of Buddhism and Ambedkar's reinterpretation, but whether or not these constitute some "essential" Buddhism to be passed down from movement to movement is unclear. Furthermore, stressing this aspect of Ambedkar's writing when analysing it in the context of other Buddhist traditions may be overly limiting. This is not to deny the importance of showing that Ambedkar's interpretation is, in many ways, legitimate from the standpoint of the Buddha's teachings. Such a project is a necessary part of religious dialogue and reinterpretation. However, one must not lose sight of the "essential" Navayana when determining its relationship to "essential" Buddhism. In this sense it would be a shame if we fail to capitalize on its most salient characteristic: a confident and rational departure from inherited patterns of thought.

Finally, the study of Navayana Buddhism needs to be as interdisciplinary as possible. Why limit the study of Navayana Buddhism to certain disciplines when Ambedkar himself was unencumbered by the traditional boundaries between political, personal, and spiritual empowerment? The modern Buddhist movement in India may be as fundamentally related to economics and development as it is to politics and religion. Take, for example, Amartya Sen's well-known *Development as Freedom*. Seen in this light, Ambedkar's project might be understood as a project of human development through religious conversion.

Focusing for a moment on the subject of religion and development, two additional suggestions can be made. First, those who wish to study development in India might take the impact of Navayana Buddhism into account. Has conversion had a significant material impact on practitioners' lives and if so, how? Given the fact that Ambedkar's view of religious conversion is integrally tied to his goals of social identity as Dalit and the past and present connotations that are associated with this. Although thus far the body of writing that examines Ambedkar and Navayana Buddhism has been a positive development with respect to Navayana Buddhism, perhaps now is a good time to remind ourselves that we must be careful not to intellectualize.

Navayana Buddhism to the extent that we lose sight of the fact that it is fundamentally a religion by and for the politically and socially oppressed, empowerment for Dalits, it seems like a missed opportunity not to consider this religious movement within the greater scheme of Indian development. This may be true despite the oft-prevailing view of religion as an anathema to progressive societal transformation. Second, the context in which Navayana Buddhist practice takes place must not be forgotten by outside observers.

QUOTATION OF AMBEDKAR

Men are mortal. So are ideas. An idea needs propagation as much as a plant needs watering. Otherwise both will wither and die.

The conception of secular state is derived from the liberal democratic tradition of west. No institution which is maintained wholly out of state funds shall be used for the purpose of religious instruction irrespective of the question whether the religious instruction is given by the state or any other body.

If you ask me, my ideal would be the society based on liberty, equality and fraternity. An ideal society should be mobile and full of channels of conveying a change taking place in one part to other parts.

To idealise the real which more often than not is full of inequities is a very selfish thing to do. It is only when a person finds a personal advantage in things, as they are that he tries to idealise the real. To proceed to make such an ideal real is nothing short of criminal. It means perpetuating inequity on the ground that whatever is settled is settled for all times. Such a view is opposed to all morality. No society with ideal conscience has ever accepted it. On the contrary whatever progress in improving the terms of associated life between individuals and classes has been made in the course of history, is due entirely to the recognition of the ethical doctrine that whatever is wrongly settled is never settled and must be resettled.

A historian ought to be exact, sincere and impartial; free from passion, unbiased by interest, fear, resentment or affection; and faithful to the truth, which is the mother of history the preserver of great actions, the enemy of oblivion, the witness of the past, the director of the future.

In every country the intellectual class is the most influential class. This is the class which can foresee, advise and lead. In no country does the mass of the people live the life for intelligent thought and action. It is largely imitative and follows the intellectual class. There is no exaggeration in saying that the entire destination of the country depends upon its intellectual class. If the intellectual class is honest and independent, it can be trusted to take the initiative and give a proper lead when a crisis arises. It is true that the intellect by itself is no virtue. It is only a means and the use of a means depends upon the ends which an intellectual person pursues. An intellectual man can be a good man but he may easily be a rogue. Similarly an intellectual class may be a band of high-souled persons, ready to help, ready to emancipate erring humanity or it may easily be a gang of crooks or a body of advocates of narrow clique from which it draws its support.

My final words of advice to you are educate, agitate and organize; have faith in yourself. With justice on our side I do not see how we can loose our battle. The battle to me is a matter of joy. The battle is in the fullest sense spiritual. There is nothing material or social in it. For ours is a battle not for wealth or for power. It is battle for freedom. It is the battle of reclamation of human personality.

You must abolish your slavery yourselves. Do not depend for its abolition upon god or a superman. Remember that it is not enough that a people are numerically in the majority. They must be always watchful, strong and self-respecting to attain and maintain success. We must shape our course ourselves and by ourselves.

Untouchability shuts all doors of opportunities for betterment in life for Untouchables. It does not offer an Untouchable any opportunity to move freely in society; it compels him to live in dungeons and seclusion; it prevents him from educating himself and following a profession of his choice.

Untouchability has ruined the Untouchables, the Hindus and ultimately the nation as well. If the depressed classes gained their self-respect and freedom, they would contribute not only to their own progress and prosperity but by their industry intellect and courage would contribute also to the strength and prosperity of the nation.

If the tremendous energy Untouchables are at present required to fritter away in combating the stigma of Untouchability had been saved them, it would have been applied by them to the promotion of education and development of resources of their nation as a whole.

There have been many Mahatmas in India whose sole object was to remove Untouchability and to elevate and absorb the depressed classes, but everyone has failed in their mission. Mahatmas have come, Mahatmas have gone but the Untouchables have remained as Untouchables.

From the point of view of annihilation of caste, the struggle of the saints did not have any effects on society. The value of a man is axiomatic and self-evident; it does not come to him from the gilding of Bhakti. The saints did not struggle to establish this point. On the contrary their struggle had very unhealthy effect on the depressed classes. It provided the Brahmins with an excuse to silence them by telling them that they would be respected if they attained the status of Chokhamela.

It is mischievously propagated by Hindu scriptures that by serving the upper classes the Sudras achieve salvation. Untouchability is another appellation of slavery. No race can be raised by destroying its self-respect. So if you really want to uplift the Untouchables, you must treat them in the social order as free citizens, free to carve out their destiny.

What you have lost others have gained. Your humiliations are a matter of pride with others. You are made to suffer wants, privations and humiliations not because it was preordained by the sins committed in your previous birth, but because of the overpowering tyranny and treachery of those who are above you. You have no lands because others have usurped them; you have no posts because others have monopolised them. Do not believe in fate; believe in your strength.

Learn to live in this world with self-respect. You should always cherish some ambition of doing something in this world. But remember that the age of selflessness has ended. A new epoch is set in. All things are now possible because of your being able to participate in the politics and legislature of your country.

Some people think that religion is not essential to the society. I do not hold this view. I consider the foundations of religion are essential to the society. At the roots of Hindu social system lies a Dharma as prescribed in the Manusmriti. Such being the case I do not think it is possible to abolish the inequality in the Hindu society unless foundations of the Smriti-religion is removed and a better one laid in its place. I however, despair of Hindu society, being able to reconstruct itself on such a better foundation.

My religious conversion is not inspired by any material motive. This is hardly anything I cannot achieve even while remaining an Untouchable. There is no other feeling than that of a spiritual feeling underlying my religious conversion. Hinduism does not appeal to my conscience. My self-respect cannot assimilate Hinduism. In your case change of religion is imperative for worldly as well as spiritual ends. Do not care for the opinion of those who foolishly ridicule the idea of conversion for material ends. Why should you live under the fold of that religion which has deprived you of honour, money, food and shelter?

I tell you, religion is for man and not man for religion. If you want to organise, consolidate and be successful in this world, change this religion. The religion that does not recognise you as a human being, or give you water to drink, or allow you to enter in temples is not worthy to be called a religion. The religion that forbids you to receive education and comes in the way of your material advancement is not worthy of the appellation 'religion'. The religion that does not teach its followers to show humanity in dealing with its co-religionists is nothing but a display of a force. The religion that teaches its followers to suffer the touch of animals but not the touch of human beings is not a religion but a mockery. The religion that compels the ignorant to be ignorant and the poor to be poor is not a religion but a visitation!

The basic idea underlying religion is to create an atmosphere for the spiritual development of the individual. This being the situation, it is clear that you cannot develop your personality at all in Hinduism.

In Hinduism, conscience, reason and independent thinking have no scope for development.

It is your claim to equality which hurts them. They want to maintain the status quo. If you continue to accept your lowly status ungrudgingly, continue to remain dirty, filthy, backward, ignorant, poor and disunited, they will allow you to live in peace. The moment you start to raise your level, the conflict starts. Untouchability is not transitory or temporary feature; it is eternal, it is lasting. Frankly it can be said that the struggle between the Hindus and the Untouchables is a never-ending conflict. It is eternal because the religion which assigns you the lowest status in society is itself divine and eternal according to the belief of the so-called high caste Hindus. No change warranted by change of time and circumstances is possible.

I have never claimed to be a universal leader of suffering humanity. The problem of the untouchables is quite enough for my slender strength. I do not say that other causes are not equally noble. But knowing that life is short, one can only serve one cause and I have never aspired to do more than serve the Untouchables.

Every man must have a philosophy of life, for everyone must have a standard by which to measure his conduct. And philosophy is nothing but a standard by which to measure.

Negatively I reject the Hindu social philosophy propounded in Bhagavad Gita, based as it is on the Triguna of Sankhya Philosophy which in my judgement is a cruel perversion of the philosophy of Kapila, and which had made the caste system of graded inequality the law of Hindu social life.

Positively, my social philosophy may be said to be enshrined in three words: liberty, equality and fraternity. Let no one however say that I have borrowed my philosophy from the French Revolution. I have not. My philosophy has its roots in religion and not in political science. I have derived them from the teachings of my master, the Buddha.

Indians today are governed by two different ideologies. Their political ideal set in the preamble of the Constitution affirms a life of liberty, equality and fraternity. Their social ideal embodied in their religion denies them.

Unlike a drop of water which loses its identity when it joins the ocean, man does not lose his being in the society in which he lives. Man's life is independent. He is born not for the development of the society alone, but for the development of his self.

Freedom of mind is the real freedom. A person whose mind is not free though he may not be in chains, is a slave, not a free man. One whose mind is not free, though he may not be in prison, is a prisoner and not a free man. One whose mind is not free though alive, is no better than dead. Freedom of mind is the proof of one's existence.

What is the proof to judge that the flame of mental freedom is not extinguished in the mind of person? To whom can we say that his mind is free. I call him free who with his conscience awake realises his rights, responsibilities and duties. He who is not a slave of circumstances and is always ready and striving to change them in his flavour, I call him free. One who is not a slave of usage, customs, of meaningless rituals and ceremonies, of superstitions and traditions; whose flame of reason has not been extinguished, I call him a free man. He who has not surrendered his free will and abdicated his intelligence and independent thinking, who does not blindly act on the teachings of others, who does not blindly accept anything without critically analysing and examining its veracity and usefulness, who is always prepared to protect his rights, who is not afraid of ridicule and unjust public criticism, who has a sound conscience and self-respect so as not become a tool in the hands of others, I call him a free man. He who does not lead his life under the direction of others, who sets his own goal of life according to his own reasoning and decides for himself as to how and in what way life should be lead, is a free man. In short, who is a master of his own free will, him alone I call a free man.

Caste cannot be abolished by inter caste dinners or stray instances of inter caste marriages. Caste is a state of mind. It is a disease of mind. The teachings of the Hindu religion are the root cause of this disease. We practice casteism and we observe Untouchability because we are enjoined to do so by the Hindu religion. A bitter thing cannot be made sweet. The taste of anything can be changed. But poison cannot be changed into nectar.

What struck me most was that my community still continues to accept a position of humiliation only because caste Hindus persist in dominating over them. You must rely on your own strength, shake off the notion that you are in any way inferior to any community.

Constitutional morality is not a natural sentiment. It has to be cultivated. We must realise that our people have yet to learn it. Democracy in India is only a top dressing on an Indian soil which is essentially undemocratic.

Majorities are of two sorts: (1) communal majority and (2) political majority. A political majority is changeable in its class composition. A political majority grows. A communal majority is born. The admission to a political majority is open. The door to a communal majority is closed. The politics of political majority are free to all to make and unmake. The politics of communal majority are made by its own members born in it.

The minorities in India have loyally accepted the rule of the majority which is basically a communal majority and not a political majority. It is for the majority to realise its duty not to discriminate against minorities. Whether the minorities will continue or will vanish must depend upon this habit of majority. The moment the majority looses the habit of discriminating against the minority, the minorities can have no ground to exist. They will vanish.

We want our own people, people who will fight tooth and nail for our interest and secure privilege for the underprivileged; people who will undo the wrongs done to our people; people who will voice our grievances fearlessly; people who can think, lead and act; people with principles and character. Such people should be sent to the legislatures. We must send such people to Legislatures who will be slaves to none but remain free to their conscience and get our grievances redressed.

Why does a human body become deceased? The reason is that as long as the human body is not free from suffering, mind cannot be happy. If a man lacks enthusiasm, either his body or mind is in a deceased condition.... Now what saps the enthusiasm in man? If there is no enthusiasm, life becomes drudgery—a mere burden to be dragged. Nothing can be achieved if there is no enthusiasm. The main reason for this lack of enthusiasm on the part of a man is that an individual looses the hope of getting an opportunity to elevate himself. Hopelessness leads to lack of enthusiasm. The mind in such cases becomes deceased.... When is enthusiasm created? When one breaths an atmosphere where one is sure of getting the legitimate reward for one's labour, only then one feels enriched by enthusiasm and inspiration.

The fundamental principle of Buddhism is equality... Buddhism was called the religion of Sudras. There was only one man who raised his voice against separatism and Untouchability and that was Lord Buddha. The teachings of Buddha are eternal, but even then Buddha did not proclaim them to be infallible. The religion of Buddha has the capacity to change according to times, a quality which no other religion can claim to have...Now what is the basis of Buddhism? If you study carefully, you will see that Buddhism is based on reason. There is an element of flexibility inherent in it, which is not found in any other religion.

I am myself a believer in Animas (non-violence). But I make a distinction between Animas and meekness. Meekness is weakness and weakness is voluntarily imposed upon oneself is not a virtue. I am believer in Animas but in the sense defined by the saint Takuma. Takuma has quite rightly said that Animas consisted of two things: (1) love and kindness towards all creatures and (2) destruction of evil doers. The second part of this definition is often lost sight of that the doctrine of Animas becomes so ridiculous.

Religion must mainly be a matter of principles only. It cannot be a matter of rules. The moment it degenerates into rules, it ceases to be a religion, as it kills responsibility which is an essence of the true religious act.

We must begin by acknowledging that there is a complete absence of two things in Indian Society. One of these is equality. On the social plane we have an India based on the principles of graded inequality, which means elevation for some and degradation for others. On the economic plane we have a society in which there are some who have immense wealth as against many who live in abject poverty.

The second thing we are wanting in is the recognition of the principle of fraternity. What does fraternity mean? Fraternity means a sense of common brotherhood of all Indians, all Indians being one people. It is a principle that gives solidarity to social life. It is difficult thing to achieve. It seems to me that there lies a heavy duty to see that democracy does not vanish from the earth as a governing principle of human relationship. If we believe in it, we must both be true and loyal to it. We must not only be staunch in our faith in democracy but we must resolve to see that whatever we do, we do not help the enemies of democracy to uproot the principles of liberty, equality and fraternity. It follows that we must strive along with other democratic countries to maintain the basis of democratic civilization. If democracy lives we are sure to reap the benefit of it. If democracy dies it will be our doom. On that there can be no doubt.

The basis of my politics lies in the proposition that the Untouchables are not a subdivision or subsection of Hindus, and that they are a separate and distinct element in the national life of India. The true function of law consists in repairing the faults in society. Unfortunately ancient societies never dared to assume the function of repairing their own defects; consequently they decayed. This country has seen the conflict between ecclesiastical law and secular law long before Europeans sought to challenge the authority of the Pope. Kautilya's Arthshastra lays down the foundation of secular law. In India unfortunately ecclesiastical law triumphed over secular law. In my opinion this was the one of the greatest disasters in the country. The unprogressive nature of the Hindu society was due to the notion that the law cannot be changed.

Civilization has never been a continuous process. There were states and societies which at one time had been civilised. In the course of time something happened which made these societies stagnant and decayed. This could be illustrated by India's history itself. There could be no doubt that one of the countries which could boast of ancient civilization is India. When the inhabitants of Europe were living under the barbaric conditions, this country had reached the highest peak of civilization, it had parliamentary institutions when the people of Europe were mere nomads.

I measure the progress of a community by the degree of progress which women have achieved.

Justice has always evoked ideas of equality, of proportion of compensation. Equity signifies equality. Rules and regulations, right and righteousness are concerned with equality in value. If all men are equal, then all men are of the same essence, and the common essence entitles them of the same fundamental rights and equal liberty... In short justice is another name of liberty, equality and fraternity.

Anyone who studies working of the system of social economy based on private enterprise and pursuit of personal gain will realise how it undermines, if it does not actually violate the individual rights on which democracy rests. How many have to relinquish their rights in order to gain their living? How many have to subject themselves to be governed by private employers?

I hate injustice, tyranny, pompousness and humbug, and my hatred embraces all those who are guilty of them. I want to tell my critics that I regard my feelings of hatred as a real force. They are only the reflexes of love I bear for the causes I believe in and I am in no way ashamed of it.

Indifferentism is the worst kind of disease that can affect people. Political tyranny is nothing compared to the social tyranny and a reformer who defies society is a more courageous man than a politician who defies Government.

Every man who repeats the dogma of Mill that one country is no fit to rule another country must admit that one class is not fit to rule another class. One cannot have any respect or regard for men who take the position of the reformer and then refuse to see the logical consequences of that position, let alone following them out in action. History shows that where ethics and economics come in conflict, victory is always with economics. Vested interests have never been known to have willingly divested themselves unless there was sufficient force to compel them.

Slavery does not merely mean a legalised form of subjection. It means a state of society in which some men are forced to accept from others the purposes which control their conduct. This condition obtains even where there is no slavery in the legal sense. It is found where as in caste system, some persons are forced to carry on the prescribed callings which are not their choice.

India is a peculiar country and her nationalists and patriots are a peculiar people. A patriot and a nationalist in India is one who sees with open eyes his fellow men treated as being less than man. But his humanity does not rise in protest. He knows that men and women for no cause are denied their rights. But it does not prick his civil sense of helpful action. He finds a whole class of people shut out from public employment. But it does not rouse his sense of justice and fair play. Hundreds of evil practices that injure man and society are perceived by him. But they do not sicken him with disgust. The patriot's one cry is power for him and his class. I am glad I do not belong to that class of patriots. I belong to that class which takes its stand on democracy and which seeks to destroy monopoly in every form. Our aim is to realise in practice our ideal of one man one value in all walks of life—political, economical and social.

There is no nation of Indians in the real sense of the world, it is yet to be created. In believing we are a nation, we are cherishing a great delusion. How can people divided into thousand of castes be a nation? The sooner we realise that we are not yet a nation, in a social and psychological sense of the world, the better for us. It is not enough to be electors only. It is necessary to be lawmakers; otherwise those who can be lawmakers ill be the masters of those who can only be electors.

Walter Bagehot defined democracy as 'Government by discussion'. Abraham Lincoln defined democracy as 'A Government of the people, by the people and for the people'.

My definition of democracy is—A form and a method of Government whereby revolutionary changes in the social life are brought about without bloodshed. That is the real test. It is perhaps the severest test. But when you are judging the quality of the material you must put it to the severest test. Democracy is not merely a form of Government. It is primarily a mode of associated living, of conjoint communicated experience. It is essentially an attitude of respect and reverence towards our fellow men.

A democratic form of Government presupposes a democratic form of a society, The formal framework of democracy is of no value and would indeed be a misfit if there was no social democracy. It may not be necessary for a democratic society to be marked by unity, by community of purpose, by loyalty to public ends and by mutuality of sympathy. But it does unmistakably involve two things. The first is an attitude of mind, and attitude of respect and equality towards their fellows. The second is a social organisation free from rigid social barriers. Democracy is incompatible and inconsistent with isolation and exclusiveness resulting in the distinction between the privileged and the unprivileged. Democracy is not a Form of Government, but a form of social organisation.

What we must do is not to content ourselves with mere political democracy. We must make our political democracy a social democracy as well. Political democracy cannot last unless there is at the base of it, a social democracy. What does social democracy mean? It means a way of life which recognises liberty, equality and fraternity as the principles of life. These principles of liberty, equality and fraternity are not to be treated as separate items. They form a union in the sense that, to divorce one from the other is to defeat the very purpose of democracy. Liberty cannot be divorced from equality, nor can liberty and equality be divorced from fraternity.

Without social union, political unity is difficult to be achieved. If achieved, it would be as precarious as a summer sapling, liable to be uprooted by the gust of wind. With mere political unity, India may be a state. But to be a state is not to be a nation and a state which is not a nation has small prospects of survival in the struggle of existence. This is especially true where nationalism—the most dynamic force of modern times, is seeking everywhere to free itself by the destruction and disruption of all mixed states. The danger to a mixed and composite state, therefore lies not so much in external aggression as in the internal resurgence of nationalities which are fragmented, entrapped, suppressed and held against their will.

The idea of fundamental rights has become a familiar one since their enactment in the American Constitution and in the Constitution framed by the Revolutionary France. The idea of making a gift of fundamental rights to every individual is no doubt very laudable. The question is how to make them effective? The prevalent view is that once the rights are enacted in law then they are safeguarded.

This again is an unwarranted assumption. As experience proves, rights are protected not by law but by social and moral conscience of the society. If social conscience is such that it is prepared to recognise the rights which law proposes to enact, rights will be safe and secure. But if the fundamental rights are opposed by the community, no Law, no Parliament, no Judiciary can guarantee them in the real sense of the world. What is the use of Fundamental rights to the Untouchables in India? As Burke said, there is no method found for punishing the multitude. Law can punish a single solitary recalcitrant criminal. It can never operate against the whole body of people who choose to defy it. Social conscience is the only safeguard of all rights, fundamental or non-fundamental.

Rights are real only if they are accompanied by remedies. It is no use giving rights if the aggrieved person has no legal remedy to which he can resort when his rights are invaded.

Lost rights are never regained by appeals to the conscience of the usurpers, but by relentless struggle.... Goats are used for sacrificial offerings and not lions.

Life should be great rather than long.

For a successful revolution it is not enough that there is discontent. What is required is a profound and thorough conviction of the justice, necessity and importance of political and social rights.

I feel that the constitution is workable, it is flexible and it is strong enough to hold the country together both in peacetime and in wartime. Indeed, if I may say so, if things go wrong under the new Constitution, the reason will not be that we had a bad Constitution. What we will have to say is that Man was vile.

Equality may be a fiction but nonetheless one must accept it as a governing principle. What are we having this liberty for? We are having this liberty in order to reform our social system, which is full of inequality, discrimination and other things, which conflict with our fundamental rights.

Our object in framing the Constitution is rally twofold: (1) To lay down the form of political democracy, and (2) To lay down that our ideal is economic democracy and also to prescribe that every Government whatever is in power shall strive to bring about economic democracy. The directive principles have a great value, for they lay down that our ideal is economic democracy.

If I find the constitution being misused, I shall be the first to burn it. On the 26th January 1950, we are going to enter into a life of contradictions. In politics we will have equality and in social and economic life we will have inequality. In politics we will be recognising the principle of one man one vote and one vote one value. In our social and economic life, we shall by reason of our social and economic structure, continue to deny the principle of one man one value.

How long shall we continue to live this life of contradictions? How long shall we continue to deny equality in our social and economic life? If we continue to deny it for long, we will do so only by putting our political democracy in peril. We must remove this contradiction at the earliest possible moment else those who suffer from inequality will blow up the structure of democracy which this Constituent Assembly has so laboriously built up.

There can be no gain saying that political power in this country has too long been the monopoly of the few, and the many are not beasts of burden but also beasts of prey.

The monopoly has not merely deprived them of their chance of betterment, it has sapped them of what may be called the significance of life. Those downtrodden classes are tired of being governed. They are impatient to govern themselves. This urge of self-realisation in the downtrodden must not be allowed to devolve into class struggle or class war. It would lead to the division of the House.

That would indeed be a day of disaster. For, as has been well-said by Abraham Lincoln: "A house divided against cannot stand very long". Therefore the sooner room is made for realisation of their aspiration, the better for the few, the better for the country, the better for the independence and the better for the continuance of its democratic structure. This can only be done by the establishment of equality and fraternity in all walks of life.

It is disgraceful to live at the cost of one's self-respect. Self-respect is the most vital factor in life. Without it, man is a cipher. To live worthily with self-respect, one has to overcome difficulties. It is out of hard and ceaseless struggle alone that one derives strength, confidence and recognition. Cultivation of mind should be the ultimate aim of human existence.

Sincerity is the sum of all moral qualities.

Man is mortal. Everyone has to die some day or the other. But one must resolve to lay down one's life in enriching the noble ideals of self-respect and in bettering one's human life. We are not slaves. Nothing is more disgraceful for a brave man than to live life devoid of self-respect. Emerson has said that consistency is a virtue of an ass.

No thinking human being can be tied down to a view once expressed in the name of consistency. More important than consistency is responsibility. A responsible person must learn to unlearn what he has learned. A responsible person must have the courage to rethink and change his thoughts. Of course there must be good and sufficient reason for unlearning what he has learned and for recasting his thoughts. There can be no finality in rethinking.

John Dewey said: "Every society gets encumbered with what is trivial, with what is dead wood from the past and what is positively perverse. As a society becomes more enlightened, it realises that it is responsible not to conserve and transmit the whole of its achievement, but only such as makes a better future society." There is nothing fixed, nothing eternal, nothing sanatan; everything is changing, change is the law of life for individuals as well as for society. In a changing society there must be constant revolution of old values.

No civilised society of today presents more survivals of primitive times than does the Indian society. Its religion is essentially primitive and its tribal code, in spite of the advance of time and civilization, operates in all its pristine vigour even today. Indian society still savours of the clan system, even though there are no clans.

An ideal society should be mobile, should be full of channels for conveying a change taking place in one part to other parts. In an ideal society there should be many interests consciously communicated and shared. The strength of a society depends upon the presence of points of contacts, possibilities of interaction between different groups that exist in it. These are what Carlyle calls "Organic filaments", *i.e.* the elastic threads which helps to bring the disintegrating elements together and to reunite them. Heroes and hero-worship is a hard fact in India's political life. I agree that hero-worship is demoralising for the devotee and dangerous to the country. I welcome the criticism so far as it conveys the caution that you must know your man is really great before you start worshipping him.

This unfortunately is not an easy task. For in these days with the Press in hand it is easy to manufacture Great Men. Carlyle used a happy phrase when he described the Great Men of history as so many bank notes. Like bank notes they represent gold.

What we have to see that they are not forged notes. I admit that we ought to be more cautious in our worship of Great Men. For in this country we have arrived at such a stage when alongside the notice boards saying "Beware of pickpockets", we need to have notice boards saying "Beware of Great Men". Even Carlyle who defended the worship of Great Men warned his readers how: "Multitudes of Great Men have figured in history who were false and selfish".

Hero-worship in the sense of expressing our unbound admiration is one thing. To obey the hero is a totally different kind of worship. There is nothing wrong in the former while the latter is no doubt a most pernicious thing. The former is man's respect for which is noble and of which the great men are only an embodiment.

The latter is the serf's fealty to his lord. The former is consistent with respect, but the latter is a sign of debasement. The former does not take away one's intelligence to think and independence to act. The latter makes one perfect fool. The former involves no disaster to the state. The latter is a source of positive danger to it.

In India, 'Bhakti' or what may be called the path of devotion or hero-worship plays a part in politics unequalled in magnitude by the part it plays in the politics of any other of the world. 'Bhakti' in religion may be a road to salvation of the soul. But in politics, 'Bhakti' or hero-worship is a sure road to degradation and to eventual dictatorship.

Who shall rule—wealth or man? Which shall lead—money or intellect? Who shall fill the public stations—educated and patriotic free men or the feudal serf's of the corporate capital? For the president, Indian politics, at any rate the Hindu part of it, instead of being spiritualised has become grossly commercialised, so much so that it has become a byword for corruption.

Many men of culture are refusing to concern themselves in this cesspool. Politics has become a kind of sewage system intolerably unsavoury and insanitary. To become a politician is like going to work in the drain.

History bears out the proposition that political revolutions have always been preceded by social and religious revolutions. Social reform in India has few friends and many critics. Law and order are the medicine of the body politic and when the body politic gets sick, medicine must be administered.

The world owes much to rebels who would dare to argue in the face of the pontiff (high priest) and insist that he is not infallible.

A people and their religion must be judged by social standards based on social ethics. No other standard would have any meaning if religion is held to be necessary good for the well-being of the people.

Ethnologists are of the opinion that men of pure race exist nowhere and that there has been admixture of all races in all parts of the world—especially is this the case with the people if India. Mr. D.R. Bhandarkar has stated: "There is hardly a class or caste in India which has not a foreign strain in it. There is as an admixture of alien blood not only among the warrior classes—the Rajputs and Marathas—but among the Brahmins who are under the happy delusion that they are free from all foreign elements.

The question is not whether a community lives or dies, the question is on what plane does it live. There are different modes of survival. But all are not equally honourable. For an individual as well as a society, there is a gulf between merely living and living worthily. To fight in a battle and live in a glory is one mode. To beat a retreat to surrender and to live the life of a captive is also a mode of survival.